THE MILES KELLY
CHILDREN'S
ATLAS

THE MILES KELLY
CHILDREN'S
ATLAS

Malcom Watson

Consultant: Clive Carpenter

First published as hardback in 2007 by Miles Kelly Publishing Ltd
Bardfield Centre, Great Bardfield, Essex, CM7 4SL, UK

Copyright © Miles Kelly Publishing Ltd 2007

This edition updated and published 2010

2 4 6 8 10 9 7 5 3 1

Author: Malcolm Watson
Consultant: Clive Carpenter

Map Artworker: Julian Baker (J B ILLUSTRATIONS)
Mountain High Maps® Copyright © 1993 Digital Wisdom, Inc.

Editorial Director: Belinda Gallagher
Art Director: Jo Brewer
Editor: Amanda Askew
Editorial Assistant: Carly Blake
Designers: Simon Lee, Elaine Wilkinson
Cover Designer: Simon Lee
Reprographics: Stephan Davis,
Liberty Newton, Ian Paulyn
Production Manager: Elizabeth Collins
Assets Manager: Bethan Ellish

ISBN 978-1-84810-288-0

Printed in Thailand

British Library Cataloguing-in-Publication Data
A catalogue record for this book is available from the British Library

Made with paper from a sustainable forest

www.mileskelly.net
info@mileskelly.net

www.factsforprojects.com
The one-stop homework helper – pictures, facts, videos, projects and more

THE MILES KELLY
CHILDREN'S
ATLAS
CONTENTS

Using the atlas

Divided into continental areas, this atlas explores the world with amazing facts, statistics and photographs. Highly detailed maps show important cultural and geographical features, such as major towns, places of interest, mountain ranges and rivers.

1 Graticule
The coloured frame that runs around each map. It changes colour for each continental area and provides grid references that enable you to locate features on the map easily.

2 Main heading
Introduces the main countries on the page.

3 Locator globe
Highlights where in the world the countries are.

4 Introduction
Gives an insight into some of the countries that are mapped.

5 Scale
Shows the scale of the map in kilometres and miles.

6 Map
Shows towns, territories and islands, plus physical features such as mountain ranges.

7 Did You Know?
Amazing facts about people and places.

8 Image
Each photograph is accompanied by a detailed caption.

North Africa

4 The Sahara Desert dominates this region at 6000 km in width and 2000 km from north to south. Only a narrow strip of land stands next to the Mediterranean Sea, but the fertile valleys of the Atlas Mountains and the banks of the Nile river have enough water to grow crops.

Algeria, Libya and Tunisia have be wealthy by selling oil and natural Europe. Egypt was the richest cou in the world when the pharaohs ru more than 3000 years ago. Egypt's well-preserved tombs and temples, especially the Great Pyramid of Giza attract many tourists.

Did You Know?
The Sahara Desert region was wet and fertile 8000 years ago. As the climate has become drier, the desert has expanded.

8 In north Africa, many civilizations live in fortified cities, or ksars. *Aït Benhaddou* is situated near Marrakech [E2], Morocco. Few families live here now as they have moved to modern villages nearby. Scenes from films including Alexander (2004) and The Mummy (1999) have been shot here.

In the next minute... ...the Sun will evaporate the equivalent of 110 million bottles of water from the Nile river.

KEY TO MAPS

Country border	State border	Disputed border	Country capital	State capital	Town
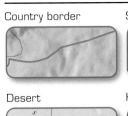	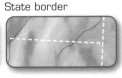	Tarfaya WESTERN	**Madrid** ●	Lincoln ■	● Rock Springs

Desert	Highest peak	River	Dependency/territory	Research station	Place of interest
SAHARA	▲ *Tahat Peak* *2918 m*	*Amazon*	*FALKLAND ISLANDS* *(UK)*	Casey (Australia)	◆ *Mount* *Rushmore*

NORTH AFRICA • AFRICA

◁ *Located on the Nile river, Cairo [F13] is the biggest city in Africa. Built in AD 988, **Al-Azhar University** is the second oldest university in the world, after the University of Al Karaouine Fez, Morocco. Al-Azhar Mosque stands alongside the university.*

14 Facts and Stats

- Egypt's population of 72.8 million would fill 728 Olympic stadiums. Libya's population of five million would only fill 50 stadiums.
- Cairo [F13] is the biggest city with 12.2 million people. This would fill 122 Olympic stadiums and is ten times the size of Tripoli [E8].
- The average income per person in Libya is £6000, compared to a world average of £3500.

10 Search and Find

Algeria	**Morocco**
● Algiers C6	● Rabat D3
Egypt	**Tunisia**
● Cairo. F13	● Tunis D7
Libya	
● Surt E9	
● Tripoli E8	

13 World Record
The Saharan sand sea of Algeria has the highest sand dunes in the world at 465 m in height.

15 Extreme Weather
The hottest temperature ever recorded was 58°C in Libya's Sahara Desert.

MEDITERRANEAN SEA

Tripoli
Zawiyah • Misurata •
Surt • Gulf of Sidra • Benghazi • Darnah
• Ajdabiya • Tubruq

GREAT SAND SEA

Alexandria • Tanta • Port Said
QATTARA DEPRESSION • **Cairo** • Suez Canal
Giza • Suez
Sinai Peninsula
Nile • Gulf of Suez
WESTERN DESERT • Sharm al Sheikh
• El Minya
• Al Ghardaqah
Asyut
• Qena
• Luxor

LIBYA

FEZZAN
LIBYAN DESERT

EGYPT

ISRAEL
Gulf of Aqaba
RED SEA

GILF KEBIR PLATEAU
• Aswan
Lake Nasser

CHAD
SUDAN

11 THE DISTANCE separating Morocco from Spain, Europe, at the Strait of Gibraltar's [C3] narrowest point is only 13 km.

12 EGYPT has huge pyramids, built more than 3000 years ago. Each one held the body of a king.

◁ *Desert tribe people, such as the Berbers and Tuaregs, travel by camel from oasis to oasis across the Sahara Desert to trade cloth, salt and spices.*

9 In the next minute...
Fascinating information about what is happening across the world in only one minute.

10 Search and Find
Each country or state is listed with its capital city and a grid reference.

11 The distance...
Measures the distance from one point to another and how long it would take to travel.

12 Place of interest
Provides extra information about a well-known sight or attraction.

13 World Record
Details a world record that a country holds.

14 Facts and Stats
Helps you to understand facts and figures. The highest peaks are compared to the Eiffel Tower in Paris, France, which is 320 m in height. Rivers are compared to the Nile river, Africa, which is 6670 km in length. Population is compared to an Olympic stadium, which would hold 100,000 people.

15 Extreme Weather
Details the highest and lowest temperatures, dramatic storms or high rainfall.

63

Planet Earth

Earth is a huge ball of rock with two-thirds of its surface covered by seas and oceans. The third planet from the Sun in the Solar System, Earth is the only planet where life is known to exist, due to an atmosphere rich in oxygen and the water on its surface. Beneath the Earth's thin, solid crust is the liquid mantle, and at the centre is the core. The outer part of the core is liquid, but the inner core is solid metal.

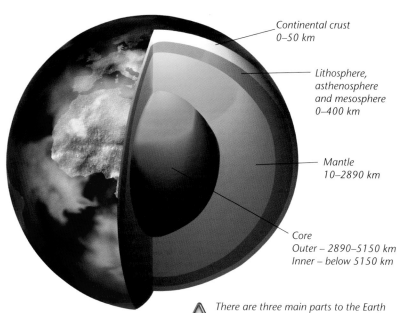

Continental crust
0–50 km

Lithosphere, asthenosphere and mesosphere
0–400 km

Mantle
10–2890 km

Core
Outer – 2890–5150 km
Inner – below 5150 km

△ There are three main parts to the Earth – the crust, mantle and core. Although the inner core reaches a temperature of 7000°C, it remains solid because the pressure is 6000 times greater than on the surface.

SPINNING EARTH

The Earth spins on its axis – an imaginary line through its centre – at a speed of more than 1600 km/h. It doesn't spin straight up, but leans to one side. As the Earth spins, the view of the Sun from different places on Earth constantly changes. This brings day and night, and the seasons.

▽ In December, the South Pole leans towards the Sun. Places in the southern half of the world have summer. At the same time, places in the northern half have winter.

Seasons
There are four seasons – spring, summer, autumn and winter. Each season brings a change in temperature and weather. The changes in the seasons occur because the Earth tilts towards the Sun. When the Northern Hemisphere tilts towards the Sun, the northern part of the world has summer and the south has winter. Six months later, the opposite occurs – the Southern Hemisphere tilts towards the Sun. Then the north has winter and the south has summer. The tropics around the centre of the Earth are slightly different. They only have two seasons – wet and dry.

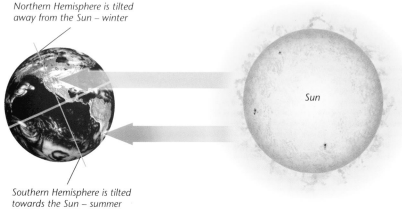

Northern Hemisphere is tilted away from the Sun – winter

Sun

Southern Hemisphere is tilted towards the Sun – summer

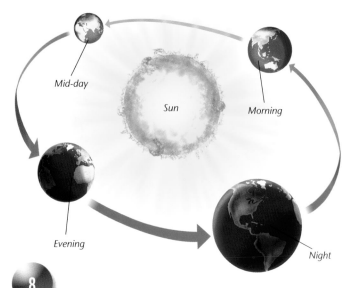

Mid-day

Sun

Morning

Evening

Night

◁ When it is daylight on the half of the Earth facing towards the Sun, it is night on the half of the Earth facing away from it. As the Earth rotates, so the day and night halves shift gradually around the world.

Night and day
The Earth spins a complete turn on its axis every 24 hours. This gives us night and day. The Sun is the source of light for daytime. When it is night, it is dark because the Sun is shining on the opposite side of the Earth. When it is evening or early morning, the Sun is moving away or towards our part of the Earth.

Shaping the land

The Earth's crust is made up of pieces called tectonic plates, which are constantly moving, changing the shape of the land. This can create mountains and volcanoes, as well as cause natural disasters, such as earthquakes. Rocks can also be broken down or worn away by the weather, such as wind and rain, or by the movement of water, such as waves.

A volcano erupts, shooting molten magma into the air.

A sea arch, formed by waves wearing away the rock.

PLATE TECTONICS

The Earth's crust is split into several parts called tectonic plates. The plates float on the molten lava underneath, causing them to constantly move.

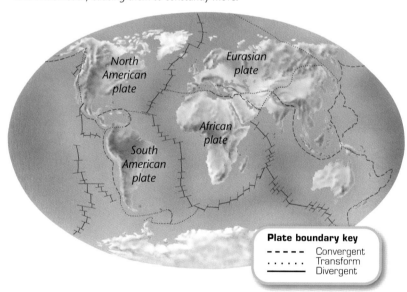

North American plate

Eurasian plate

African plate

South American plate

Plate boundary key
- - - - - Convergent
. . . . . . Transform
———— Divergent

Divergent plate boundaries

Where two plates move away from each other, molten rock, or magma, rises to fill the gap. This usually occurs beneath the oceans, forming a spreading ocean ridge, such as the mid-Atlantic ridge.

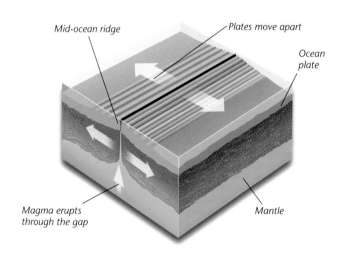

Mid-ocean ridge

Plates move apart

Ocean plate

Magma erupts through the gap

Mantle

Convergent plate boundaries

When two plates crash together, they crumple up and form major mountain chains, such as the Andes, as well as volcanoes. The Earth's crust is thin, so if cracks appear, the magma shoots up as the lava of a volcano. When an ocean plate is driven down into the Earth's magma, it is called subduction.

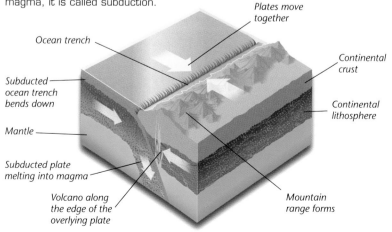

Ocean trench

Plates move together

Continental crust

Subducted ocean trench bends down

Continental lithosphere

Mantle

Subducted plate melting into magma

Volcano along the edge of the overlying plate

Mountain range forms

Transform plate boundaries

If two plates push past each other, pressure can build up, creating a break, or fault, which often causes an earthquake. Some earthquakes are so powerful that buildings collapse. Landslides can also occur, causing great damage. Undersea earthquakes can cause the massive waves of a tsunami, such as the tsunami that struck southeast Asia in 2004, killing 190,000 people.

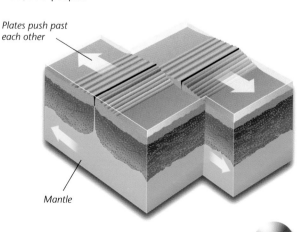

Plates push past each other

Mantle

Climate

The Earth's climate is very simple. Near the Equator, the temperture is hot, and closer to the poles, the temperature is cold. All year round, daytime temperatures at the Equator are around 33°C and there are no seasons. At the poles, the temperature is usually below freezing, and in winter there are long hours of darkness and temperatures drop to −40°C. Rain and snowfall patterns are more complex. Countries at the Equator experience heavy rain, but the poles have very little rainfall.

Global warming

The increased level of carbon dioxide in the atmosphere causes global warming because the gas traps the Sun's heat. Carbon dioxide is emitted when carbon fuels are burnt – this happens in cars and factories. The effects of global warming are becoming evident. Large areas of ice around Antarctica have already disappeared. The Sahara Desert is expanding and droughts are more common in Australia, causing rivers, such as the Murray, to dry up (see below). Sea levels are slowly rising, threatening cities such as New York City and low-lying countries such as Bangladesh with flooding. Using alternative sources of energy, such as wind and solar power, is vital to slow down these changes.

TYPES OF CLIMATE

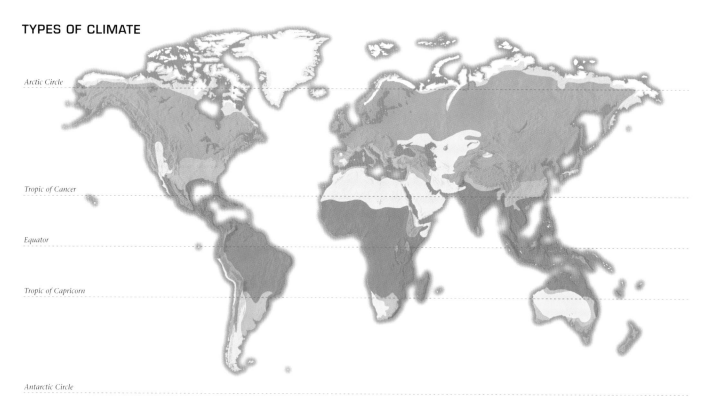

Arctic Circle

Tropic of Cancer

Equator

Tropic of Capricorn

Antarctic Circle

Polar and tundra
The lands around the Arctic Ocean and Antarctica are normally covered in snow. Northern Canada and Russia have a brief summer where the snow melts and the top layer of soil thaws to create a boggy ground called tundra.

Desert
Just north and south of the Equator lie desert areas. They have high daytime summer temperatures and are warm even in winter. Rain is very rare. Few plants grow and crops are only farmed where there are sources of water.

Cool temperate
Near the Arctic Circle, winters are cold and snowy, and summers are short. Closer to the Equator winters are milder, with little snow and warm summers. Forests are abundant and farming is common in the southern areas.

Warm temperate
In areas around the Mediterranean Sea and in some parts of North America, summers are hot and dry and winters are cool, but mild. Rainfall varies, so farming centres around growing citrus and olive trees.

Tropical
Close to the Equator, countries experience high temperatures and high rainfall for almost every month of the year. More animals and plants live in the tropical rainforests of the Amazon, central Africa and Indonesia than any other region.

Mountainous
Mountains have their own climate and snow can even be found at the Equator. At 5000 m in height, the temperature is 30°C colder than at sea level. Mountains also have more rainfall than the land surrounding them.

Population

The population of the world reached 6.7 billion in 2008. With more than 250 babies being born each minute, and many people living longer due to a better quality of life, the population of the world is increasing rapidly. This rise puts pressure on the world's natural resources, and many cities are becoming overcrowded as people move in search of work. China is the most populated country with 1.24 billion people. Tokyo, the capital of Japan, is the largest city in the world with a population of 37.36 million.

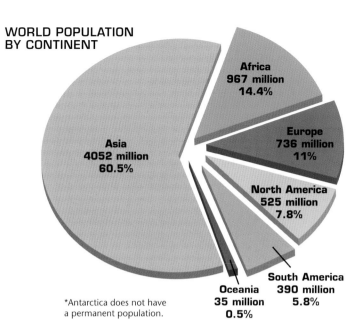

WORLD POPULATION BY CONTINENT

Asia 4052 million 60.5%
Africa 967 million 14.4%
Europe 736 million 11%
North America 525 million 7.8%
South America 390 million 5.8%
Oceania 35 million 0.5%

*Antarctica does not have a permanent population.

TOP 10 COUNTRIES BY POPULATION DENSITY

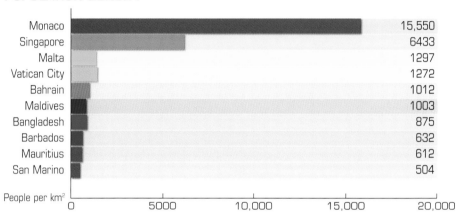

	People per km²
Monaco	15,550
Singapore	6433
Malta	1297
Vatican City	1272
Bahrain	1012
Maldives	1003
Bangladesh	875
Barbados	632
Mauritius	612
San Marino	504

People per km² 0   5000   10,000   15,000   20,000

TOP 10 COUNTRIES BY POPULATION

1	China	1,240,000,000
2	India	1,148,000,000
3	USA	304,060,000
4	Indonesia	222,192,000
5	Brazil	183,889,000
6	Pakistan	162,508,000
7	Russia	142,754,000
8	Nigeria	140,003,000
9	Bangladesh	129,247,000
10	Japan	127,931,000

TOP 20 CITIES BY POPULATION

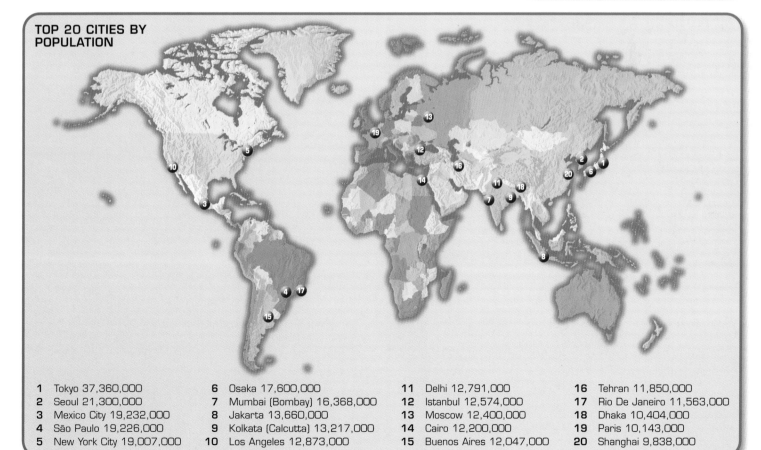

1 Tokyo 37,360,000	6 Osaka 17,600,000	11 Delhi 12,791,000	16 Tehran 11,850,000
2 Seoul 21,300,000	7 Mumbai (Bombay) 16,368,000	12 Istanbul 12,574,000	17 Rio De Janeiro 11,563,000
3 Mexico City 19,232,000	8 Jakarta 13,660,000	13 Moscow 12,400,000	18 Dhaka 10,404,000
4 São Paulo 19,226,000	9 Kolkata (Calcutta) 13,217,000	14 Cairo 12,200,000	19 Paris 10,143,000
5 New York City 19,007,000	10 Los Angeles 12,873,000	15 Buenos Aires 12,047,000	20 Shanghai 9,838,000

The Physical World

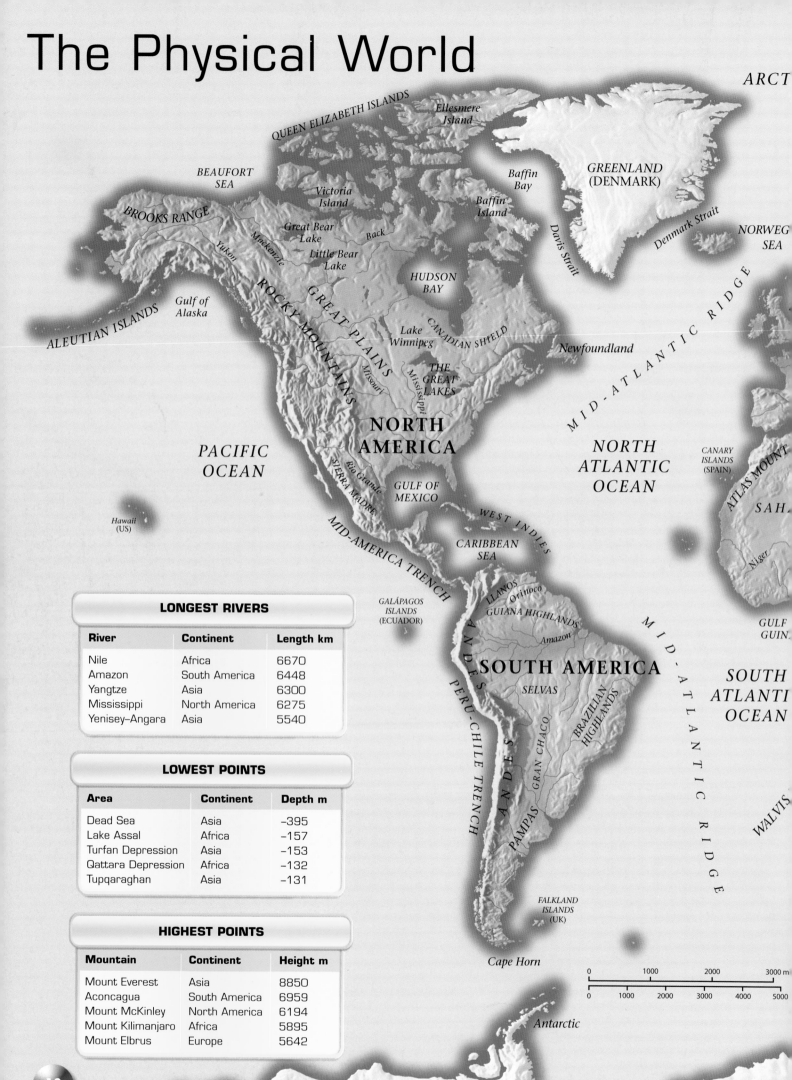

LONGEST RIVERS

River	Continent	Length km
Nile	Africa	6670
Amazon	South America	6448
Yangtze	Asia	6300
Mississippi	North America	6275
Yenisey–Angara	Asia	5540

LOWEST POINTS

Area	Continent	Depth m
Dead Sea	Asia	−395
Lake Assal	Africa	−157
Turfan Depression	Asia	−153
Qattara Depression	Africa	−132
Tupqaraghan	Asia	−131

HIGHEST POINTS

Mountain	Continent	Height m
Mount Everest	Asia	8850
Aconcagua	South America	6959
Mount McKinley	North America	6194
Mount Kilimanjaro	Africa	5895
Mount Elbrus	Europe	5642

CEAN

Franz Josef Land

LBARD
RWAY)

Novaya Zemlya

Severnaya Zemlya

LAPTEV SEA

NEW SIBERIAN
ISLANDS

EAST
SIBERIAN
SEA

BARENTS
SEA

*KARA
SEA*

LAPLAND

CENTRAL
SIBERIAN
PLATEAU

Dvina

Yenisey

Nizhnyaya Tunguska

Lena

BERING
SEA

LTIC SEA

EUROPEAN PLAIN

Volga

Ob

SIBERIAN
LOWLAND

Yenisey

Ob

Angara

Lena

Aldan

SEA OF
OKHOTSK

EUROPE

URAL MOUNTAINS

ASIA

Dnieper

Ural

Irtysh

SAYAN MOUNTAINS

Lake
Baikal

CARPATHIAN
MOUNTAINS

*Arat
Sea*

Lake
Balkhash

GOBI
DESERT

KURIL TRENCH

Danube

BLACK SEA

CASPIAN SEA

TIEN MOUNTAINS

SEA OF
JAPAN

ITERRANEAN SEA

ZAGROS MOUNTAINS

Euphrates

Tigris

HINDU KUSH

KUNLAN MOUNTAINS

Indus

TIBETAN
PLATEAU

Huang

Chang Jiang

EAST CHINA
SEA

PACIFIC
OCEAN

SERT

Nile

RED SEA

NUBIAN
DESERT

*Arabian
Peninsula*

ARABIAN
SEA

HIMALAYAS

Ganges

DECCAN

Irrawaddy

Mekong

SOUTH
CHINA
SEA

MICRONESIA

GULF OF ADEN

BAY OF
BENGAL

FRICA

ETHIOPIAN
HIGHLANDS

PHILIPPINE SEA

Uele

Congo

CONGO
BASIN

GREAT RIFT VALLEY

Lake
Victoria

CELEBES
SEA

MELANESIA

Kasai

MID-INDIAN RIDGE

EAST INDIES

JAVA TRENCH

CORAL
SEA

KALAHARI
DESERT

INDIAN
OCEAN

GREAT SANDY
DESERT

Orange

GREAT
VICTORIAN
DESERT

GREAT DIVIDING RANGE

OCEANIA

SOUTHWEST INDIAN RIDGE

SOUTHEAST INDIAN RIDGE

Cape of
Good Hope

SOUTHERN
OCEAN

Great
Australian
Bight

TASMAN
SEA

WORLD'S OCEANS

Ocean	Area km²
Pacific	165,240,000
Atlantic	82,440,000
Indian	73,440,000
Southern	23,325,000
Arctic	14,090,000

LARGEST DESERTS

Desert	Continent	Area km²
Sahara	Africa	8,600,000
Arabian	Asia	2,300,000
Australian	Australia	1,550,000
Gobi	Asia	1,300,000
Kalahari	Africa	930,000

LARGEST INLAND WATER BODIES

Lake	Continent	Area km²
Caspian Sea	Asia–Europe	371,800
Superior	North America	82,000
Victoria	Africa	69,500
Huron	North America	59,600
Michigan	North America	58,000

The Political World

KEY TO CARIBBEAN

1. DOMINICAN REPUBLIC
2. *PUERTO RICO* (US)
3. *VIRGIN ISLANDS* (US)
4. *SABA* (NETHERLANDS)
5. *ST. EUSTATIUS* (NETHERLANDS)
6. *ANGUILLA* (UK)
7. *ST. MARTIN* (FRANCE AND NETHERLANDS)
8. *ST. BARTHELÉMY* (FRANCE)
9. ANTIGUA AND BARBUDA
10. ST. KITTS AND NEVIS
11. *MONTSERRAT* (UK)
12. *GUADALOUPE* (FRANCE)
13. DOMINICA
14. *MARTINIQUE* (FRANCE)
15. ST. LUCIA
16. ST. VINCENT AND THE GRENADINES
17. BARBADOS
18. GRENADA
19. TRINIDAD AND TOBAGO
20. *BONAIRE* (NETHERLANDS)
21. *CURAÇAO* (NETHERLANDS)
22. *ARUBA* (NETHERLANDS)

KEY TO EUROPE

23. RUSSIAN FEDERATION
24. LITHUANIA
25. NETHERLANDS
26. BELGIUM
27. LUXEMBOURG
28. GERMANY
29. CZECH REPUBLIC
30. SLOVAKIA
31. MOLDOVA
32. ROMANIA
33. HUNGARY
34. AUSTRIA
35. LIECHTENSTEIN
36. SWITZERLAND
37. SLOVENIA
38. CROATIA
39. BOSNIA AND HERZEGOVINA
40. SERBIA
41. MONTENEGRO
42. KOSOVO
43. MACEDONIA
44. ALBANIA
45. SAN MARINO
46. VATICAN CITY
47. MONACO
48. ANDORRA
49. MALTA
50. EQUATORIAL GUINEA
51. SÃO TOMÉ AND PRÍNCI[PE]
52. REPUBLIC OF THE CON[GO]
53. *CABINDA* (ANGOLA)

COLOUR KEY

- ANTARCTICA
- NORTH AMERICA
- SOUTH AND CENTRAL AMERICA
- EUROPE
- AFRICA
- ASIA
- OCEANIA

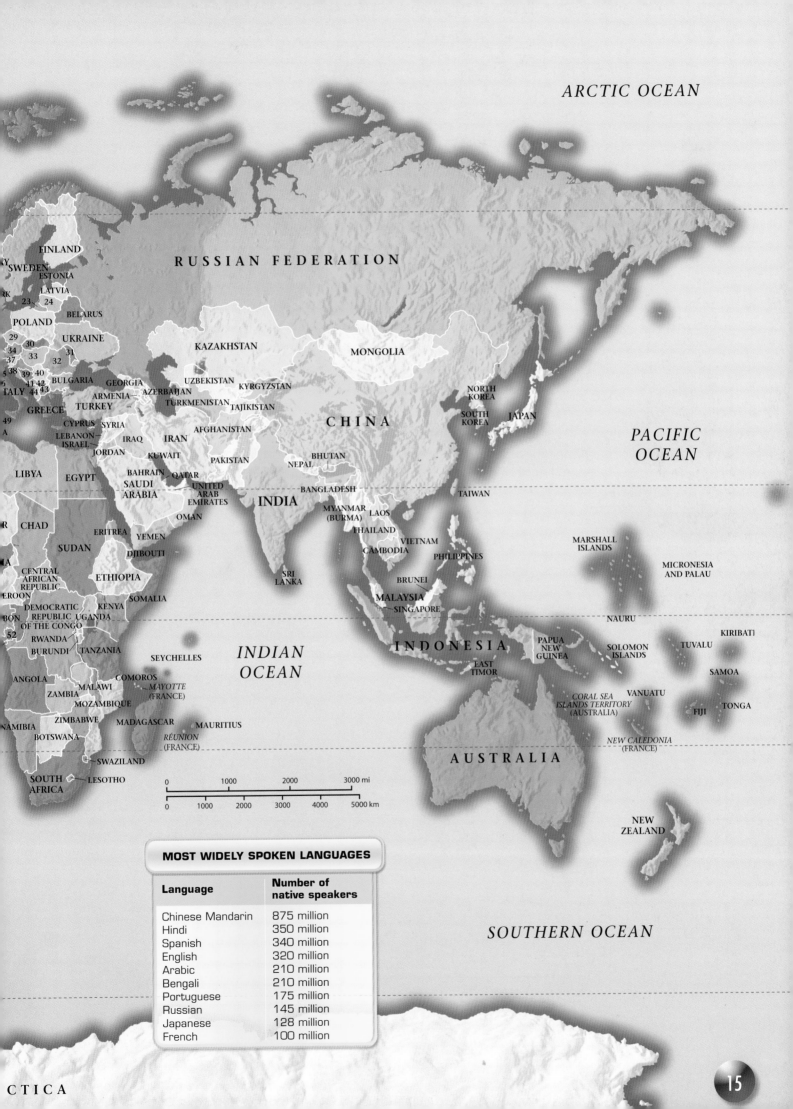

ARCTIC OCEAN

PACIFIC OCEAN

INDIAN OCEAN

SOUTHERN OCEAN

MOST WIDELY SPOKEN LANGUAGES

Language	Number of native speakers
Chinese Mandarin	875 million
Hindi	350 million
Spanish	340 million
English	320 million
Arabic	210 million
Bengali	210 million
Portuguese	175 million
Russian	145 million
Japanese	128 million
French	100 million

Antarctica

Antarctica is 98 percent covered by ice that is about 1.6 km thick. Although it is the coldest place on Earth, the region is heavily affected by global warming. The climate is becoming warmer due to an increased level of carbon dioxide, which traps the Sun's heat. Large areas of ice that cover the sea around Antarctica have already broken away and melted. Deep under the ice lie vast amounts of oil, coal and gold, but mining is prohibited.

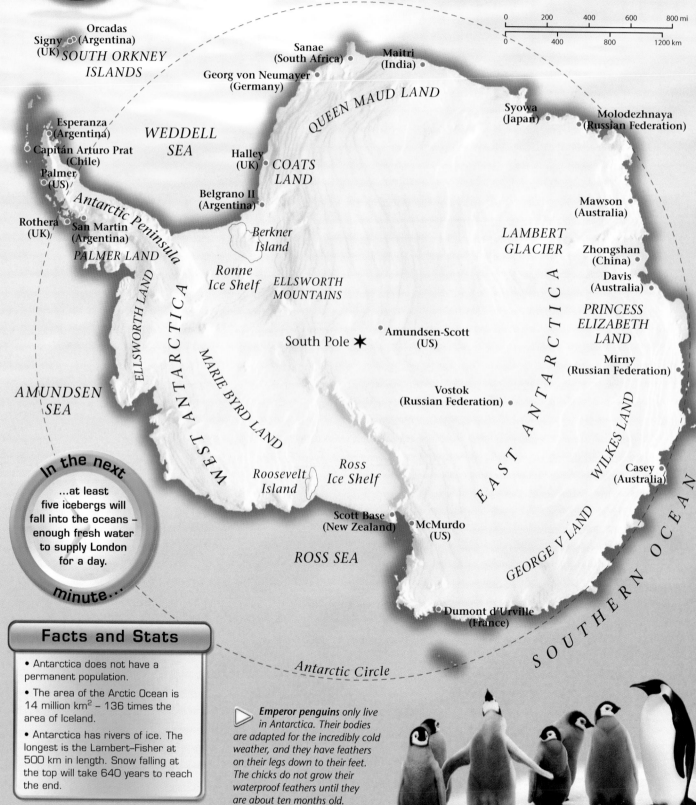

Signy (UK)
Orcadas (Argentina)
SOUTH ORKNEY ISLANDS

Sanae (South Africa)
Maitri (India)
Georg von Neumayer (Germany)

Syowa (Japan)
Molodezhnaya (Russian Federation)

QUEEN MAUD LAND

Esperanza (Argentina)
WEDDELL SEA
Capitán Arturo Prat (Chile)
Halley (UK)
COATS LAND
Palmer (US)

Mawson (Australia)

Antarctic Peninsula

Belgrano II (Argentina)

LAMBERT GLACIER

Rothera (UK)
San Martin (Argentina)
PALMER LAND

Berkner Island

Zhongshan (China)
Davis (Australia)

Ronne Ice Shelf
ELLSWORTH MOUNTAINS

PRINCESS ELIZABETH LAND

ELLSWORTH LAND

ELLSWORTH LAND

South Pole ✳
Amundsen-Scott (US)

Mirny (Russian Federation)

AMUNDSEN SEA

WEST ANTARCTICA

MARIE BYRD LAND

Vostok (Russian Federation)

EAST ANTARCTICA

Roosevelt Island
Ross Ice Shelf

WILKES LAND

Casey (Australia)

Scott Base (New Zealand)
McMurdo (US)

ROSS SEA

GEORGE V LAND

SOUTHERN OCEAN

Dumont d'Urville (France)

Antarctic Circle

0 200 400 600 800 mi
0 400 800 1200 km

In the next minute...

...at least five icebergs will fall into the oceans – enough fresh water to supply London for a day.

Facts and Stats

• Antarctica does not have a permanent population.

• The area of the Arctic Ocean is 14 million km² – 136 times the area of Iceland.

• Antarctica has rivers of ice. The longest is the Lambert–Fisher at 500 km in length. Snow falling at the top will take 640 years to reach the end.

▷ **Emperor penguins** only live in Antarctica. Their bodies are adapted for the incredibly cold weather, and they have feathers on their legs down to their feet. The chicks do not grow their waterproof feathers until they are about ten months old.

Arctic Ocean

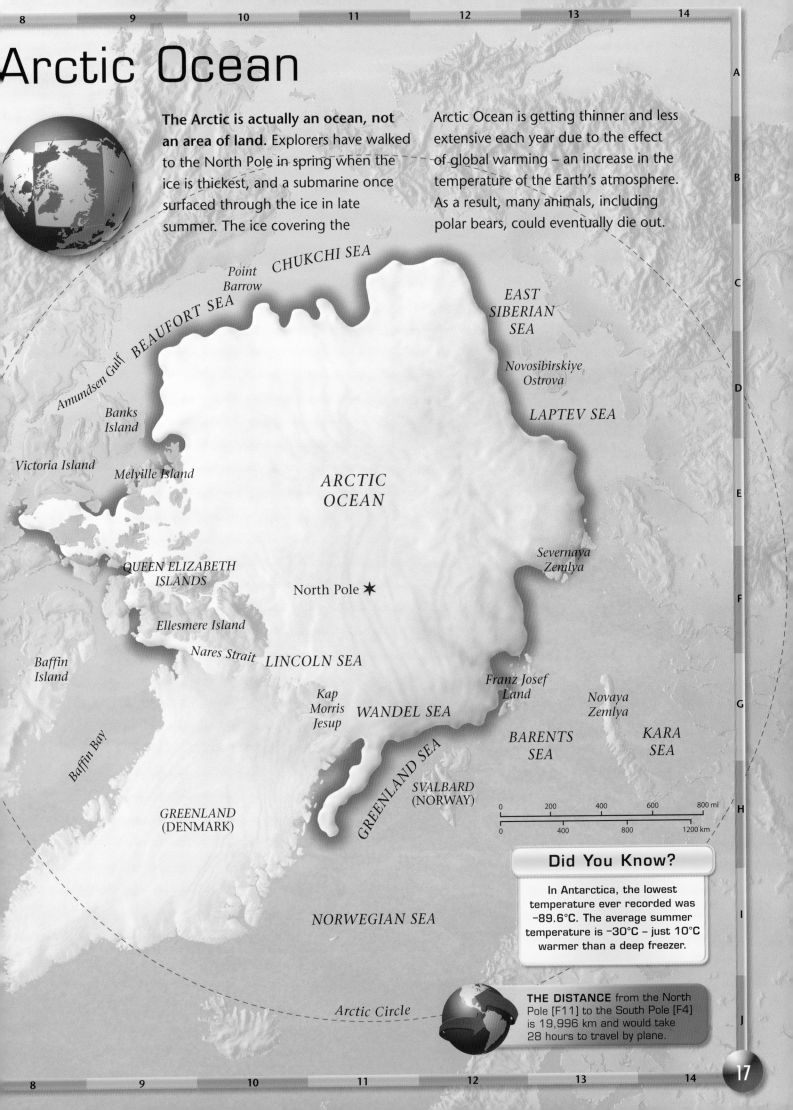

The Arctic is actually an ocean, not an area of land. Explorers have walked to the North Pole in spring when the ice is thickest, and a submarine once surfaced through the ice in late summer. The ice covering the Arctic Ocean is getting thinner and less extensive each year due to the effect of global warming – an increase in the temperature of the Earth's atmosphere. As a result, many animals, including polar bears, could eventually die out.

CHUKCHI SEA

Point Barrow

EAST SIBERIAN SEA

BEAUFORT SEA

Amundsen Gulf

Novosibirskiye Ostrova

Banks Island

LAPTEV SEA

Victoria Island

Melville Island

ARCTIC OCEAN

QUEEN ELIZABETH ISLANDS

Severnaya Zemlya

North Pole ✶

Ellesmere Island

Nares Strait

LINCOLN SEA

Baffin Island

Kap Morris Jesup

WANDEL SEA

Franz Josef Land

Novaya Zemlya

BARENTS SEA

KARA SEA

Baffin Bay

GREENLAND SEA

SVALBARD (NORWAY)

GREENLAND (DENMARK)

0	200		400	600	800 mi
0		400		800	1200 km

Did You Know?

In Antarctica, the lowest temperature ever recorded was −89.6°C. The average summer temperature is −30°C – just 10°C warmer than a deep freezer.

NORWEGIAN SEA

Arctic Circle

THE DISTANCE from the North Pole [F11] to the South Pole [F4] is 19,996 km and would take 28 hours to travel by plane.

North America

ARCTIC OCEAN

Alaska
(US)

CANADA

PACIFIC
OCEAN

UNITED STATES
OF AMERICA

ATLANTIC
OCEAN

MEXICO

Hawaii
(US)

COUNTRY FACTFILE

Country	Life expectancy	Population in thousands	Population growth %	Population as urban %	Literacy %	Area km²	Population density per km²	Capital city	Currency	Languages
Canada	81	33,505	0.8	80	99	9,970,610	3.4	Ottawa	Canadian Dollar	English, French
Mexico	76	103,264	1.1	77	91	1,958,201	52.7	Mexico City	Mexican Peso	Spanish
United States of America	78	304,060	1	82	99	9,629,091	31.5	Washington D.C.	US Dollar	English, Spanish

NB: Central America can be found as part of the South and Central America section.

Northeast USA

The northeast is the centre of the United States' industry and commerce with many large manufacturing companies. Ford and General Motor vehicles, as well as coal mines, steel works, the New York Stock Exchange, Washington White House and the Senate buildings are all situated here. Modern black music started in Cleveland and Detroit, whilst away from the cities there are many beaches, rivers, forests and lakes.

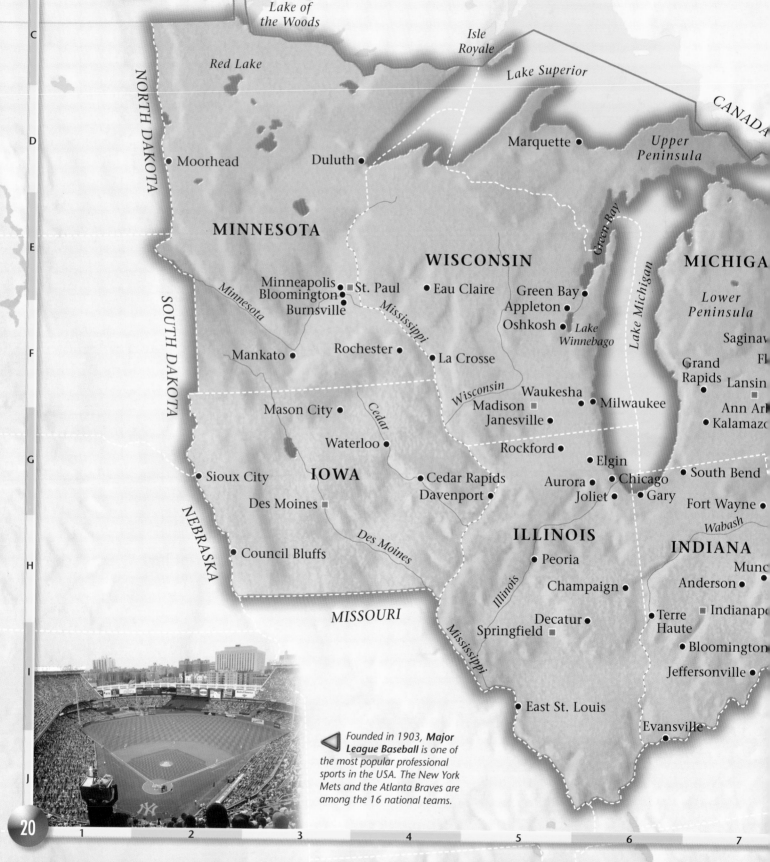

Lake of the Woods

Isle Royale

Lake Superior

CANADA

NORTH DAKOTA

Red Lake

Marquette

Upper Peninsula

• Moorhead

Duluth •

MICHIGA

MINNESOTA

WISCONSIN

Green Bay

Lower Peninsula

SOUTH DAKOTA

Minneapolis
Bloomington
Burnsville

St. Paul

Eau Claire

Green Bay
Appleton
Oshkosh

Lake Winnebago

Saginaw

Fl

Mississippi

Grand Rapids

Lansin

Minnesota

Mankato •

Rochester

La Crosse

Wisconsin

Ann Ar

Kalamazo

Mason City •

Cedar

Waukesha
Madison
Janesville

Milwaukee

Waterloo •

Rockford •

Elgin

South Bend

NEBRASKA

Sioux City •

IOWA

Cedar Rapids
Davenport

Aurora •

Chicago

Gary

Fort Wayne

Des Moines

Council Bluffs •

Des Moines

ILLINOIS

Joliet

Wabash

INDIANA

Peoria

Munc

Champaign

Anderson •

MISSOURI

Illinois

Decatur •

Terre Haute

Indianapo

Springfield

Mississippi

• East St. Louis

Bloomington

Jeffersonville

Evansville

Founded in 1903, **Major League Baseball** is one of the most popular professional sports in the USA. The New York Mets and the Atlanta Braves are among the 16 national teams.

Search and Find

- Washington D.C. H11

Connecticut
- Hartford F12

Delaware
- Dover G11

Illinois
- Springfield. I5

Indiana
- Indianapolis . . . H7

Iowa
- Des Moines . . . G3

Maine
- Augusta D13

Maryland
- Annapolis . . . H11

Massachusetts
- Boston E13

Michigan
- Lansing F7

Minnesota
- St. Paul E3

New Hampshire
- Concord E13

New Jersey
- Trenton G12

New York
- Albany E12

Ohio
- Columbus H8

Pennsylvania
- Harrisburg. . . G11

Rhode Island
- Providence. . . E13

Vermont
- Montpelier. . . D12

West Virginia
- Charleston I9

Wisconsin
- Madison F5

Facts and Stats

- The biggest city is New York City [F12] with 19 million people. This would fill 190 Olympic stadiums.
- The biggest lake is Lake Superior [C5] at 82,000 km^2. This is only 20 percent smaller than Iceland.
- Mount Washington [D12] is the highest mountain at 1917 m – six times higher than the Eiffel Tower.

Did You Know?

The five Great Lakes between USA and Canada are Michigan, Superior, Ontario, Huron and Erie. They contain one-fifth of the world's fresh water – 22.8 quadrillion litres.

In the next ...204 million litres of water will crash over Niagara Falls [F9] – enough for one million baths. **minute...**

THE DISTANCE from New York City [F12] to London across the Atlantic Ocean is 4800 km and would take seven hours by plane.

THE STATUE OF LIBERTY, Ellis Island [F12], was made in France and shipped to USA in 1884. There are 354 steps leading to the top.

Scale: 0 — 50 — 100 — 150 — 200 mi / 0 — 100 — 200 — 300 km

Map labels:
Presque Isle, MAINE, Bangor, Penobscot, Gulf of Maine, Newport, Mount Washington 1917 m, Augusta, Lewiston, Portland, VERMONT, Burlington, Montpelier, NEW HAMPSHIRE, Portsmouth, Concord, Manchester, Lowell, CANADA, ADIRONDACK MOUNTAINS, Watertown, NEW YORK, MASSACHUSETTS, Boston, Cape Cod, Worcester, Springfield, Lake Ontario, Syracuse, Utica, Schenectady, Troy, Providence, Rochester, Albany, RHODE ISLAND, Niagara Falls, Buffalo, CONNECTICUT, Hartford, New Haven, Port Huron, Bridgeport, Long Island, Stamford, Erie, Scranton, Paterson, New York City, Warren, Lake Erie, Newark, Ellis Island, Detroit, Allegheny, Susquehanna, NEW JERSEY, Jersey City, ATLANTIC OCEAN, Cleveland, Youngstown, Allentown, Reading, Toledo, Akron, PENNSYLVANIA, Trenton, Canton, Philadelphia, Pittsburgh, Harrisburg, Vineland, Atlantic City, Wilmington, OHIO, Wheeling, Dover, Morgantown, Baltimore, DELAWARE, Columbus, MARYLAND, Annapolis, Dayton, Kettering, Washington D.C., WEST VIRGINIA, APPALACHIAN MOUNTAINS, cinnati, Charleston, Huntington, VIRGINIA, NTUCKY, Lake Huron

Southeast USA

The warm climate of Florida and the Gulf of Mexico coastal areas makes southeast USA popular with tourists. There is Disney World in Florida for fun, Cape Canaveral for space rocket launches, Miami for beaches, New Orleans for jazz, Nashville for country music and the Mississippi river for boat trips. Farming is the main occupation – mainly of tobacco, oranges, rice, peanuts, vegetables and cotton. There are many oil and gas rigs in the Gulf of Mexico to generate energy resources.

GRACELAND, Nashville [C8], is the home of Elvis Presley (1935–1977) and is visited by more than 600,000 fans a year.

THE DISTANCE from the source to the mouth of the Mississippi–Missouri river is 6275 km and would take 20 days floating on a raft.

Extreme Weather

Hurricane Katrina, the largest hurricane ever recorded in the USA, caused 80 percent of New Orleans [H6] to flood. More than one million people were evacuated and 1300 died.

The **Kentucky Derby** takes place in Louisville [B8] on the first Saturday of May. The race is 2 km in length and more than 150,000 spectators attend the two-week-long festival every year.

World Record

The largest space rocket launch site in the world is at Cape Canaveral [H11].

IOWA

ILLINOIS

St. Joseph

Independence
Kansas City
Columbia
Jefferson City
St. Louis

Owensboro

KANSAS

MISSOURI
Cape Girardeau
Paducah

Springfield
Clarksvill

OZARK PLATEAU

OKLAHOMA

ARKANSAS
Fort Smith
Memphis

Little Rock
Hot Springs
Pine Bluff
Mississippi
Yazoo

Ouachita
Greenville
Tuscalo

Texarkana
El Dorado
MISSISSIPPI

TEXAS
Monroe
Meridian

Shreveport
Jackson

Pearl

LOUISIANA
Natchez
Hattiesburg

Red
Alexandria
Prichar
Mob
Biloxi

Baton Rouge
Lafayette
Lake Charles
Metairie
New Orleans

Marsh Island

Mississippi Delta

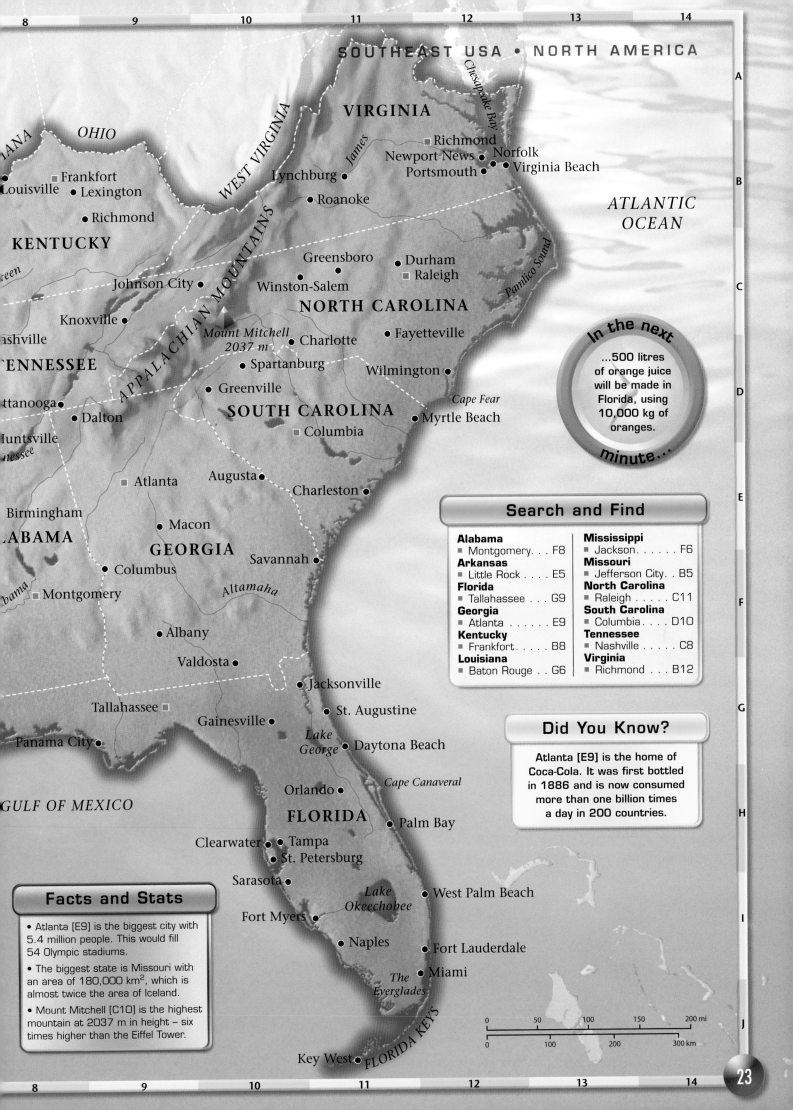

ATLANTIC OCEAN

GULF OF MEXICO

States and cities shown:

OHIO

KENTUCKY
Louisville
Frankfort
Lexington
Richmond

WEST VIRGINIA

VIRGINIA
Chesapeake Bay
Richmond
Newport News
Norfolk
Portsmouth
Virginia Beach
Lynchburg
Roanoke
James

TENNESSEE
Nashville
Knoxville
Johnson City
Chattanooga
Dalton
Huntsville

APPALACHIAN MOUNTAINS

NORTH CAROLINA
Greensboro
Durham
Raleigh
Winston-Salem
Fayetteville
Charlotte
Mount Mitchell 2037 m
Spartanburg
Wilmington
Pamlico Sound
Cape Fear

SOUTH CAROLINA
Greenville
Myrtle Beach
Columbia

ALABAMA
Birmingham
Montgomery

GEORGIA
Atlanta
Augusta
Charleston
Macon
Columbus
Savannah
Albany
Valdosta
Altamaha

FLORIDA
Tallahassee
Panama City
Jacksonville
St. Augustine
Gainesville
Lake George
Daytona Beach
Cape Canaveral
Orlando
Palm Bay
Clearwater
Tampa
St. Petersburg
Sarasota
Lake Okeechobee
West Palm Beach
Fort Myers
Naples
Fort Lauderdale
Miami
The Everglades
FLORIDA KEYS
Key West

In the next

...500 litres of orange juice will be made in Florida, using 10,000 kg of oranges.

minute...

Search and Find

Alabama		**Mississippi**	
Montgomery	F8	Jackson	F6
Arkansas		**Missouri**	
Little Rock	E5	Jefferson City	B5
Florida		**North Carolina**	
Tallahassee	G9	Raleigh	C11
Georgia		**South Carolina**	
Atlanta	E9	Columbia	D10
Kentucky		**Tennessee**	
Frankfort	B8	Nashville	C8
Louisiana		**Virginia**	
Baton Rouge	G6	Richmond	B12

Did You Know?

Atlanta [E9] is the home of Coca-Cola. It was first bottled in 1886 and is now consumed more than one billion times a day in 200 countries.

Facts and Stats

• Atlanta [E9] is the biggest city with 5.4 million people. This would fill 54 Olympic stadiums.

• The biggest state is Missouri with an area of 180,000 km², which is almost twice the area of Iceland.

• Mount Mitchell [C10] is the highest mountain at 2037 m in height – six times higher than the Eiffel Tower.

0   50   100   150   200 mi
0   100   200   300 km

Northwest USA and Alaska

Inland areas in northwest USA are either stunning mountain scenery or vast ranches. Washington's Seattle is the only large urban area, with the Boeing aircraft factory, and the headquarters of Microsoft, UPS, Starbucks and Amazon. The USA's biggest apple-growing region stretches from the Pacific Ocean to the Great Plains of the Dakotas. Alaska is the USA's largest state. However, vast areas are uninhabited due to long, severe winters. Alaska is one of the leading oil-producing regions in the world.

In the next ...Wyoming will produce 300 tonnes of coal – enough to produce electricity to power ten million TVs. minute...

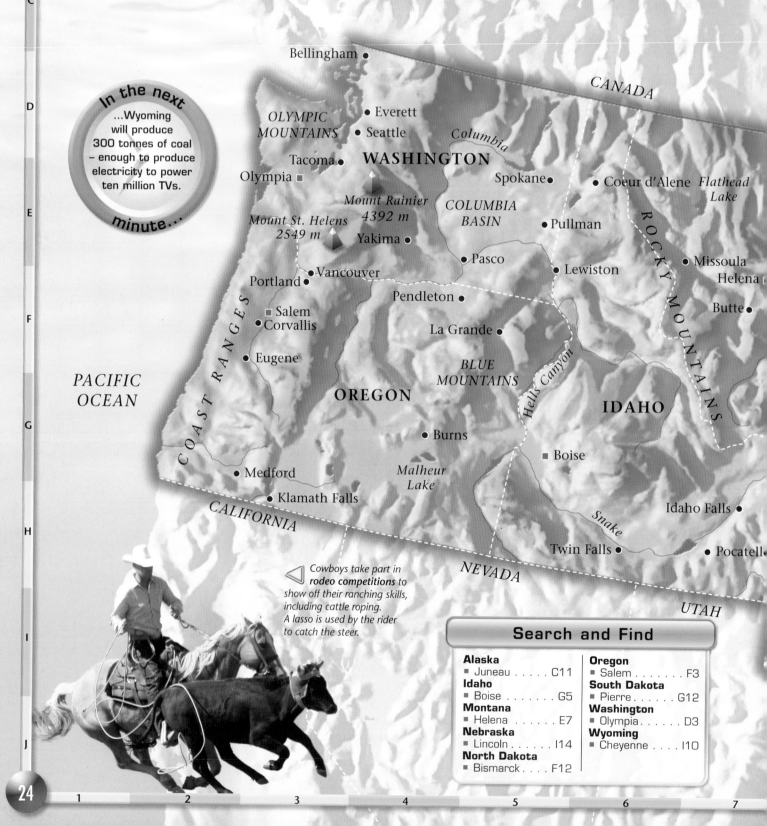

Bellingham

CANADA

OLYMPIC MOUNTAINS

Everett
Seattle

Columbia

Tacoma

WASHINGTON

Olympia

Spokane
Coeur d'Alene   Flathead Lake

Mount Rainier 4392 m

COLUMBIA BASIN

Pullman

Mount St. Helens 2549 m

Yakima

Missoula
Helena

Pasco

Lewiston

Butte

Vancouver

Portland

Pendleton

ROCKY MOUNTAINS

Salem
Corvallis

La Grande

Eugene

BLUE MOUNTAINS

Hells Canyon

COAST RANGES

OREGON

IDAHO

PACIFIC OCEAN

Burns

Boise

Medford

Malheur Lake

Idaho Falls

Klamath Falls

Snake

CALIFORNIA

Twin Falls

Pocatell

NEVADA

UTAH

Cowboys take part in **rodeo competitions** to show off their ranching skills, including cattle roping. A lasso is used by the rider to catch the steer.

Search and Find

ALASKA

CHUKCHI SEA

Wainwright
Point Hope •
• Barrow

St. Lawrence
Island
St. Matthew
Island

Noatak

Colville

BERING SEA

Nome •

Koyukuk

St. Paul
Island
Nunivak
Island
Hooper Bay

Yukon

Kobuk

Fort Yukon •

NEAR
ISLANDS

St. George
Island

Bethel •
• Kwethluk

Tanana •

• Alakanuk

Mount McKinley
6194 m

Fairbanks •

RAT
ISLANDS

ALEUTIAN ISLANDS

Dillingham •

ANDREANOF
ISLANDS

FOX
ISLANDS

Unimak
Island

Kenai
Seward

• Anchorage

• Cordova

• Kodiak

Kodiak
Island

Gulf of
Alaska

Yakutat •

PACIFIC
OCEAN

Juneau □

Sitka •

CANADA

Ketchikan •

0 100 200 300 400 500 mi
0 200 400 600 800 km

0 50 100 150 200 mi
0 100 200 300 km

eat Falls

Fort Peck
Lake

Missouri

• Williston

• Minot

Grand Forks •

MONTANA

Lake
Sakakawea

NORTH DAKOTA

G R E A T

Miles City •

Bismarck □ Jamestown •

Fargo •

MINNESOTA

zeman • Billings

P L A I N S

Lake
Oahe

• Aberdeen

Watertown •

wstone
nal Park

• Cody

BIGHORN
MOUNTAINS

• Gillette

Cheyenne

□ Pierre

SOUTH DAKOTA

kson

Rapid City •
◆
Mount
Rushmore

White

Lake
Francis
Case

Sioux Falls •

WYOMING

• Casper

Niobrara

• Yanktown

SAND HILLS

Norfolk •

IOWA

• Rock Springs

Loup

Laramie •
Cheyenne □

NEBRASKA

Omaha •

COLORADO

North Platte •

Grand Island •

Lincoln □

Platte

• Hastings

THE DISTANCE of the USA's Pacific coastline is 12,268 km and would take a migrating whale about 50 days to swim.

KANSAS

25

Southwest USA and Hawaii

PACIFIC
OCEAN

The nation's most dramatic landscape belongs to southwest USA, which is covered by the Rocky Mountains. Southern California, Nevada and Arizona are desert – the driest place being Death Valley. Texas is the home of the oil industry, and Nevada's Las Vegas attracts tourists visiting casinos and nearby scenery, such as the Grand Canyon. California has boomed due to the Hollywood film studios, Silicon Valley's large number of computer firms, and some of the most productive farmland in the country. Tropical Hawaii is a popular surfing and beach island 4800 km southwest of California.

Map labels:

OREGON
IDA...
Mount Shasta 4322 m
Eureka
Redding
Winnemucca
Humboldt
Elko
Reno
Carson City
COAST RANGES
Sacramento
Santa Rosa
NEVADA
Oakland
Stockton
San Francisco
Modesto
Yosemite National Park
Palo Alto
Sunnyvale
San Jose
Tonopah
GREAT BASIN
Salinas
Fresno
SIERRA NEVADA
Monterey
Mount Whitney 4418 m
Cedar City
San Luis Obispo
Bakersfield
Las Vegas
DEATH VALLEY
Hoover Dam
Grand Ca...
CALIFORNIA
ARIZO...
Santa Barbara
Oxnard
Pasadena
San Bernardino
Los Angeles
Riverside
Long Beach
Anaheim
Presc...
Oceanside
San Diego
Phoenix
Gila
Yuma

Search and Find

Hawaii map:

Mount Kawaikini 1598 m
Kauai
Kapaa
Niihau
KAUAI CHANNEL
Oahu
Waialua
Wahiawa
Kaneohe
Honolulu
Kalaupapa
Molokai
Maui
Lanai City
Wailuku
Lanai
Kahoolawe
ALENUIHAHA CHANNEL
PACIFIC OCEAN
Mauna Kea 4205 m
Hilo
HAWAII
Mauna Loa 4169 m

0   50   100   150 mi
0   100   200 km

Did You Know?

If California were its own country, it would have the eighth largest economy in the world.

Facts and Stats

- Texas is 678,051 km² in area – 6.5 times the area of Iceland.
- Los Angeles [F5] is the biggest city with 12.9 million people. This would fill 129 Olympic stadiums.
- Mount Whitney [D5] is the highest mountain at 4418 m in height – 14 times higher than the Eiffel Tower.

The Colorado river has carved a gorge over millions of years to form the **Grand Canyon** [E7]. It is up to 446 km in length and 1.6 km in depth.

In the next ...the Hoover Dam's [E6] power station will generate enough electricity to power 34.6 million light bulbs. **minute...**

THE DISTANCE across the Rocky Mountains [E9] is 1700 km and once took horse-drawn wagon trains more than six months to travel.

Canada

Canada is the second largest country in the world. The Rocky Mountains of western Canada reach more than 3600 m above sea level and create stunning scenery. Tourists sail along the coast to see icebergs and to view migrating whales. The largest Canadian cities are Toronto and Montreal in the east, and Vancouver in the west. Quebec differs from the rest of Canada because of the large French-speaking population that lives there. Canada has a wealth of natural resources, including wood and petroleum, and is one of the top ten richest nations.

Did You Know?

Canada has 10 percent of the world's forests. These are inhabited by a wide range of wildlife, including bears and moose.

Facts and Stats

- Canada is the second largest country in the world with an area of 10 million km² – 97 times the area of Iceland.
- Toronto [J11] is the biggest city with a population of 5.5 million – this would fill 55 Olympic stadiums.

ARCTIC OCEAN

BEAUFORT SEA

Ba
Isl

• Inuvik

ALASKA (US)

Mackenzie

Kugluktuk

• Dawson

Norman
Wells •

YUKON
TERRITORY

MACKENZIE MOUNTAINS

NORTHWEST
TERRITORIE

Mount Logan
5959 m

□ Whitehorse

Yellowknife ■

Gulf of
Alaska

Fort Resolution •

Fort Smith

PACIFIC
OCEAN

BRITISH
COLUMBIA

ROCKY

COAST

C A

Peace

QUEEN CHARLOTTE
ISLANDS

• Hazelton
• Prince Rupert

• Peace Rive

• Grande Prairie

Prince
George

MOUNTAINS

ALBERTA

■ Edmo

Fraser

• Red D

Vancouver
Island

• Kamloops

• Calgary

Vancouver •
Victoria ■

Medicine Hat

Lethbridge •

MOUNTAINS

•

UNITED STA

Deep in the Canadian Rockies is **Banff National Park** in Alberta, which was founded in 1885, and is Canada's oldest national park. Peyto Lake is a popular attraction as the water turns turquoise in colour as the surrounding glaciers melt.

▷ **Aurora Borealis** *can be seen in the Northern Hemisphere. Also known as the Northern Lights, the bands of shimmering light are caused by atmospheric particles crashing into the Earth's atmosphere.*

Search and Find

Alberta		**Nova Scotia**	
▪ Edmonton	H7	▪ Halifax	I13
British Columbia		**Nunavut**	
▪ Victoria	I5	▪ Iqaluit	F11
Canada		**Ontario**	
● Ottawa	I12	▪ Toronto	J11
Manitoba		**Prince Edward**	
▪ Winnipeg	I9	**Islands**	
New Brunswick		▪ Charlottetown	I13
▪ Fredericton	I13	**Quebec**	
Newfoundland and		▪ Quebec	I12
Labrador		**Saskatchewan**	
▪ St. John's	H14	▪ Regina	I8
Northwest		**Yukon Territory**	
Territories		▪ Whitehorse	F5
▪ Yellowknife	F7		

In the next …Canadians will consume 25 litres of maple syrup – a natural sugar from the sugar maple tree. **minute…**

GREENLAND (DENMARK)

Axel Heiberg Island

Ellesmere Island

Bathurst Island

Devon Island

Prince of Wales Island

Baffin Bay

Baffin Island

...oria ...nd

● Iqalukyuuttiaq

NUNAVUT

Southampton Island

Iqaluit ▪

● Salliit

LABRADOR SEA

Hudson Strait

Kangiqtiniq (Rankin Inlet) ●

Coats Island

Mansel Island

Ungava Peninsula

Feuilles

HUDSON BAY

Nain ●

LABRADOR

● Churchill

Churchill

Nelson

James Bay

La Grande Rivière

Goose Bay ●

NEWFOUNDLAND AND LABRADOR

● Flin Flon

...rince ...lbert

MANITOBA

Severn

ONTARIO

Fort Albany ●

QUEBEC

Anticosti Island

● Gander
St. John's ▪
Newfoundland

ST. PIERRE AND MIQUELON (FRANCE)

...askatoon

Albany

Chicoutimi ●

Gaspé ●

PRINCE EDWARD ISLANDS

● Regina
...se

Winnipeg ▪

Quebec ▪

NEW BRUNSWICK

Fredericton ▪

● Charlottetown

Brandon

Trois-Rivières

St. John

● Halifax

● Thunder Bay

Sherbrooke ●

Bay of Fundy

NOVA SCOTIA

...MERICA

Sudbury ●

Montreal ●

Ottawa ⬤

Georgian Bay

ATLANTIC OCEAN

Toronto ▪ ● Oshawa

Kitchener ● ● Hamilton

● London

● Windsor

🌐 **THE DISTANCE** from St. John's [H14] to Vancouver [I6] is further than St. John's to Prague, Europe.

Mexico

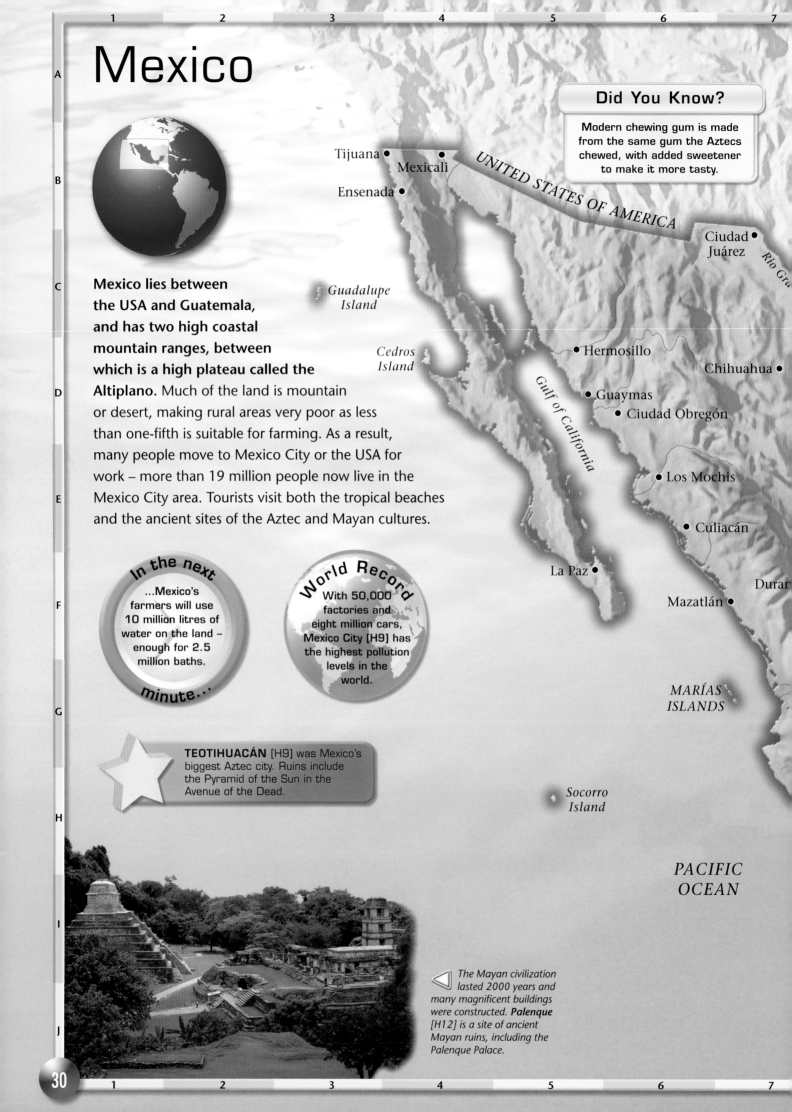

Did You Know?

Modern chewing gum is made from the same gum the Aztecs chewed, with added sweetener to make it more tasty.

Mexico lies between the USA and Guatemala, and has two high coastal mountain ranges, between which is a high plateau called the Altiplano. Much of the land is mountain or desert, making rural areas very poor as less than one-fifth is suitable for farming. As a result, many people move to Mexico City or the USA for work – more than 19 million people now live in the Mexico City area. Tourists visit both the tropical beaches and the ancient sites of the Aztec and Mayan cultures.

In the next ...Mexico's farmers will use 10 million litres of water on the land – enough for 2.5 million baths. **minute...**

World Record With 50,000 factories and eight million cars, Mexico City [H9] has the highest pollution levels in the world.

TEOTIHUACÁN [H9] was Mexico's biggest Aztec city. Ruins include the Pyramid of the Sun in the Avenue of the Dead.

Tijuana
Mexicali
Ensenada

UNITED STATES OF AMERICA

Ciudad Juárez

Río Gra

Guadalupe Island

Cedros Island

Gulf of California

Hermosillo

Chihuahua

Guaymas
Ciudad Obregón

Los Mochis

Culiacán

La Paz

Durar

Mazatlán

MARÍAS ISLANDS

Socorro Island

PACIFIC OCEAN

The Mayan civilization lasted 2000 years and many magnificent buildings were constructed. *Palenque* [H12] is a site of ancient Mayan ruins, including the Palenque Palace.

The stories of the ancient Mexican cultures are retold through ornately dressed **folk dancers**. The costumes and performances represent ancient Mayan dances for the gods.

Facts and Stats

• Mexico City [H9] has a population of 19.2 million people – this would fill 192 Olympic stadiums.

• The Rio Grande [C7] is 3060 km in length – less than half the length of the Nile river.

• The highest mountain is Volcan Pico de Orizaba [H10] at 5700 m in height. It is 18 times higher than the Eiffel Tower.

THE DISTANCE from east to west across Mexico City [H9] is only 30 km, but it takes more than three hours by car at peak times.

The Xochimilco area of Mexico City [H9] has many **ancient canals**. During festivals, boats are covered with flowers to attract tourists.

UNITED STATES OF AMERICA

Nuevo Laredo

ez Palacio • Monclova
rreón • Monterrey • Reynosa • Matamoros
Saltillo •

MEXICO

Ciudad Victoria

Ciudad Madero
San Luis Potosí • Tampico
Aguascalientes •

León • Querétaro
Guadalajara
Pachuca
Teotihuacán • Ecatepec
Morelia • Toluca
lima
Mexico City • Cuernavaca • Puebla • Orizaba
Volcan Pico de Orizaba 5700 m

Chilpancingo •
Oaxaca •
Acapulco •

GULF OF MEXICO

Bay of Campeche

Veracruz
Coatzacoalcos • Villahermosa
Palenque
Tuxtla Gutiérrez •

Mérida • Cancún •
Chichén Itzá
Cozumel Island
Yucatán Peninsula
Chetumal •

GUATEMALA BELIZE

Gulf of Tehuantepec

0 100 200 300 mi
0 200 400 km

South and Central America

BAHAMAS

CUBA

DOMINICAN
REPUBLIC

BELIZE

GUATEMALA

HONDURAS

EL SALVADOR

NICARAGUA

COSTA RICA

PANAMA

VENEZUELA

GUYANA

SURINAME

COLOMBIA

ECUADOR

PERU

BRAZIL

BOLIVIA

PACIFIC
OCEAN

CHILE

PARAGUAY

URUGUAY

ATLANTIC
OCEAN

ARGENTINA

KEY
1 HAITI
2 JAMAICA
3 ST. KITTS AND NEVIS
4 ANTIGUA AND BARBUDA
5 DOMINICA
6 ST. LUCIA
7 ST. VINCENT AND THE GRENADINES
8 GRENADA
9 BARBADOS
10 TRINIDAD AND TOBAGO

COUNTRY FACTFILE

Country	Life expectancy	Population in thousands	Population growth %	Population as urban %	Literacy %	Area km²	Population density per km²	Capital city	Currency	Languages
Antigua and Barbuda	75	77	1.3	92	86	442	174	St. John's	East Caribbean Dollar	English, Creole
Argentina	77	39,356	1.1	92	97.2	2,766,890	14.2	Buenos Aires	Argentine Peso	Spanish
Bahamas	66	304	0.5	87	96	13,939	21.8	Nassau	Bahamian Dollar	English, Creole
Barbados	74	272	0.4	52	99.7	430	632.6	Bridgetown	Barbadian Dollar	English, Bajan (Creole)
Belize	68	322	2.2	52	77	22,965	14	Belmopan	Belizean Dollar	English, Creole, Spanish
Bolivia	67	10,028	1.8	66	87	1,098,581	9.1	La Paz, Sucre	Boliviano	Spanish, Quechua, Aymara
Brazil	72	183,889	1.2	83	88.6	8,547,404	21.5	Brasília	Real	Portuguese
Chile	77	15,116	0.9	88	95.7	756,626	20	Santiago, Valparaiso	Chilean Peso	Spanish
Colombia	73	43,942	1.4	74	90.4	1,414,568	38.5	Bogotá	Colombian Peso	Spanish
Costa Rica	78	4299	1.4	65	96	51,100	84.1	San José	Costa Rican Colon	Spanish
Cuba	77	11,239	0.2	74	99.8	110,861	101.4	Havana	Cuban Peso	Spanish
Dominica	76	71	0.2	71	94	739	96.1	Roseau	East Caribbean Dollar	English, French Creole
Dominican Republic	74	8562	1.5	69	87	48,443	176.7	Santo Domingo	Domincan Peso	Spanish
Ecuador	75	12,157	1.5	66	91	269,178	45.2	Quito	US Dollar	Spanish, Quechua
El Salvador	72	6875	1.7	61	80.2	21,041	326.7	San Salvador	US Dollar	Spanish
Grenada	66	103	0.5	34	96	344	299.4	St. George's	East Caribbean Dollar	English, French Creole
Guatemala	70	11,237	2.1	48	69.1	108,889	103.2	Guatemala City	Quetzal	Spanish
Guyana	67	751	0.2	36	98.8	215,083	3.5	Georgetown	Guyanese Dollar	English, Creole
Haiti	61	9013	1.8	47	52.9	27,750	324.8	Port-au-Prince	Gourde	French, Creole
Honduras	69	6535	2	48	80	112,088	58.3	Tegucigalpa	Lempira	Spanish
Jamaica	74	2608	0.8	53	87.9	10,991	237.2	Kingston	Jamaican Dollar	English, Creole
Nicaragua	72	5142	1.8	57	67.5	130,670	39.4	Managua	Gold Cordoba	Spanish
Panama	77	3228	1.5	73	91.9	75,990	42.5	Panama City	Balboa, US Dollar	Spanish, English
Paraguay	76	5163	2.4	60	94	406,752	12.8	Asunción	Guarani	Spanish, Guarani
Peru	71	28,221	1.2	71	92.9	1,285,216	22	Lima	Nuevo Sol	Spanish, Quechua
St. Kitts and Nevis	73	46	0.8	43	97.8	269	170.6	Basseterre	East Caribbean Dollar	English, Creole
St. Lucia	76	158	0.4	48	90.1	617	256.1	Castries	East Caribbean Dollar	English, French Creole
St. Vincent and the Grenadines	74	103	-0.3	55	96	398	264.8	Kingstown	East Caribbean Dollar	English, Creole
Suriname	74	493	1.1	75	89.6	163,270	3	Paramaribo	Suriname Dollar	Dutch, Sranantonga, Hindi
Trinidad and Tobago	71	1262	−0.1	72	98.6	5128	246.1	Port-of-Spain	Trinidad and Tobago Dollar	English
Uruguay	76	3445	0.5	92	98	176,215	19.5	Montevideo	Uruguayan Peso	Spanish
Venezuela	74	27,483	1.5	93	93	912,050	30.1	Caracas	Bolivar	Spanish

Central America and the Caribbean

Central America is a narrow area of land where the mountain chain continues from Antarctica up to Alaska. The only gap, which joins the Atlantic and Pacific Oceans, is the Panama Canal. The manmade canal shortens the journey between the oceans by 13,000 km. The Caribbean islands are mainly agricultural, but their sandy beaches, warm seas and links to the USA and Europe make them popular tourist destinations. Venezuela is one of the world's leading oil producers and is much wealthier than Colombia and Guyana.

In many places in Central America, **weaving** is still done by hand rather than by machine. Colourful rugs and tapestries from the region are sold around the world.

Havana
Guanabacoa
Pinar del Río
Cárdenas
Santa Clara
Nueva Gerona
Cienfuegos
Sancti Spíri
Isla de la
Juventud
Camagüe
CU

MEXICO

BELIZE
Belize City
MAYA
MOUNTAINS
Belmopan
Quezaltenango
San Antonio
GUATEMALA
San Pedro
Guatemala
Sula
La Ceiba
City
El Progreso
Escuintla
HONDURAS
San Salvador
Tegucigalpa
EL SALVADOR
Chinandega
Estelí
León
NICARAGUA
Managua

CAYMAN
ISLANDS
(UK)
Montego Ba
JAMAICA
Sp
T

COSTA RICA
San José
Puntarenas
Limón
Cerro Chirripó
Grande 3819 m
Panama
Canal
Colón
David
San Miguelito
PANAMA
Panama City
Gulf of
Panama

Gulf of
Darien
Barran
Cartager
CORDILLERA CENTRAL
Sincele
Mont

Medellí
Quibdó
Manizales
Pereira
Armenia
Buenaventura
Ibagu
Cali
Popayán
Pasto
CORDILLE
ECUADOR

Search and Find

0   100   200   300   400 mi
0   200   400   600 km

Facts and Stats

• Colombia has a population of 44 million people – this would fill 440 Olympic stadiums.

• The life expectancy of people in Haiti is only 61 years, compared to 77 years in Cuba and a world average of 68 years.

• The average income per person in Haiti is £560 and £10,200 in the Bahamas, compared to a world average of £3500.

8 9 10 11 12 13 14

A

There are two lakes in the craters of the **Poas volcano**, Costa Rica. Due to geothermal activity, it is believed that the lakes are turning into geysers. Since 1828, the volcano has erupted 39 times.

ssau

B

BAHAMAS

TURKS AND CAICOS ISLANDS (UK)

olguín
amo • Guantánamo
go Cap-Haïtien •
ba Gonaïves •
DOMINICAN REPUBLIC
Santiago • San Francisco de Macorís

C

La Vega •
ort-au-Prince
ston • La Romana •
Les Cayes Jacmel
Santo Domingo
HAITI

VIRGIN ISLANDS (US) ANGUILLA (UK)
ST. MARTIN (NETH. AND FRANCE)
ST. BARTHÉLÉMY (FRANCE)
ST. EUSTATIUS (NETH.)

PUERTO RICO (US) *SABA (NETH.)*
Basseterre •
ST. KITTS AND NEVIS
MONTSERRAT (UK)
ANTIGUA AND BARBUDA
St. John's •

D

CARIBBEAN SEA

GUADELOUPE (FRANCE)
DOMINICA
Roseau •
MARTINIQUE (FRANCE)
Castries •
ST. LUCIA

...Venezuela will extract enough oil from the Earth to make 220,000 litres of petrol.

In the next minute...

E

ARUBA (NETHERLANDS)
CURAÇAO (NETHERLANDS)
BONAIRE (NETHERLANDS)

ST. VINCENT AND THE GRENADINES
Kingstown •
GRENADA
St. George's •
BARBADOS
Bridgetown •

World Record
At more than 979 m in height, Angel Falls [G11] is the highest waterfall in the world.

a Pico Cristobal Colon 5800 m
lad
• Maracaibo
Barquisimeto •
Valera •
• Acarigua
• Guanare
• Barinas
Port-of-Spain
Caracas • Cumaná
• Valencia • Barcelona
TRINIDAD AND TOBAGO

F

cuta •
• San Cristóbal
• Bucaramanga
rancabermeja
Ciudad Bolívar •
• Ciudad Guayana

G

• Tunja
Río Meta
VENEZUELA
Angel Falls ◆
• Puerto Ayacucho
GUIANA HIGHLANDS
Georgetown •
Paramaribo •
FRENCH GUIANA (FRANCE)

Bogotá
• Villavicencio
BRAZIL
GUYANA
SURINAME

H

COLOMBIA
Río Vaupés
Río Apaporis
BRAZIL
BRAZIL

I

Caquetá

Did You Know?

The Bermuda Triangle is an area in the Atlantic Ocean, northeast of the Caribbean. Many ships and aircraft have disappeared here without a trace.

PERU

THE DISTANCE from one end of the Panama Canal [F6] to the other is only 77 km, but it saves 18 days sailing time.

J

8 9 10 11 12 13 14

South America

Stretching from the tropical forests of the Amazon to just a short distance from icy Antarctica, South America is a continent of contrasts. The Andes stretch the length of the continent, but the main feature is the Amazon rainforest. The rainforest is home to more plant and animal species than any other habitat in the world. However, more than 52,000 km² of the rainforest is destroyed each year to make room for farmland. The forest not only provides a home to many animals, but it is also the source of many plant-derived medicines. By absorbing carbon dioxide, the forest helps to reduce global warming.

◁ At 6448 km in length, the **Amazon river** crosses the full width of Brazil. A wide range of wildlife live in the river, including the endangered boto, or Amazon river dolphin.

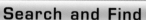

Search and Find

Argentina
- Buenos Aires . . G8

Bolivia
- La Paz D7
- Sucre E7

Brazil
- Brasília D10

Chile
- Santiago G7

- Valparaíso G6

Ecuador
- Quito B5

Paraguay
- Asunción E8

Peru
- Lima. D5

Uruguay
- Montevideo . . . G8

In the next ...9000 tonnes of the Amazon rainforest will be destroyed – about 100 trees and other plants. minute...

▷ The statue of Jesus, **Christ the Redeemer**, stands at the top of Mount Corcovado, Rio de Janeiro [E10]. At 38 m in height, it is one of the most famous landmarks in the world.

VENEZU

Esmeraldas •
• Ibarra
Manta • • **Quito**
Portoviejo • • Ambato
Guayaquil • • Riobamba
Negro
COLOMBIA
Amazon
ECUADOR
• Iquitos
AMAZO
BASIN
Piura •
Chiclayo •
Pucallpa •
Porto Velho
Trujillo •
Chimbote •
• Rio Branc
PERU
Huacho •
Callao • **Lima** • Huancayo
Ayacucho • • Cusco
Ica •
BOLIV
Lake
Titicaca
Juliaca • • Puno
Arequipa •
Cochaba
La Paz
Oruro •
Sucre
Arica •
Nevado Sajama
6520 m • Potosí
Iquique •
Tarija
Calama • San Salv
ATACAMA de Ju
Antofagasta • DESERT

PACIFIC OCEAN

CHILE
San Miguel
de Tucumán
ARG
La Serena •
Coquimbo •
• Córd
San Juan •
Godoy Cruz •
Viña del Mar •
• Cu
Valparaíso • • Mendoz
Santiago • Cerro
Rancagua • Aconcagu
6959 m
Talcahuano • • Chillán
Concepción •
Los Ángeles •
Temuco • Neuqu
Valdivia •
Osorno •
Puerto Montt •
Comod
Rivada
PATAGONIA
Puer
Mad
Río
Gallo
Punta Arenas •
Ushu

8 9 10 11 12 13 14

A
B
C
D
E
F
G
H
I
J

GUYANA
SURINAME
FRENCH GUIANA (FRANCE)

Amapá

Macapá

Marajó Island

Belém

São Luis

Parnaíba

Amazon

Manaus

Altamira

Santarém

Fortaleza

Marabá

Imperatriz

Teresina

Mossoró

Natal

Campina Grande

João Pessoa

Araguaína

Juazeiro do Norte

Recife

BRAZIL

Tocantins

Juazeiro

Maceio

Aracaju

Feira de Santana

Salvador

Cuiabá

Taguatinga

Brasília

Itabuna

Anápolis

MATO GROSSO PLATEAU

Goiânia

Campo Grande

Uberlândia

Uberaba

Governador Valadares

Rio Préto

Belo Horizonte

Vitoria

Nova Iguaçu

Pedro Juan Caballero

Campinas

São Paulo

Niteroi

Rio de Janeiro

ARAGUAY

sunción

Ciudad del Este

Santos

Curitiba

CO esistencia

Corrientes

Florianópolio

TINA

Porto Alegre

Salto

Rivera

Pelotas

ta Fe

Rivera

Rio Grande

sario

URUGUAY

ATLANTIC OCEAN

omas

Buenos Aires

Montevideo

amora

La Plata

ahía lanca

Mar del Plata

unta Alta

0 200 400 600 800 mi
0 400 800 1200 km

FALKLAND ISLANDS (UK)

SOUTH GEORGIA (UK)

Horn

Did You Know?

The Amazon river holds two-thirds of all the flowing water in the world and is 270 km in width where it meets the sea.

Extreme Weather

Chile's Atacama Desert [E7] has an average rainfall of less than 0.5 mm a year. The city of Calama [E7] has never recorded a single drop. It's too dry for animals to survive.

USHUAIA [J7] is the most southern city in the world. It has a ski resort and a base for supply ships to Antarctica.

THE DISTANCE from Chile to the next land mass of Australia is 10,400 km and would take 12 hours by plane.

One of the largest **street carnivals** in the world is held every February in Rio de Janeiro [E10]. People dress in elaborate costumes and parades take place in the city centre. More than 200,000 people take part.

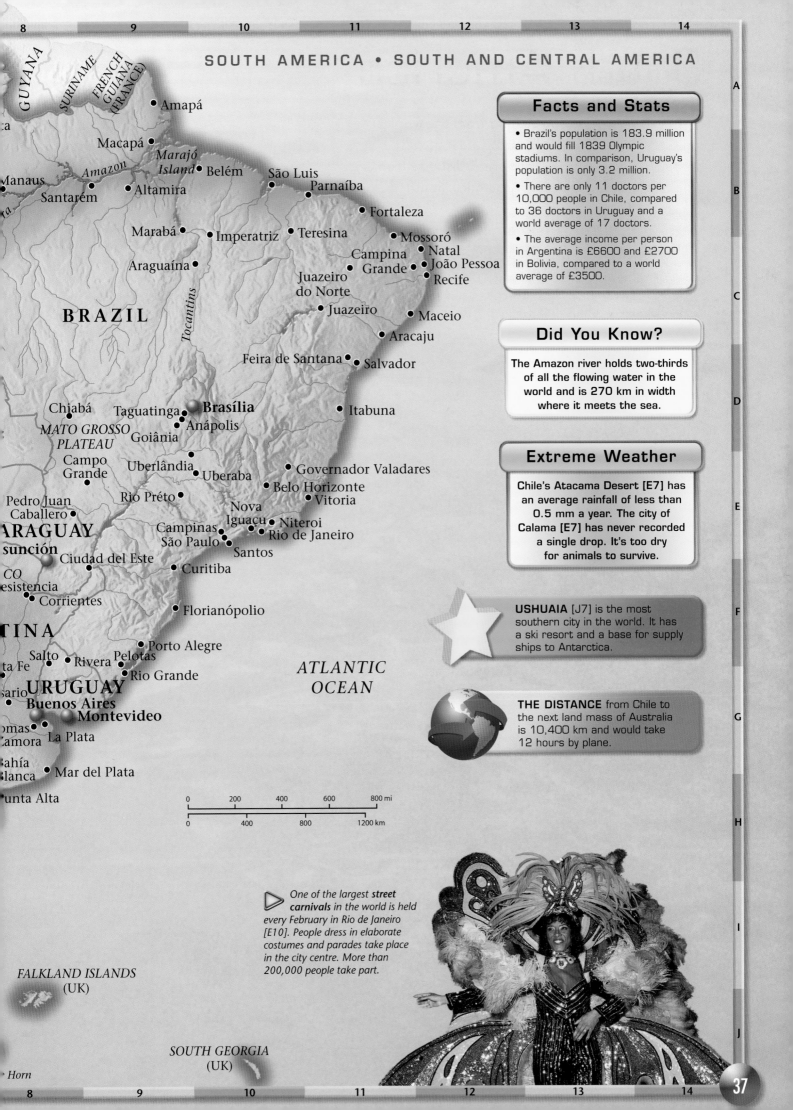

Europe

ARCTIC OCEAN

ICELAND

FINLAND

NORWAY SWEDEN

ESTONIA

LATVIA

RUSSIAN
FEDERATION

DENMARK

1

2

UNITED
KINGDOM

POLAND

BELARUS

REPUBLIC OF
IRELAND

3

GERMANY

4

UKRAINE

5

11

6

*ATLANTIC
OCEAN*

FRANCE

12

10

7

8

13

14

15

16

9

23

17

18

ROMANIA

SPAIN

24

19

20 21

22

BULGARIA

GEORGIA

26

AZERBAIJAN

PORTUGAL

ITALY

GREECE

25

KEY

1 RUSSIAN FEDERATION	14 MONACO
2 LITHUANIA	15 SLOVENIA
3 NETHERLANDS	16 CROATIA
4 BELGIUM	17 BOSNIA AND HERZEGOVINA
5 LUXEMBOURG	18 SERBIA
6 CZECH REPUBLIC	19 MONTENEGRO
7 SLOVAKIA	20 KOSOVO
8 MOLDOVA	21 MACEDONIA
9 HUNGARY	22 ALBANIA
10 AUSTRIA	23 SAN MARINO
11 LIECHTENSTEIN	24 VATICAN CITY
12 SWITZERLAND	25 MALTA
13 ANDORRA	26 ARMENIA

COUNTRY FACTFILE

Country	Life expectancy	Population in thousands	Population growth %	Population as urban %	Literacy %	Area km²	Population density per km²	Capital city	Currency	Languages
Albania	78	3069	0.5	47	98.7	28,748	106.8	Tiranë	Lek	Albanian
Andorra	83	83	1.1	95	100	468	177.6	Andorra la Vella	Euro	Catalan, Spanish
Armenia	73	3230	-0.03	70	99.4	29,743	108.6	Yerevan	Dram	Armenian
Austria	80	8332	0.05	67	98	83,858	99.3	Vienna	Euro	German
Azerbaijan*	67	8630	0.8	57	98.8	86,600	99.7	Baku	Manat	Azeri
Belarus	71	9751	-0.4	73	99.6	207,546	47	Minsk	Belarusian Rouble	Belarusian, Russian
Belgium	79	10,667	0.1	97	99	30,528	349.4	Brussels	Euro	Dutch, French
Bosnia and Herzegovina	79	3842	0.3	47	96.7	51,129	75.1	Sarajevo	Marka	Croat, Serb
Bulgaria	73	7679	-0.8	70	98.2	110,993	69.2	Sofia	Lev	Bulgarian
Croatia	75	4436	-0.05	58	98.1	56,542	78.5	Zagreb	Kuna	Croat
Czech Republic	77	10,381	-0.09	75	99	78,864	131.6	Prague	Czech Koruna	Czech
Denmark	78	5476	0.3	87	99.1	43,094	127.1	Copenhagen	Danish Krone	Danish
Estonia	73	1341	-0.6	69	99.8	45,227	29.7	Tallinn	Estonian Kroon	Estonian, Russian
Finland	79	5300	0.1	67	100	338,145	15.7	Helsinki	Euro	Finnish, Swedish
France	81	61,399	0.5	77	99	547,030	112.2	Paris	Euro	French
Georgia	77	4632	-0.3	68	99	69,492	66.7	Tbilisi	Lari	Georgian
Germany	79	82,218	-0.05	88	99	357,021	230.3	Berlin	Euro	German
Greece	80	11,214	0.1	61	96	131,957	85	Athens	Euro	Greek
Hungary	73	10,045	-0.3	68	99.4	93,030	108	Budapest	Forint	Hungarian
Iceland	81	313	0.7	93	99	102,819	3	Reykjavik	Icelandic Krona	Icelandic
Ireland, Republic of	78	4240	1.1	61	99	70,285	60.3	Dublin	Euro	English, Irish (Gaelic)
Italy	80	59,619	-0.05	68	98.4	301,277	197.9	Rome	Euro	Italian
Kosovo	78	2,100	-0.5	40	91.9	10,887	192.9	Pristina	Euro	Albania
Latvia	72	2271	-0.6	69	99.7	64,610	35.1	Riga	Latvian Lat	Latvian, Russian
Liechtenstein	80	35.4	0.7	45	100	160	221.3	Vaduz	Swiss Franc	German
Lithuania	75	3336	-0.3	68	99.6	65,301	51.5	Vilnius	Litas	Lithuanian, Russian
Luxembourg	79	484	1.2	88	100	2586	187.2	Luxembourg	Euro	Letzeburgish, German, French
Macedonia	75	2023	0.3	67	96.1	25,713	78.7	Skopje	Macedonian Denar	Macedonian, Albanian
Malta	79	410	0.4	94	92.8	316	1297.5	Valletta	Euro	Maltese, English
Moldova	71	3958	-0.08	48	99.1	33,873	116.8	Chisinau	Moldovan Leu	Romanian (Moldovan), Russian, Ukrainian
Monaco	80	31.1	0.4	100	99	2	15,550	Monaco	Euro	French, Monegasque, Italian
Montenegro	75	620	-0.9	60	97	13,812	44.9	Podgorica	Euro	Serb, Albanian
Netherlands	79	16,487	0.4	91	99	41,526	397	Amsterdam, The Hague	Euro	Dutch, Frisian
Norway	80	4779	0.3	77	100	323,878	14.8	Oslo	Norwegian Krone	Norwegian
Poland	76	38,116	-0.05	66	99.8	312,685	121.9	Warsaw	Zloty	Polish
Portugal	78	10,618	0.3	64	93.3	92,391	114.9	Lisbon	Euro	Portuguese
Romania	72	21,623	-0.1	55	97.3	237,500	91	Bucharest	Leu	Romanian
Russian Federation	66	142,754	-0.5	78	99.4	17,075,400	8.4	Moscow	Rouble	Russian, Tatar, Ukrainian
San Marino	82	30.8	1.1	94	96	61	504.9	San Marino	Euro	Italian
Serbia	74	7382	-0.5	52	96.4	77,474	95.3	Belgrade	Serbian Dinar	Serb, Hungarian
Slovakia	75	5401	0.1	57	99.6	49,036	110.1	Bratislava	Euro	Slovak, Hungarian
Slovenia	77	2010	-0.1	51	99.7	20,273	99.1	Ljubljana	Euro	Slovenian
Spain	80	46,158	0.07	78	97.9	504,782	91.4	Madrid	Euro	Spanish (Castilian), Catalan, Basque, Gallego
Sweden	81	9183	0.2	83	99	449,964	20.4	Stockholm	Swedish Krona	Swedish
Switzerland	81	7593	0.3	73	99	41,285	183.9	Bern	Swiss Franc	German, French, Italian
Ukraine	68	46,373	-0.6	68	99.4	603,700	76.8	Kiev	Hryvnia	Ukrainian, Russian
United Kingdom	79	60,975	0.3	90	99	244,088	249.8	London	British Pound	English
Vatican City	N/A	0.56	N/A	100	100	0.44	1272.7	Vatican City	Euro	Italian, Latin

* Although Azerbaijan is a member of some European organizations, it is historically and culturally part of western Asia
NB: Cyprus is part of Europe, but the mapping can be found in the Asia section

The British Isles

The United Kingdom (England, Scotland, Wales and Northern Ireland) and the Republic of Ireland make up the British Isles. The UK has become one of the most influential and prosperous countries in the world. By 1900, the British Empire ruled many countries, including Canada, South Africa, India and Australia, which is why so many nations speak English. Ireland declared independence in 1919, but it only came into effect in 1922. Scotland, Wales and Northern Ireland now have their own parliaments. Manufacturing was once the major industry, but most wealth is now generated by banking, insurance and high-tech equipment.

The **Giant's Causeway** [E7] in Northern Ireland is made up of 40,000 columns created by a volcanic eruption. The columns measure up to 12 m in height. According to legend, the giant Finn McCool began to build the causeway towards Scotland, but he fell asleep before he finished it.

Search and Find

England
- London H10

Northern Ireland
- Belfast F7

Republic of Ireland
- Dublin G7

Scotland
- Edinburgh E8

Wales
- Cardiff H8

THE DISTANCE from Land's End [I7] to John o'Groats [C9] once took a cyclist 41 hours and a runner 12 days to complete.

ATLANTIC OCEAN

OUTER HEBRIDES

Lewi

Sk

Giant's Causewa

Londonde

NORTHERN
IRELAND

B

Sligo

Arm

REPUBLIC
OF IRELAND

Drogheda

IR
S

Galway

Shannon

Liffey

Du

WICKLOW
MOUNTAINS

Limerick

Carrantuohill
1041 m

Waterford

Cork

ST. GEORGE'S CHAN

Edinburgh [E8], Scotland, is the second most visited city after London. More than 13 million people are attracted to the city each year to see historical sights, such as Edinburgh Castle, or to attend the Edinburgh Festival in August.

ISLES OF
SCILLY   Land's
End

SHETLAND
ISLANDS

Lerwick

ORKNEY
ISLANDS

John o'Groats

▷ **Snowdonia National Park** [G8], Wales, was created in 1951 and covers 2142 km² of land. More than 26,000 people actually live within the area and it receives more than six million visitors a year. The area is a mixture of forest, open land, coast and mountains – making it popular with hikers.

Inverness

COTLAND

Ben Nevis
1343 m

APIAN MOUNTAINS

Aberdeen

Perth   Dundee

Falkirk

asgow   Edinburgh

Ayr

NORTH
SEA

Scale:
0   50   100   150 mi
0   100   200 km

THE TOWER OF LONDON [H10] has been a castle, a royal palace, a prison, a zoo and the home of the crown jewels.

Newcastle
upon Tyne

Carlisle   Sunderland

Scafell Pike
977 m

Middlesbrough

E
1AN
K)

York

Blackpool   Leeds   Hull

owdon   Liverpool   Manchester
085 m

Chester   Sheffield

ENGLAND

Wrexham   Stoke-on-Trent

Trent

WALES

Aberystwyth   Derby   Nottingham

Leicester   Peterborough

Birmingham   Norwich

Coventry

Ouse

AMBRIAN
OUNTAINS

Wye   Severn

Northampton   Cambridge

Ipswich

ansea   Gloucester   Colchester

Cardiff   Swindon   Oxford

Bristol   Thames   **London**

Avebury Stone Circle ◆   Reading

◆ Stonehenge   Dover

Southampton   Portsmouth

Exeter   Bournemouth   Brighton

Plymouth

Isle of
Wight

ENGLISH CHANNEL

Guernsey
CHANNEL Jersey
ISLANDS (UK)

In the next minute...
...133 passengers will arrive or depart from London's Heathrow Airport, one of the busiest airports in the world.

Facts and Stats

• London [H10] is the biggest city with 8.3 million people. This would fill 83 Olympic stadiums.

• The Shannon [G6] is the longest river at 386 km in length. However, it is more than 17 times shorter than the Nile river.

• Ben Nevis [D8] is the highest mountain at 1343 m in height – four times higher than the Eiffel Tower.

Did You Know?

Avebury Stone Circle [I9] is 6000 years old, and is the largest ancient stone monument in the world.

▷ The **Millennium Bridge**, London [H10], was opened in 2000, and is used as a pedestrian footbridge. It has been designed to hold 5000 people at any one time. St. Paul's Cathedral is situated at its north end and the Tate Modern art gallery is at the south end.

Scandinavia

Norway, Sweden, Denmark, Finland and Iceland are Europe's most northerly and least populated countries. Mainland Scandinavia stretches from Norway's mountainous Atlantic coast in the west to Finland's low-lying forested countryside in the east. More than one-third lies within the Arctic Circle where, during a 73-day winter period, the Sun never rises. Norway and Iceland are not members of the European Union. Living standards are high due to vast natural resources, such as oil, gas, timber and iron. Scandinavia has a reputation for stylish designs with brands such as Bang and Olufsen, Ikea and Volvo.

In the next ...minute...

...Sweden will make more than two million matches – enough to fill 40,000 boxes.

World Record

Finland has more of its territory covered by lakes than any other country – 187,888 lakes cover 10 percent of the country.

Facts and Stats

- Sweden's population of 9.2 million would fill 92 Olympic stadiums.
- The life expectancy of people in Sweden is 81 years, compared to 78 years in Denmark and a world average of 68 years.
- The average income per person in Norway is £19,900, compared to a world average of £3500.

Did You Know?

The first Legoland was opened in Billund [I6], Denmark, in 1968. On average, every person in the world owns 52 Lego bricks.

◁ **Sognefjord [F5], Norway,** is the second largest fjord in the world. Towns are situated on the fjord and the stunning scenery attracts many tourists, which helps to support the economy.

Lofoten Island

Bode

ATLANTIC OCEAN

Kristiansund •

Ålesund •

Trondheim   Östersun

NORWAY

Sognefjord   ▲ Galdhøpiggen 2469 m

Bergen •   • Voss

• Lillehammer

Hamar •

Haugesund •

Stavanger •

Oslo

Drammen •

Skien •   Fredrikstad   Karlstad

Öre

Kristiansand •

Linköpi

Skagerrak

Göteborg   Borås

NORTH SEA

Jönköp

Ålborg •   *Kattegat*

Halmstad   Vä

DENMARK

• Randers

Århus •   • Helsingborg   Karlsham

Billund •

Esbjerg •

Copenhagen

Karlskr

• Odense   • Lund

Kolding •   • Roskilde   Malmö

BORNHOLM (DENMARK

GERMANY

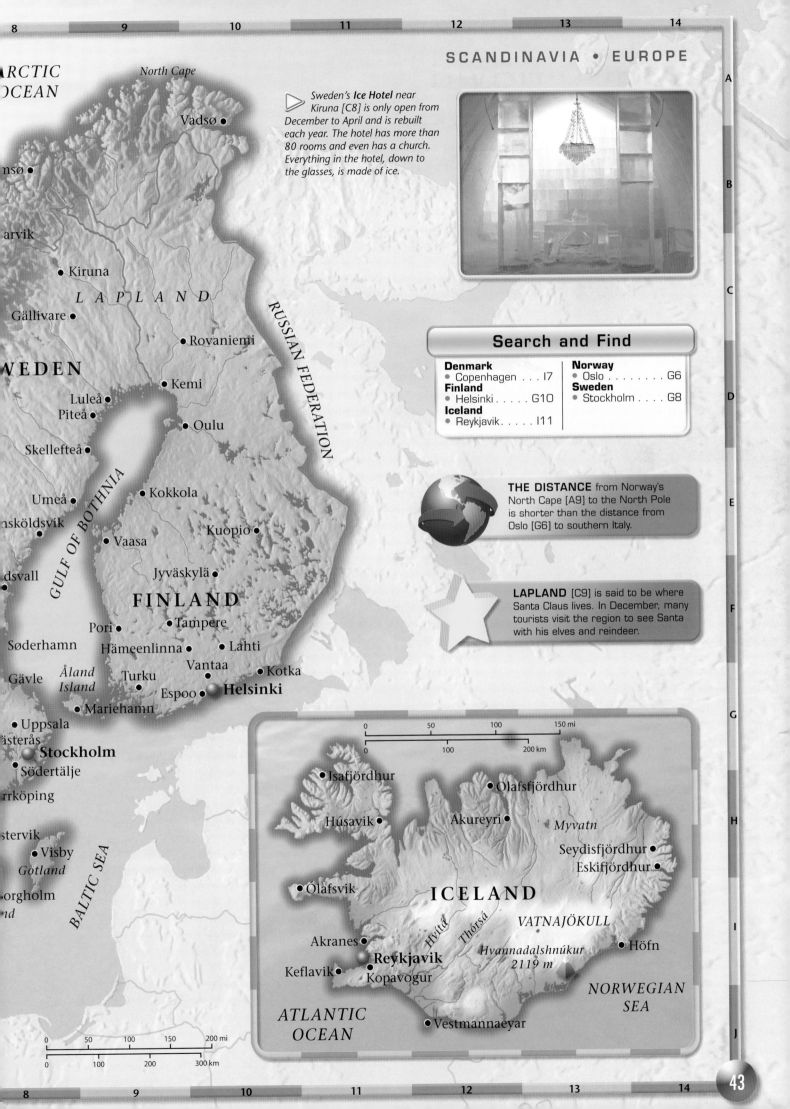

ARCTIC
OCEAN

North Cape

Vadsø •

nsø •

arvik

• Kiruna

L A P L A N D

Gällivare •

WEDEN

• Rovaniemi

RUSSIAN FEDERATION

• Kemi

Luleå •
Piteå •

• Oulu

Skellefteå •

• Kokkola

Umeå •

Kuopio •

nsköldsvik •

• Vaasa

dsvall •

• Jyväskylä

FINLAND

• Tampere

Pori •

Söderhamn •   Hämeenlinna •   • Lahti

Åland   • Vantaa   • Kotka
Gävle •   *Island*   Turku •

Espoo • • **Helsinki**

• Mariehamn

• Uppsala

ästerås •

• **Stockholm**

• Södertälje

rrköping

stervik •

• Visby
Gotland

GULF OF BOTHNIA

orgholm
nd

BALTIC SEA

> Sweden's **Ice Hotel** near Kiruna [C8] is only open from December to April and is rebuilt each year. The hotel has more than 80 rooms and even has a church. Everything in the hotel, down to the glasses, is made of ice.

Search and Find

Denmark		Norway	
• Copenhagen . . . I7		• Oslo G6	
Finland		**Sweden**	
• Helsinki G10		• Stockholm G8	
Iceland			
• Reykjavik I11			

THE DISTANCE from Norway's North Cape [A9] to the North Pole is shorter than the distance from Oslo [G6] to southern Italy.

LAPLAND [C9] is said to be where Santa Claus lives. In December, many tourists visit the region to see Santa with his elves and reindeer.

0   50   100   150 mi
0   100   200 km

• Isafjördhur

• Olafsfjördhur

Húsavik •   Akureyri •   *Myvatn*

Seydisfjördhur •
Eskifjördhur •

Ólafsvik •

ICELAND

VATNAJÖKULL

Hvítá *Thórsá*

Akranes •   *Hvannadalshnúkur*   • Höfn
                   2119 m

Keflavik • • **Reykjavik**
           • Kopavogur

*NORWEGIAN
SEA*

*ATLANTIC
OCEAN*

• Vestmannaeyar

0   50   100   150   200 mi
0   100   200   300 km

Spain and Portugal

The Iberian Peninsula is occupied by Spain and Portugal. Africa is less than 16 km from the Strait of Gibraltar, and to the north Spain is bordered by France and the mountain state of Andorra. Spain also includes the Balearic Islands in the Mediterranean Sea and the Canary Islands, Tenerife and Gran Canaria, which lie 100 km west of Africa in the Atlantic Ocean. Well-known for olive, orange and lemon groves, as well as hot weather and sandy beaches, these countries attract millions of tourists each year.

The costas of Spain are popular coastal regions. **Costa Brava [C13]** in northeast Spain is in the vicinity of Barcelona. S'Agaró is an exclusive resort, and its hotels have even been used in films.

THE DISTANCE from the east to the west side of the border between Spain and Gibraltar [I7] is only 800 m.

BILBAO [B9] is home to many museums including the Fine Arts Museum and the world-famous Guggenheim Museum.

Facts and Stats

- Spain's population of 46.2 million would fill 462 Olympic stadiums. However, the population of Andorra is only 67,000 and would only fill half a stadium.
- The life expectancy of people in Spain is 80 years, compared to a world average of 68 years.
- The average income per person in Andorra is £20,000, compared to a world average of £3500.

Did You Know?

Sardines are the most popular Portuguese seafood. The average consumption for a person is 6 kg a year.

El Ferrol
La Coruña
Gijón
Ov
Lugo
Santiago de Compostela
CANTABRIAN
Sil
León
Orense
Vigo
Braga
Zamor
Guimaraes
Duero
Tormes
Porto
Salamanca
Aveiro
SIER
Coimbra
Tajo (T
Tajo (Tagus)
Cáceres
Santarém
PORTUGAL
Mérida
Estoril   Lisbon
Badajoz
Almada
Setúbal
Évora
Beja
Guadiana
Guadalq
Lagos
Seville
ATLANTIC OCEAN
Faro
Huelva
Moron de la Frontera
Arcos
Jerez de la Frontera
Ron
Cádiz
GIBRAL
(UK
Algeciras
Strait of Gibra
CEU
(SPA
MOROCC

8 9 10 11 12 13 14

A

BAY OF BISCAY

Santander

San Sebastián

Bilbao

FRANCE

Vitória-Gasteiz   Pamplona

Pico de Aneto 3405 m

ANDORRA

Logroño

P Y R E N E E S

Andorra la Vella

Burgos

Gállego

Girona

Palencia

Ebro

Cinca

Manresa

Mataró

Soria

Saragossa

Lleida

Terrasa

Costa Brava

Barcelona

lladolid

Duero

Reus   Tarragona

Costa Dorada

Tortosa

ovia

la

Morella

Menorca

GREDOS

Guadalajara

Teruel

Mallorca

Mahón

Alcalá de Henares

Madrid

Castellón de la Plana

Palma

Cuenca

Turia

oledo   Aranjuez

Sagunto

Costa del Azahar

BALEARIC ISLANDS

Valencia

SPAIN

Júcar

Gulf of Valencia

Ibiza

Albacete

Ibiza

Ciudad Real

Alcoy

Benidorm

Formentera

Segura

Alicante

Elche

Costa Blanca

Linares

0   50   100 mi

Murcia

rdoba

0   80   160 km

Jaén

Lorca   Cartagena

H

Genil

In the next

...the bark of Portugal's and Spain's cork trees will produce enough cork for 136,000 wine bottles.

minute...

Granada

SIERRA NEVADA

Motril   Almería

rbella   Málaga

Costa del Sol

I

M E D I T E R R A N E A N   S E A

Bullfighting is popular in Spain. **Toreros** are performers who fight and kill bulls. There are various types, including matadors, depending on the skills used during the fight. Performances and costumes are elaborate, attracting tourists from all over the world.

MELILLA (SPAIN)

J

France and Monaco

The third largest country in Europe, **France has the fourth highest population.** Despite having a rural landscape, more than 70 percent of the population lives in cities, with more than one-sixth in Paris. France has an excellent health, education and social care system, and is the fifth wealthiest country in the world. Northern France is an industrialized, low-lying region, and the south has the snow-capped peaks of the Alps and Pyrenees as well as the sunny beaches of the Mediterranean Sea. Monaco is a tiny, independent, French-speaking country. One of the richest countries in the world, Monaco boasts more than 2000 millionaires and no taxes. Only three hours from the mainland by boat is the mountainous island of Corsica.

Search and Find

France	Monaco
● Paris C9	● Monaco H11

PARIS [C9] is one of the most visited places in the world, with attractions such as the Eiffel Tower and the Louvre.

THE DISTANCE from Calais [A9] to Dover, England, is 41 km and has been swum in less than eight hours.

ENGLISH CHANNEL

Cher

Île d'Ouessant

Brest ●

St. Malo ●

Quimper ●

Laval

Lorient ●

Rennes ●

Belle-Île

St. Nazaire ●

Angers

● Nantes

Île d'Yeu

Poiti

Île de Ré

● La Rochelle

BAY OF BISCAY

Cognac ●

Angoulê

Périgu

Bordeaux ●

Dordogne

Berg

Garonne

Mont-de-Marsan ●

Agen ●

Adour

Montau

Bayonne ●

● Pau

Tou

● Tarbes

● Lourdes

P Y R E N E E S

SPAIN

ANDORRA

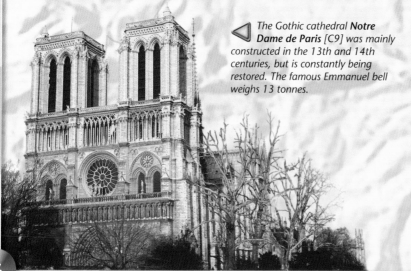

◁ The Gothic cathedral **Notre Dame de Paris** [C9] was mainly constructed in the 13th and 14th centuries, but is constantly being restored. The famous Emmanuel bell weighs 13 tonnes.

In the next ...France will provide the UK with enough electricity to power one light bulb in every home. **minute...**

8   9   10   11   12   13   14

Calais • • Dunkerque
Boulogne •
Roubaix •
Lille •
Lens • Valenciennes •
Seine
Dieppe •
Le Havre •
Amiens •
St. Quentin •
Rouen •

BELGIUM

Charleville Mézières •

LUXEM-
BOURG

Reims •
Seine
St. Denis •
Marne
Versailles • Paris
Chartres •
Verdun •
Châlons-en-
Champagne
Metz •

Fontainebleau •
Mans
Nancy •

Orléans •
Troyes •
Haguenau •

Tours
Auxerre •
Strasbourg •
VOSGES
MOUNTAINS

Cher
Dijon •
Saône
Mulhouse •
GERMANY

Bourges •
Besançon •
Châteauroux •

FRANCE
JURA
MOUNTAINS

Montluçon •
Chalon-sur-Saône •
SWITZERLAND

Limoges
Mâcon •

lermont-Ferrand •
Puy de Sancy
1881 m
Bourg-en-Bresse •

Mont Blanc
4807 m
Chamonix •

Lyon •
Chambéry •
St. Étienne •
Rhône

A
L
P
S

MASSIF
CENTRAL
Grenoble •
Tarn
Valence •
ITALY

Montélimar •

Castres •
Nîmes •
Avignon •
Béziers •
Montpellier •
Arles •
rcassonne
Sète •
Aix-en-Provence •
MONACO
Marseille •
Antibes •
Monaco
Cannes • Nice
pignan
Toulon • • St. Tropez

Gulf of Lion

Cape Corse

Bastia •

MEDITERRANEAN SEA

Corsica

Gulf of Sagone

Ajaccio •

Strait of Bonifacio

0   50   100   150 mi
0   100   200 km

Monaco has a
population of
only 31,100. The city
of **Monte Carlo** is well
known for its casinos,
harbour, glamour and
racetrack.

Facts and Stats

• The longest river is the Loire [D7]
at 1000 km in length – nearly seven
times shorter than the Nile river.

• Mont Blanc [F11] is the highest
mountain at 4807 m – 15 times
higher than the Eiffel Tower.

• The average income per person
in France is £14,600, compared
to £27,000 in Monaco and a world
average of £3500.

Did You Know?

For three weeks every summer,
more than 100 professional
cyclists take part in a 4000-km
race called the Tour de France.

World Record

Monaco has
the highest
population density
in the world with
15,500 people
per km².

Italy and the Balkans

Northern Italy is highly industrialized and produces many famous brands, such as Ferrari and Armani, while the south is mainly agricultural. Croatia, Bosnia and Herzegovina, Serbia, Montenegro, Kosovo and Macedonia were once part of Yugoslavia, but they have each become independent since 1991. Greece is one of Europe's oldest nations. The dry climate, steep slopes and thin soil limit farming to grapes, olives and citrus fruit. This area was home to the ancient Greek and Roman empires, which produced monuments such as Rome's Colosseum and the Parthenon in Athens, as well as Olympia – home to the first Olympic Games in 776 BC.

Facts and Stats

- Italy's population of 59.6 million would fill 596 Olympic stadiums. Montenegro's population of 620,000 would fill six stadiums.

- The life expectancy of people in Italy is 81 years, compared to 78 years in Albania and a world average of 68 years.

- The average income per person in Italy is £14,300, compared to £3800 in Montenegro and a world average of £3500.

In the next ...Italy will produce over 12,000 packets of pasta – that's 200 km of spaghetti! **minute...**

One of the most prominent sights in **Zagreb** [B8], the capital of Croatia, is the cathedral. The spires are 105 m in height and were built after an earthquake in 1880, which damaged much of the original structure.

Did You Know?

It costs the Italian government more money to keep the Tower of Pisa [D5] leaning than it would to straighten it.

Map labels:

SWITZERLAND · AUST · SLOVEN · Bolzano · Aosta · Como · Lecco · Trento · Kra · Monza · Bergamo · Udine · Ljublj · Novara · Milan · Brescia · Verona · Vicenza · Treviso · Trieste · FRANCE · Turin · Lodi · Piacenza · Cremona · Padua · Venice · Ko · Alessandria · Mantua · Chioggia · Rije · Parma · Adria · Pu · Genoa · Reggio nell' · Ferrara · Gulf of Venice · Savona · Emilia · Bologna · Ravenna · San Remo · La Spezia · Carrara · Forli · Massa · Pistoia · Rimini · Viareggio · Prato · SAN MARIN · Pisa · Florence · San Marino · Livorno · Empoli · Ancona · Siena · Arezzo · Piombino · Perugia · ITALY · Elba · Grosseto · Terni · Teram · Civitavecchia · Pe · Rome · VATICAN CITY (in Rome) · Latina · Campobasso · Sassari · Gaeta · Bene · Nuoro · Gulf of Gaeta · Na · Sardinia · Salerno · Cagliari · Gulf of Salerno · TYRRHENIAN SEA · Palermo · Me · Trapani · Mount Etna 3326 m · Caltanissetta · Agrigento · Cata · Sicily · Ragusa · Sir · Pantelleria · MALTA · Vall

A
B
C
D
E
F
G
H
I
J

8 9 10 11 12 13 14

▷ **The Grand Canal,** *Venice [B6], is the main waterway through the city – public transportation is by water, rather than road. Venice is slowly sinking due to rising sea levels. The main squares flood about 60 times a year.*

Search and Find

Albania
- Tiranë F10

Bosnia and Herzegovina
- Sarajevo D9

Croatia
- Zagreb B8

Greece
- Athens H12

Italy
- Rome E6

Kosovo
- Pristina E10

Macedonia
- Skopje E11

Malta
- Valletta I7

Montenegro
- Podgorica E9

San Marino
- San Marino . . . D6

Serbia
- Belgrade C10

Slovenia
- Ljubljana B7

Vatican City
- Vatican City . . . E6

Maribor
elje • Varazdin
HUNGARY
• Subotica
Mesto • Bjelovar
Zagreb Osijek
Sisak CROATIA Zrenjanin
rlovac Slavonski Brod
ihac • Prijedor Novi Sad
anja Luka Brcko Bijeljina • Pancevo
BOSNIA AND Belgrade
c HERZEGOVINA • Tuzla Sabac Smederevo
Zenica Valjevo
Sarajevo Srebrenica Kragujevac • Negotin
Uzice • Cacak Zajecar
Sibenik Foca SERBIA • Krusevac
Split Mostar
MONTENEGRO Novi Pazar • Nis
Ivangrad Kosovska • Leskovac
Niksic Mitrovica
Podgorica • Pec • Pristina
Dubrovnik Dakovica KOSOVO • Vranje
Cetinje Prizren • Kumanovo
Bar Shkodër Skopje
MACEDONIA
Tiranë Lake • Prilep BULGARIA
Durrës Ohrid Kilkís Sérrai Drama • Komotiní
Elbasan • Bitola Xánthi
ALBANIA Lake Florina • Edessa Kaválla Alexandroúpolis
Korçë Prespa Ptolemaïs Thessaloníki Thásos Samothrace
Vlorë Kastoria Veroia Mount Athos
Kozáni • Kateríni 2033 m
Metéora Mount Olympus
Ioánnina 2917 m Lemnos
Tríkala Larissa GREECE
Corfu Párga Vólos
Arta Kardhitsa Lesbos
Préveza Lamía
Skíros
Agrínion Thérmon Euboea Chios
Mesalóngion Marathon
Pátrai Thebes Káristos Sámos
Megara Piraeus Andros
Olympia Athens Ikaría
Pyrgos Árgos Tínos
Peleponnese Kéa Mykonos
Páros Náxos
Kalamata Kos
Amorgos Rhódes
Astipálaia
Neápolis Rhodes
Kíthira SEA OF CRETE
Kárpathos
Khaniá Iráklion
Crete

DRIATIC SEA
Bari
Brindisi
Taranto • Lecce
Cosenza
Crotone
Catanzaro
gio di Calabria
IONIAN SEA
Caphalonía
Zákinthos
ROMANIA

0 50 100 150 200 mi
0 100 200 300 km

🌐 **THE DISTANCE** from the town of Marathon [H12] to Athens [H12] is 42 km, and was first run by a Greek soldier 2500 years ago.

8 9 10 11 12 13 14

Germany and the Low Countries

Luxembourg, Belgium and the Netherlands are the three nations that make up the low countries.
Much of the Netherlands is below sea level, and it relies on massive sea walls called dykes and thousands of pumps to drain the land. Brussels, the capital of Belgium, is home to the European Union's main centre of government, and Antwerp is the centre of the world's diamond-cutting industry.
Luxembourg has the highest income per person in the world due to its banking industry. Germany has the third largest economy in the world after the United States and Japan, and produces machinery and cars such as BMW, Mercedes and Porsche. However, the reunification of East and West Germany in 1990 has caused unemployment and slow economic growth.

Search and Find

Belgium
• Brussels E5
Germany
• Berlin D11

Luxembourg
• Luxembourg. . . G6
Netherlands
• Amsterdam . . . D6
• The Hague. . . . D5

Amsterdam [D6] is well-known for its network of canals. The tall, leaning buildings were once used for storage. Hooks at the top of each house enabled goods to be pulled up to the top rooms.

Facts and Stats

• Germany's population of 82.8 million would fill 828 Olympic stadiums. Luxembourg's population of 484,000 would only fill 4.8 stadiums.

• Mount Zugspitze [I9] is the highest mountain at 2964 m – nine times higher than the Eiffel Tower.

• The average income per person in Luxembourg is £29,600, compared to a world average of £3500.

COLOGNE [E7] holds one of the biggest carnivals in the world. Every November, more than one million people take part in the festival.

THE DISTANCE from the source of the Rhine river [F7] in the Swiss Alps to its mouth at the North Sea is 1320 km.

Map labels:

NOR
SE

Terschelling Ameland
Vlieland Waddenzee
Texel Groni
Den Helder• Leeuwarden•
NETHERLANDS As
Alkmaar• Northeast Emme
Polder
Amsterdam
Haarlem• Flevoland • Zwolle
Leiden• Polder Apeldoorn
The Hague • Hilversum Enschede•
Utrecht• • Arnhem
Delft• Nijmegen•
Rotterdam• Waal Mür
Dordrecht•
Vlissingen• Breda• Tilburg• 's-Hertogenbosch
Zeebrugge•
Ostend• • Bruges Eindhoven•
Ghent• • Antwerp Duisburg Dortn
Roeselare• Aalst• Mechelen• Krefeld• Ess
Leuven• Düsseldorf• Wupp
Kortrijk• Genk• Solingen•
Schelde **Brussels** Hasselt• Maastricht• Colo
•Tournai Aachen•
Charleroi• Namur• • Liège Bonn
Mons• Verviers•
Meuse (Maas) • Dinant
FRANCE **BELGIUM** HUNSRÜCK Rhin
Bastogne• Kobl
LUXEMBOURG
Luxembourg • Trier
Esch-sur-Alzette•
FRANCE Kaisersla
Saarbrücken•
Karlsru
Baden-B.

B
F
Freibur
im Brei

SW

Scale:
0 50 100 150 200 mi
0 100 200 300 km

A

Sylt
DENMARK
• Flensburg
• Schleswig
Kiel Bay
Fehmarn
Kiel •
Mecklenburg
Bay
Rügen

B

AN ISLANDS
• Cuxhaven
Lübeck •
Rostock •
Greifswald •

lmshaven
• Bremerhaven
• Hamburg
• Schwerin

C

nburg
• Bremen
• Lüneburg
Neubrandenburg •

Ems

Elbe

brück
• Hannover
Wolfsburg •
Brandenburg •
Berlin

D

• Bielefeld
• Braunschweig
• Hameln
POLAND

mm
Magdeburg •
• Potsdam

• Paderborn
Frankfurt an der Oder •

Dessau •

E

• Göttingen
Elbe
Cottbus •

Kassel •
Halle •
GERMANY
Görlitz •

gen
Eisenach •
Weimar •
Meissen •
Leipzig •
Erfurt •
Dresden •

F

• Giessen
Jena •
Chemnitz •
Freital •
Gera •
• Fulda
Zwickau •

n
• Frankfurt am Main
Plauen •
CZECH REPUBLIC

inz
Offenbach
Main

G

• Darmstadt
Bamberg •
ms
• Bayreuth

nheim
• Würzburg

vigshafen

delberg
Fürth •• Nuremberg
BOHEMIAN FOREST

• Heilbronn

H

> **Cologne Cathedral** *[E7] is one of the tallest and most magnificent Gothic buildings in the world. Its construction began in the 13th century, but wasn't completed until the late 19th century. The cathedral has 12 bells, and 509 steps lead to the top of the south tower, nearly 100 m above the ground.*

forzheim
Regensburg •
• Stuttgart

Tübingen
• Ingolstadt
• Reutlingen

I

SWABIAN JURA
Passau •
• Ulm
Danube
• Augsburg

• Munich

BAVARIAN ALPS
Lake Constance
Mount Zugspitze 2964 m

J

AND
Berchtesgaden •

AUSTRIA

Did You Know?

Each year, Belgium produces and sells 172,000 tonnes of chocolate in more than 2130 chocolate shops.

In the next
...the Netherlands will make 1280 kg of cheese – enough for 64,000 cheese slices.
minute...

World Record
Germany has the highest paper recycling rate in the world – more than 75 percent of their paper is reused.

Switzerland and Austria

Landlocked Switzerland, Austria and Liechtenstein are dominated by the Alps, creating stunning mountain scenery. Millions of tourists are attracted to the natural beauty, spectacular mountain vistas and popular Alpine skiing. Switzerland guards its independence and was not involved in either of the two World Wars. As a neutral, independent state, Switzerland is the home of the United Nations and many charitable and banking organizations. As a result, it is a very wealthy country. Many composers come from Austria, including Mozart, Haydn, Schubert and Strauss.

◁ **The Belvedere Palace,** Vienna [E13], was built in the 17th and 18th centuries. Archduke Franz Ferdinand was the last person to live at the palace. It is now a museum and gallery, exhibiting many important collections, including the works of Renoir, Monet and Van Gogh.

In the next ...41,000 kg of chocolate will be eaten worldwide. The Swiss are the world's biggest consumers. **minute...**

FRANCE

Basel
Rhine
Schaffhausen
Aarau
Baden
Winterthur
Olten
Lake Constance
GERMANY
Solothurn
Zürich
Biel
St. Gallen
Bregenz
Neuchâtel
Zug
Feldkirch
Innsbruck
Lake Neuchâtel
Lucerne
Bern
SWITZERLAND
Vaduz
Yverdon
Thun
LIECHTENSTEIN
St. Anton
Fribourg
Interlaken
Chur
Galtür
Lausanne
Saanen
Andermatt
LEPONTINE ALPS
Davos
Lake Geneva
Montreux
BERNESE ALPS
Geneva
Sion
Brig
St. Moritz
Mount Dufourspitze 4634 m
Bellinzona
Zermatt
Locarno
Mount Matterhorn 4478 m
ITALY
ITALY
Lugano

Did You Know?

The Swiss invented the quartz watch, wristwatch and waterproof watch. Switzerland produces expensive watches, such as Rolex, and watch-making is its third largest industry.

▷ **Leukerbad,** in the heart of the Bernese Alps [G3], is the largest thermal spa in Europe. Dating back to Roman times, the complex contains 3.9 million litres of water and is surrounded by picturesque mountain scenery.

BERN [F3] is the city where Albert Einstein worked, the Toblerone chocolate bar is made, and Emmental cheese is manufactured.

THE DISTANCE of the St. Moritz [G5] bobsleigh run is 1585 m and it takes just 70 seconds to travel from one end to the other.

Search and Find

Austria
- Vienna E13

Liechtenstein
- Vaduz F5

Switzerland
- Bern F3

Extreme Weather

In 1999, the biggest avalanche in Austria for 400 years smashed into the town of Galtür [G6], killing 31 people.

0   50   100 mi
0   80   160 km

CZECH REPUBLIC

SLOVAKIA

Zwettl Stadt

Inn

Braunau

Linz

Krems

Danube

Wels

Amstetten

Klosterneuburg

Steyr

Sankt Pölten

Vienna

Gmunden

Baden

Salzburg

Hallein

Bad Ischl

AUSTRIA

Enns

Wiener Neustadt

Neusiedler See

Kufstein

Kitzbühel

hwaz

Mount Grossglockner 3797 m

Kapfenberg

Leoben

NIEDERE TAUERN

Knittelfeld

HOHE TAUERN

Judenburg

Mur

HUNGARY

Graz

Gleisdorf

Spittal

Wolfsberg

ITALY

Drau

Villach

Klagenfurt

SLOVENIA

Facts and Stats

- The population of Liechtenstein is only 35,400 and wouldn't even fill half an Olympic stadium.

- Switzerland's Mount Dufourspitze [H3] is the highest mountain at 4634 m in height – 14 times higher than the Eiffel Tower.

- The average income per person in Switzerland is £16,800, compared to a world average of £3500.

▷ Switzerland is split into federal states, or cantons. Bern is the second largest Swiss canton, and is dominated by mountains, glaciers and waterfalls. The small village of **Gstaad** near Saanen [G2] is a popular ski resort with fantastic Alpine scenery.

Hungary, Romania and Bulgaria

Bulgaria and Romania became members of the European Union in 2007, with Hungary joining in 2004. These countries will now experience rapid economic growth after decades of communist rule. Romania is the largest of the three and Europe's longest river, the Danube, flows along its southern border to the Black Sea. Hungary's capital, Budapest, has a lively arts and music scene, and is host to a range of cultural and sporting festivals. The countryside is scenic with many lakes, historic towns and villages. Bulgaria also borders the Black Sea, but it is mainly mountainous and rural, and relatively undeveloped.

SLOVAKIA

AUSTRIA

Gyor •   • Esztergom   Miskolc •

• Budapest

Szombathely •

Székesfehérvár •   **HUNGARY**

Lake Balaton   Dunaujvaros   • Kecskemét

SLOVENIA

Kaposvár •   *Danube*   *Tisza*

Szeged •   Ara

Pécs •   Timisoa

CROATIA   SERBIA

Facts and Stats

• The Danube [D6/G10] is the longest river at 2860 km in length. The Nile river is twice as long.

• Mount Musala [I10] is the highest mountain at 2925 m, which is nine times higher than the Eiffel Tower.

• The average income per person in Hungary is £4600, compared to a world average of £3500.

On the bank of the Danube river in Budapest [C6] is **Hungary's Parliament building.** *Hungarian architect, Imre Steindl, designed the building, although he went blind before the project was completed. More than 40 kg of gold was used in its construction.*

Bran Castle in Romania is more commonly known as Dracula's Castle because Bram Stoker based his novel around the building. In 2007, the castle was put up for sale for £40 million.

Did You Know?

One of the few Bulgarian commercial crops is the rose. The petals are used in the perfume industry.

THE DISTANCE from the source to the mouth of the Danube river [D6/G10] is 2888 km – almost all of it is accessible to boats.

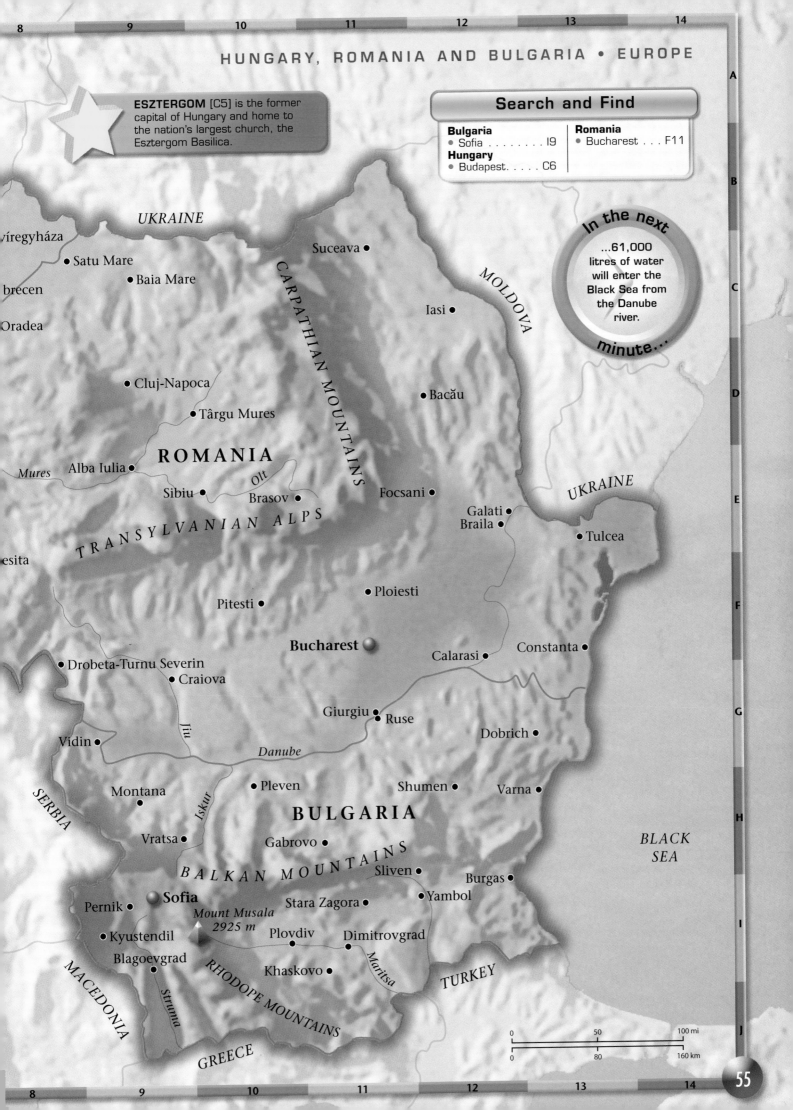

ESZTERGOM [C5] is the former capital of Hungary and home to the nation's largest church, the Esztergom Basilica.

Search and Find

Bulgaria
● Sofia I9
Hungary
● Budapest. C6

Romania
● Bucharest . . . F11

In the next
...61,000 litres of water will enter the Black Sea from the Danube river.
minute...

UKRAINE

Nyíregyháza
● Satu Mare
● Baia Mare
brecen
Oradea

CARPATHIAN MOUNTAINS

● Suceava

MOLDOVA

Iasi ●

● Cluj-Napoca
● Târgu Mures

ROMANIA

Bacău ●

UKRAINE

Mures
Alba Iulia ●
Sibiu ●
Olt
Brasov ●

Focsani ●

TRANSYLVANIAN ALPS

Galati ●
Braila ●

● Tulcea

esita

● Ploiesti

Pitesti ●

Bucharest ●

Calarasi ●

Constanta ●

● Drobeta-Turnu Severin
● Craiova

Giurgiu ●
● Ruse

Jiu

● Dobrich

Vidin ●

Danube

Montana ●

Iskur

● Pleven

Shumen ●

Varna ●

BULGARIA

Vratsa ●

Gabrovo ●

BALKAN MOUNTAINS

Sliven ●

Burgas ●

Pernik ● **Sofia** ●

Stara Zagora ●

● Yambol

Mount Musala
2925 m

● Kyustendil

Plovdiv ●

Dimitrovgrad ●

Blagoevgrad ●

RHODOPE MOUNTAINS

Khaskovo ●

Maritsa

TURKEY

MACEDONIA

Struma

GREECE

SERBIA

BLACK SEA

0   50   100 mi
0   80   160 km

Poland, Czech Republic and Slovakia

Poland, Slovakia and the Czech Republic are among the newest members of the European Union. Standards of living are much lower than western Europe and many workers have moved to the United Kingdom, Ireland and Germany for better-paid jobs. The Baltic coast of Poland is industrial with steelworks and shipyards, but low-wage rates and money from the European Union have attracted new industries. Many rural areas are untouched by progress, and horse-drawn carts are still used. Prague, the capital of the Czech Republic, is situated on the Vltava river and receives more than ten million tourists a year.

*The **Prague Astronomical Clock** [G5] is mounted on the wall of the Old Town City Hall. The astronomical dial represents the Sun and Moon. The 12 figures of the Apostles appear every hour, and all 12 are seen at 12 p.m. Finally, the calendar dial represents the months.*

In the next
...Poland will mine 190 tonnes of coal, generating enough electricity for 7.6 million light bulbs.
minute...

*Zygmunt's Column sits in the centre of **Castle Square, Warsaw** [E10]. Built in 1644, the monument represents King Zygmunt III Waza. Markets, street entertainment and concerts take place here, making it a popular tourist site.*

BALTIC SEA

Koszalin

Szczecin

Notéc

Warta

Gorzow Wielkopolski

Pozn

Zielona Gora

Ka

Oder

Legnica

Wrocla

Opole

Walbrzych

GERMANY

Liberec

Ústí nad Labem

Hradec Kralove

Karlovy Vary

Cheb

Prague

Elbe

Pardubice

Plzen

CZECH REPUBLIC

Olomouc

Vltava

Jihlava

Zli

BOHEMIAN FOREST

Brno

Ceské Budejovice

Morava

AUSTRIA

Tren

Trnav

Bratislava

Komár

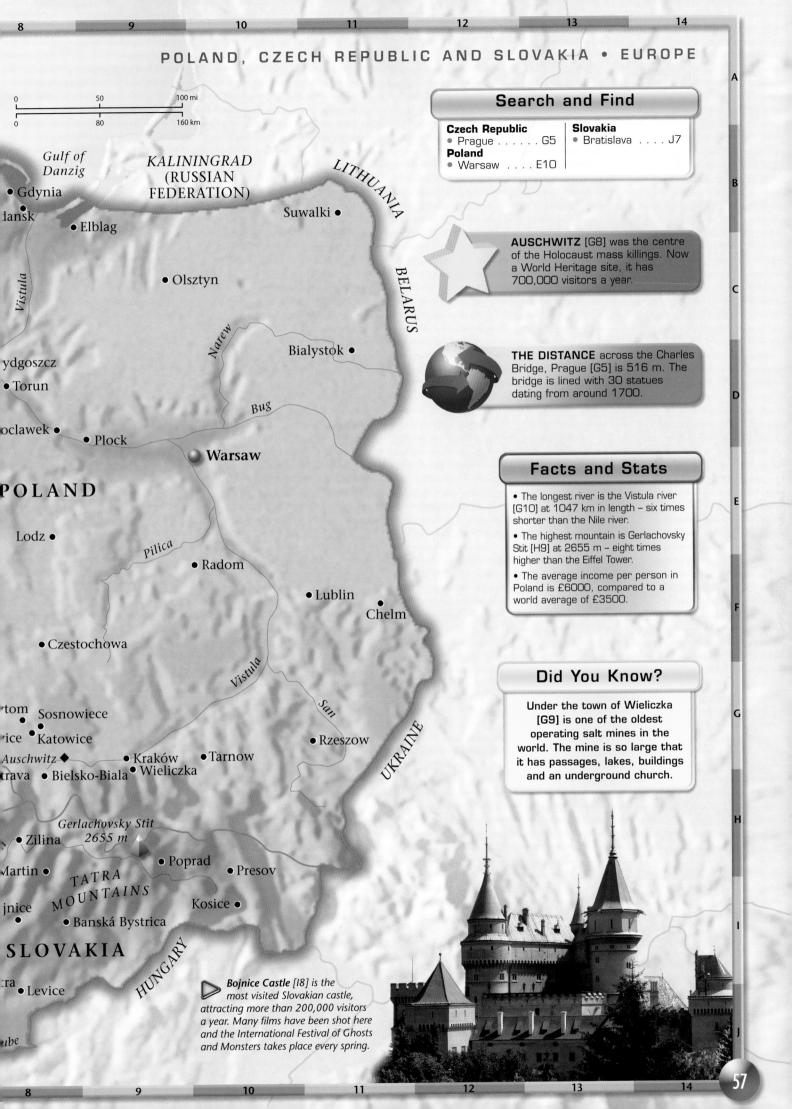

0 — 50 — 100 mi
0 — 80 — 160 km

KALININGRAD (RUSSIAN FEDERATION)

Gulf of Danzig

LITHUANIA

BELARUS

• Gdynia
• lansk
• Elblag
• Suwalki

• Olsztyn

Vistula

ydgoszcz
• Torun

Narew

• Bialystok

Bug

oclawek
• Plock
• **Warsaw**

POLAND

• Lodz

Pilica

• Radom

• Lublin
• Chelm

• Czestochowa

Vistula

San

tom
• Sosnowiece
rice • Katowice
Auschwitz ◆
trava • Bielsko-Biala
• Kraków
• Wieliczka
• Tarnow

• Rzeszow

UKRAINE

Gerlachovsky Stit 2655 m
• Zilina
Martin
• Poprad
• Presov

TATRA MOUNTAINS
jnice
• Kosice
• Banská Bystrica

SLOVAKIA

HUNGARY

ra
• Levice

ube

Search and Find

Czech Republic
● Prague G5
Poland
● Warsaw E10

Slovakia
● Bratislava J7

AUSCHWITZ [G8] was the centre of the Holocaust mass killings. Now a World Heritage site, it has 700,000 visitors a year.

THE DISTANCE across the Charles Bridge, Prague [G5] is 516 m. The bridge is lined with 30 statues dating from around 1700.

Facts and Stats

• The longest river is the Vistula river [G10] at 1047 km in length – six times shorter than the Nile river.

• The highest mountain is Gerlachovsky Stit [H9] at 2655 m – eight times higher than the Eiffel Tower.

• The average income per person in Poland is £6000, compared to a world average of £3500.

Did You Know?

Under the town of Wieliczka [G9] is one of the oldest operating salt mines in the world. The mine is so large that it has passages, lakes, buildings and an underground church.

▷ *Bojnice Castle [I8] is the most visited Slovakian castle, attracting more than 200,000 visitors a year. Many films have been shot here and the International Festival of Ghosts and Monsters takes place every spring.*

Eastern Europe

The former Soviet states of Estonia, Latvia and Lithuania are now democratic, independent countries. The area is mainly flat, low-lying land that is covered in snow during winter, but a fertile grain- and dairy-farming region in summer. Without industries to compete with western Europe, these countries remain poor. Russia controls much of Europe's natural gas supplies, but has struggled to improve its standard of living. Armenia, Azerbaijan and Georgia are part of the Caucasus range with the Caucasus Mountains providing a border between Europe and Asia.

*The town of Trakai, Lithuania, can be found west of Vilnius [G5]. Out of the area's 200 lakes, Lake Galve is the largest at 47 m in depth. Built in the 14th and 15th centuries on the lake, **Trakai Island Castle** can only be reached by a drawbridge.*

Search and Find

Armenia
- Yerevan J8

Azerbaijan
- Baku J9

Belarus
- Minsk G6

Estonia
- Tallinn E5

Georgia
- Tbilisi I8

Latvia
- Riga F5

Lithuania
- Vilnius G5

Moldova
- Chisinau H6

Russian Federation
- Moscow F7

Ukraine
- Kiev G6

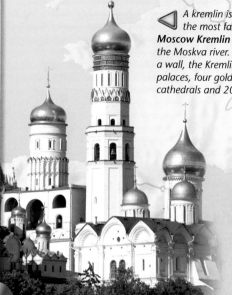

*A kremlin is a Russian castle, the most famous is the **Moscow Kremlin** [F7] on the bank of the Moskva river. Surrounded by a wall, the Kremlin includes four palaces, four golden-domed cathedrals and 20 towers.*

In the next ...Russia will sell enough natural gas to Europe to light 250 million gas fires. **minute...**

BAREN

• Murmansk

FINLAND

Onega

Lake Onega

• Petrozav

Vyborg • *Lake Ladoga*

BALTIC SEA

Gulf of Finland   • St. Petersburg

Tallinn

ESTONIA   • Novgorod

Gulf of   Tartu •   *Lake Peipus*   Rybinsk

Riga   Yaroslav

Liepaja •   **Riga**   Tver •

LATVIA

LITHUANIA   Vitsyebsk   **Moscow**

RUSSIAN
FEDERATION   **Vilnius**   • Smolensk   Ryaza

Kaliningrad   Kaunas   **BELARUS**

• Kirov

Minsk

POLAND   • Hrodna   • Bryansk

Pripyat Marshes   • Homyel   Lipe

Voronez

Rivne •   **Kiev**   *Dnieper*

Lviv •   • Khar

SLOVAKIA   **UKRAINE** Dnipropetrov

Prut   Kryvyy Rih

Dniester   Donets

MOLDOVA   Zaporizhzhya   Rosto

Chisinau   na-D

ROMANIA   Tiraspol   • Odessa   *Sea of Azov*

Crimea   Krasno

Sevastopol •

BLACK SEA

A

ARCTIC
OCEAN

Novaya Zemlya

KARA SEA

B

Extreme Weather

For seven months, the far north of Russia has temperatures below freezing and only two months above 10°C. It is too cold even for trees to grow.

Kolguyev Island

C

Facts and Stats

- The population of Russia is 143 million and would fill 1430 Olympic stadiums. It is more than 100 times larger than Estonia's population of 1.3 million.
- Russia's area is 17 million km^2 – 165 times the area of Iceland. It is the biggest country in the world.
- The average income per person in Moldova is £1500, compared to £7800 in Estonia and a world average of £3500.

• Vorkuta •

Pechora

D

khangelísk

Severnaya Dvina

• Ukhta •

E

THE DISTANCE from Vilnius [G5] to Tallinn [E5] was once covered by two million citizens in a human chain stretching more than 300 km.

• Syktyvkar

RUSSIAN FEDERATION

URAL MOUNTAINS

• Perm

F

ST. PETERSBURG [E6] has many canals and hundreds of bridges. It is sometimes called the Venice of the North.

• Izhevsk

Nizhniy Novgorod
• Kazan

• Ufa

G

Simbirsk
Tolyatti
Magnitogorsk •

Did You Know?

Armenia has its own alphabet and language. The alphabet contains 38 letters. More than 90 percent of the country speak the Armenian language.

• Penza   Samara
Orenburg
Ural
• Orsk •

Saratov

KAZAKHSTAN

Volga

0   100   200   300   400   500 mi

0   200   400   600   800 km

H

• Volgograd

• Astrakhan

CASPIAN SEA

Stavropol
• Vladikavkaz
• Grozny
unt Elbrus 5642 m

I

EORGIA
Tbilisi

RMENIA

Yerevan   Baku

AZERBAIJAN

RKEY

IRAN

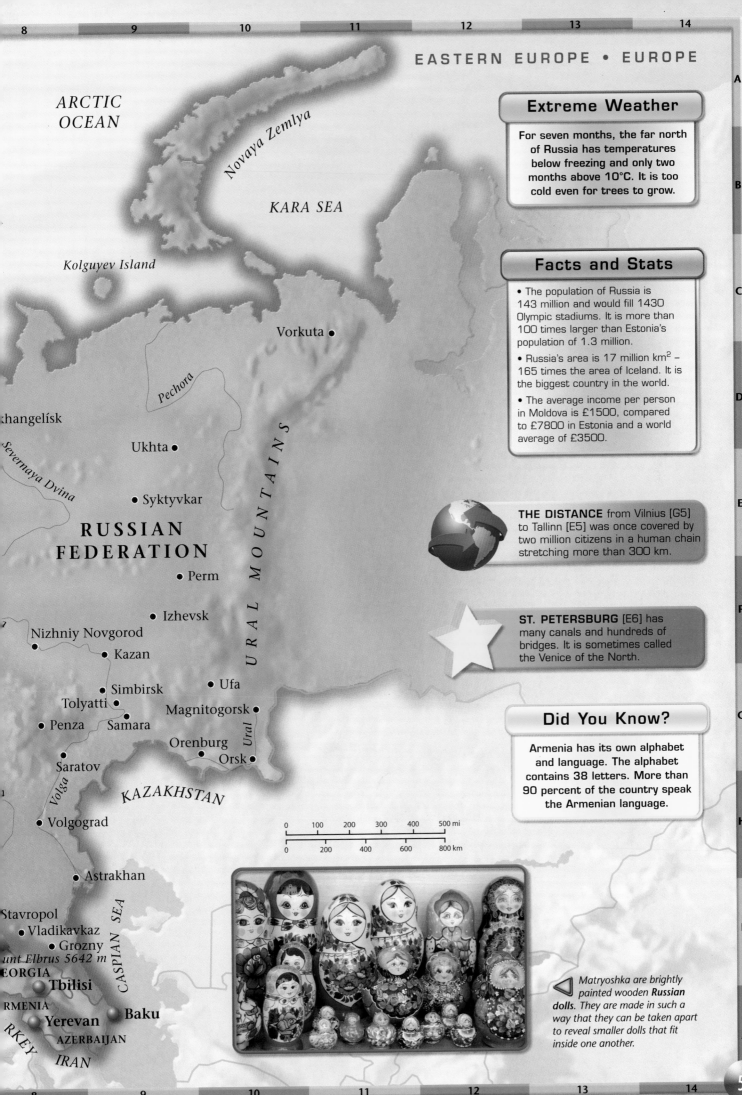

Matryoshka are brightly painted wooden Russian dolls. They are made in such a way that they can be taken apart to reveal smaller dolls that fit inside one another.

J

Africa

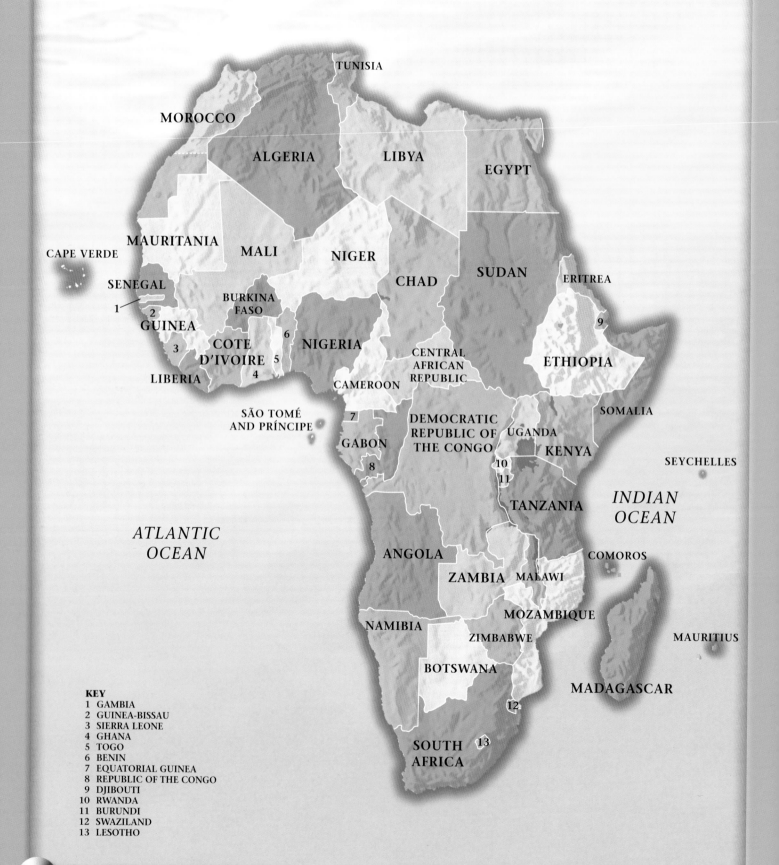

TUNISIA

MOROCCO

ALGERIA

LIBYA

EGYPT

MAURITANIA

MALI

NIGER

CHAD

SUDAN

ERITREA

CAPE VERDE

SENEGAL

1

2

GUINEA

BURKINA
FASO

9

3

6

NIGERIA

ETHIOPIA

COTE
D'IVOIRE

5

CENTRAL
AFRICAN
REPUBLIC

4

LIBERIA

CAMEROON

SOMALIA

SÃO TOMÉ
AND PRÍNCIPE

7

DEMOCRATIC
REPUBLIC OF
THE CONGO

UGANDA

GABON

KENYA

8

10

SEYCHELLES

11

ATLANTIC
OCEAN

TANZANIA

INDIAN
OCEAN

ANGOLA

COMOROS

ZAMBIA

MALAWI

MOZAMBIQUE

NAMIBIA

ZIMBABWE

MAURITIUS

BOTSWANA

12

MADAGASCAR

13

SOUTH
AFRICA

KEY
1 GAMBIA
2 GUINEA-BISSAU
3 SIERRA LEONE
4 GHANA
5 TOGO
6 BENIN
7 EQUATORIAL GUINEA
8 REPUBLIC OF THE CONGO
9 DJIBOUTI
10 RWANDA
11 BURUNDI
12 SWAZILAND
13 LESOTHO

COUNTRY FACTFILE

Country	Life expectancy	Population in thousands	Population growth %	Population as urban %	Literacy %	Area km²	Population density per km²	Capital city	Currency	Languages
Algeria	74	31,540	1.2	65	69.9	2,381,741	13.3	Algiers	Algerian Dinar	Arabic, Berber, French
Angola	38	15,566	2.1	35	67.4	1,246,700	12.5	Luanda	Kwanza	Portuguese, Umbundu
Benin	59	7841	3	43	34.7	112,622	69.6	Cotonou, Porto-Novo	CFA Franc	French, Fon, Yoruba
Botswana	62	1773	1.9	66	81.2	581,730	3	Gaborone	Pula	English, Tswana
Burkina Faso	53	14,017	3.1	19	21.8	274,122	50.1	Ouagadougou	CFA Franc	French, Mossi
Burundi	52	7384	3.3	9	59.3	27,834	265.3	Bujumbura	Burundi Franc	Kirundi, French
Cameroon	54	15,881	2.2	57	67.9	476,077	33.4	Yaoundé	CFA Franc	French, English, Fang
Cape Verde	72	509	0.6	62	76.6	4033	126.2	Praia	Cape Verdean Escudo	Portuguese, Crioulo
Central African Republic	44	3895	1.5	42	48.6	622,436	6.3	Bangui	CFA Franc	French, Sango
Chad	48	7799	2.1	24	26	1,284,000	6.1	N'Djamena	CFA Franc	French, Arabic
Comoros	63	669	2.8	32	56.6	1862	359.3	Moroni	Comoran Franc	Comorian, French, Arabic
Congo, Democratic Republic of the	54	58,300	3.2	34	67.2	2,344,856	24.9	Kinshasa	Congolese Franc	French, Lingala, Swahili
Congo, Republic of the	54	3397	2.8	63	83.8	342,000	9.9	Brazzaville	CFA Franc	French, Monokutuba, Kongo
Côte d'Ivoire (Ivory Coast)	55	17,065	2.1	49	48.7	320,783	53.2	Abidjan, Yamoussoukro	CFA Franc	French, Akan
Djibouti	43	638	1.9	85	67.9	23,200	27.5	Djibouti	Djiboutian Franc	Somali, French, Akan
Egypt	72	72,798	1.6	45	71.4	997,739	73	Cairo	Egyptian Pound	Arabic
Equatorial Guinea	62	1015	2.7	48	87	28,051	36.2	Malabo	CFA Franc	Spanish, French, Fang
Eritrea	62	3622	2.6	20	58.6	121,100	29.9	Asmara	Nakfa	Tigrinya, Arabic, Afar
Ethiopia	55	73,919	3.2	18	42.7	1,127,127	65.6	Addis Ababa	Birr	Amharic, Oromo, Tigrinya
Gabon	53	1521	1.9	81	63.2	267,667	5.7	Libreville	CFA Franc	French, Fang
Gambia	55	1365	2.7	57	40.1	10,689	127.7	Banjul	Dalasi	English, Malinke
Ghana	60	23,417	1.9	44	57.9	238,533	98.2	Accra	Cedi	Hausa, English, Akan
Guinea	57	9030	2.6	33	29.5	245,857	36.7	Conakry	Guinean Franc	Fulani, French, Malinke
Guinea-Bissau	48	1296	2	30	42.4	36,125	35.9	Bissau	CFA Franc	Crioulo, Portuguese
Kenya	58	35,112	2.7	30	85.1	582,646	60.3	Nairobi	Kenyan Shilling	Swahili, English
Lesotho	40	1881	0.1	25	84.8	30,355	62	Maseru	Loti	Sesotho, English
Liberia	42	3476	2.7	46	60	111,370	31.2	Monrovia	US Dollar, Liberian Dollar	Krio, English
Libya	77	5673	2.2	88	82.6	1,777,060	3.2	Surt, Tripoli	Libyan Dinar	Arabic
Madagascar	63	17,594	3	29	68.9	587,041	30	Antananarivo	Madagascar Ariary	Malagasy, French
Malawi	44	13,066	2.8	19	62.7	118,484	110.3	Lilongwe	Malawian Kwacha	Chichewa, English
Mali	50	11,732	2.7	30	46.4	1,248,574	9.4	Bamako	CFA Franc	French, Bambara
Mauritania	60	2906	2.4	58	51.2	1,030,700	2.8	Nouakchott	Ouguiya	Arabic
Mauritius	74	1249	0.8	48	84.4	2040	612.3	Port Louis	Mauritius Rupee	French Creole, Bhojpuri, English
Morocco	72	29,475	1.5	56	52.3	446,550	66	Rabat	Moroccan Dirham	Arabic, Berber
Mozambique	41	20,530	1.8	35	47.8	801,590	25.6	Maputo	Metical	Makua, Portuguese
Namibia	51	1830	1	37	85	824,269	2.2	Windhoek	Namibian Dollar	English, Ovambo, Nama
Niger	52	14,297	3.7	21	28.7	1,186,408	12.1	Niamey	CFA Franc	French, Hausa
Nigeria	47	140,003	2	45	68	923,103	151.7	Abuja	Naira	English, Hausa, Yoruba
Rwanda	51	8129	2.8	18	70.4	26,338	308.6	Kigali	Rwandan Franc	Rwanda, French, English
São Tomé and Príncipe	68	138	3.1	44	84.9	1001	137.9	São Tomé	Dobra	Portuguese, Crioulo
Senegal	59	11,343	2.7	47	39.3	196,712	57.7	Dakar	CFA Franc	French, Wolof
Seychelles	73	83	1	59	91.8	455	182.4	Victoria	Seychelles Rupee	Creole, English
Sierra Leone	41	4977	2.3	37	35	71,740	69.4	Freetown	Leone	English, Krio, Mende
Somalia	50	8600	2.8	37	38	637,657	13.5	Mogadishu	Somali Shilling	Somali, Arabic
South Africa	49	48,502	0.3	61	86.4	1,224,691	39.6	Cape Town, Pretoria	Rand	Xhosa, English, Zulu, Afrikaans
Sudan	51	39,154	2.1	36	61.1	2,505,815	15.6	Khartoum	Sudanese Dinar	Arabic, Dinka
Swaziland	32	954	–0.5	34	81.6	17,363	54.9	Lobamba, Mbabane	Lilangeni	Swazi, English
Tanzania	52	37,394	2	25	69.4	945,037	39.6	Dar es Salaam, Dodoma	Tanzanian Shilling	Swahili, English
Togo	59	5337	2.7	42	60.9	56,785	94	Lomé	CFA Franc	French, Ewe
Tunisia	76	10,327	1	66	74.3	163,610	63.1	Tunis	Tunisian Dinar	Arabic, French
Uganda	53	29,593	2.7	14	66.8	241,040	122.8	Kampala	Ugandan Shilling	Swahili, English, Ganda
Zambia	39	9,886	1.6	43	80.6	752,614	13.1	Lusaka	Zambian Kwacha	English, Bemba
Zimbabwe	46	11,635	1.5	37	90.7	390,757	29.8	Harare	Zimbabwean Dollar	English, Shona

North Africa

The Sahara Desert dominates this region at 6000 km in width and 2000 km from north to south. Only a narrow strip of land stands next to the Mediterranean Sea, but the fertile valleys of the Atlas Mountains and the banks of the Nile river have enough water to grow crops.

Algeria, Libya and Tunisia have become wealthy by selling oil and natural gas to Europe. Egypt was the richest country in the world when the pharaohs ruled more than 3000 years ago. Egypt's well-preserved tombs and temples, especially the Great Pyramid of Giza, attract many tourists.

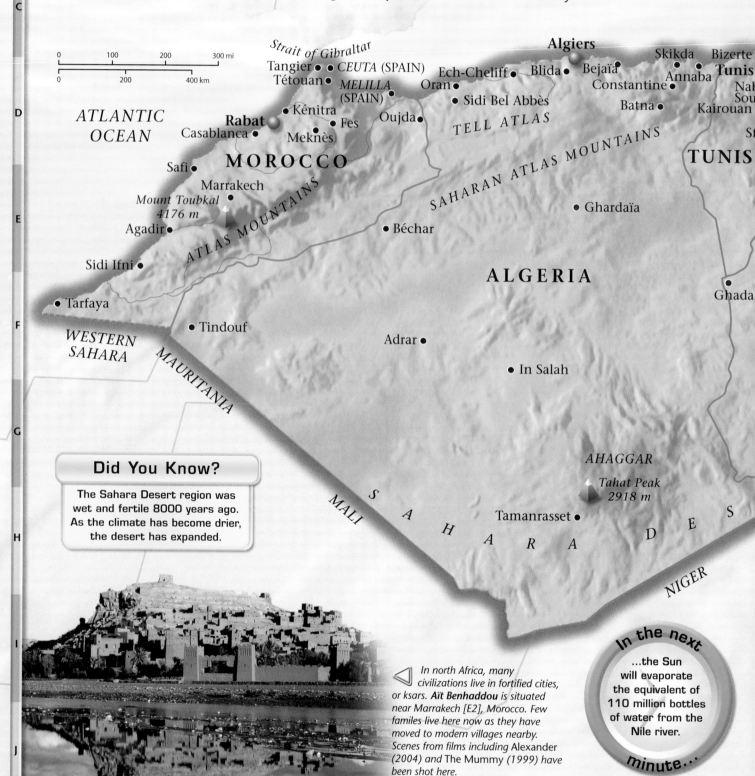

0   100   200   300 mi
0   200   400 km

ATLANTIC OCEAN

Strait of Gibraltar
Tangier ● ● *CEUTA* (SPAIN)
Tétouan ●
MELILLA (SPAIN)
Rabat ● ● Kénitra
Casablanca ● ● Fes
Meknès ●
Oujda ●
Safi ●
MOROCCO
Marrakech ●
Mount Toubkal 4176 m
Agadir ●
Sidi Ifni ●
● Tarfaya

WESTERN SAHARA

MAURITANIA

Algiers
Ech-Cheliff ● ● Blida ● Bejaïa
Oran ●
● Sidi Bel Abbès
TELL ATLAS
Skikda ●
Annaba ● **Tunis**
Constantine ●
Batna ●
Kairouan ●
Nab
Sou

SAHARAN ATLAS MOUNTAINS

● Ghardaïa

TUNIS

ATLAS MOUNTAINS

● Béchar

ALGERIA

Ghada

● Tindouf

Adrar ●

● In Salah

AHAGGAR
Tahat Peak 2918 m

Tamanrasset ●

S A H A R A   D E S

MALI

NIGER

Did You Know?

The Sahara Desert region was wet and fertile 8000 years ago. As the climate has become drier, the desert has expanded.

In north Africa, many civilizations live in fortified cities, or ksars. **Aït Benhaddou** is situated near Marrakech [E2], Morocco. Few families live here now as they have moved to modern villages nearby. Scenes from films including Alexander (2004) and The Mummy (1999) have been shot here.

In the next
...the Sun will evaporate the equivalent of 110 million bottles of water from the Nile river.
minute...

◁ Located on the Nile river, Cairo [F13] is the biggest city in Africa. Built in AD 988, **Al-Azhar University** is the second oldest university in the world, after the University of Al Karaouine Fez, Morocco. Al-Azhar Mosque stands alongside the university.

Facts and Stats

• Egypt's population of 72.8 million would fill 728 Olympic stadiums. Libya's population of five million would only fill 50 stadiums.

• Cairo [F13] is the biggest city with 12.2 million people. This would fill 122 Olympic stadiums and is ten times the size of Tripoli [E8].

• The average income per person in Libya is £6000, compared to a world average of £3500.

World Record

The Saharan sand sea of Algeria has the highest sand dunes in the world at 465 m in height.

Extreme Weather

The hottest temperature ever recorded was 58°C in Libya's Sahara Desert.

Search and Find

Algeria
• Algiers C6

Egypt
• Cairo F13

Libya
• Surt E9
• Tripoli E8

Morocco
• Rabat D3

Tunisia
• Tunis D7

MEDITERRANEAN SEA

Tripoli
Misurata
Zawiyah
Surt
Gulf of Sidra
Darnah
Benghazi
Tubruq
Ajdabiya
Alexandria
Tanta
Port Said
Suez Canal
Cairo
Giza
Suez
ISRAEL
Sinai Peninsula
Gulf of Suez
Gulf of Aqaba

GREAT SAND SEA

QATTARA DEPRESSION

Sharm al Sheikh
El Minya
Al Ghardaqah
Asyut

LIBYA

F E Z Z A N

W E S T E R N D E S E R T

EGYPT

Qena
Luxor
RED SEA

LIBYAN DESERT

Aswan

GILF KEBIR PLATEAU

Lake Nasser

CHAD

SUDAN

THE DISTANCE separating Morocco from Spain, Europe, at the Strait of Gibraltar's [C3] narrowest point is only 13 km.

EGYPT has huge pyramids, built more than 3000 years ago. Each one held the body of a king.

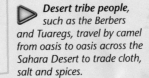

▷ **Desert tribe people,** such as the Berbers and Tuaregs, travel by camel from oasis to oasis across the Sahara Desert to trade cloth, salt and spices.

West Africa

Stretching from the heart of the Sahara Desert to the tropical forests of southern Nigeria, this region is one of the poorest in the world. In the north, Mali and Niger are plagued by drought and famine. The southern countries of Sierra Leone, Liberia, Côte d'Ivoire and Nigeria suffer with armed unrest, government corruption and religious disputes between the Islamic north and the Christian south. Oil provides 65 percent of Nigeria's income, but this fails to lift the rapidly growing population out of poverty.

Extreme Weather

Southern Nigeria has eight times as much rain as London. However, parts of northern Mali have almost no rain.

CANARY ISLANDS
(SPAIN)

Las Palmas de Gran Canaria

MOROCCO

El Aaiún

WESTERN SAHARA

ALGERIA

Dakhla

Zouérat

SAHARA

MAURITANIA

MALI

Tombouctou

Mindelo

CAPE VERDE

Praia

ATLANTIC OCEAN

Nouakchott

Senegal

St. Louis

Kaédi

Dakar • Thiès

SENEGAL

Banjul GAMBIA

Bissau

GUINEA-BISSAU

Kayes

Mopti

Djenné

Ségou

Bamako

Ouagadou

GUINEA

Conakry

Kankan

Sikasso

Bobo Dioulasso

BURKIN

Freetown SIERRA LEONE

Bo

COTE D'IVOIRE

Tama

Man

Daloa

Bouaké

Kumasi

Monrovia • Harbel

Yamoussoukro

GHAN

LIBERIA

Greenville

Abidjan

Accr

Sekondi-Tako

Cape Palmas

GULF

0   100   200   300   400 mi

0   200   400   600 km

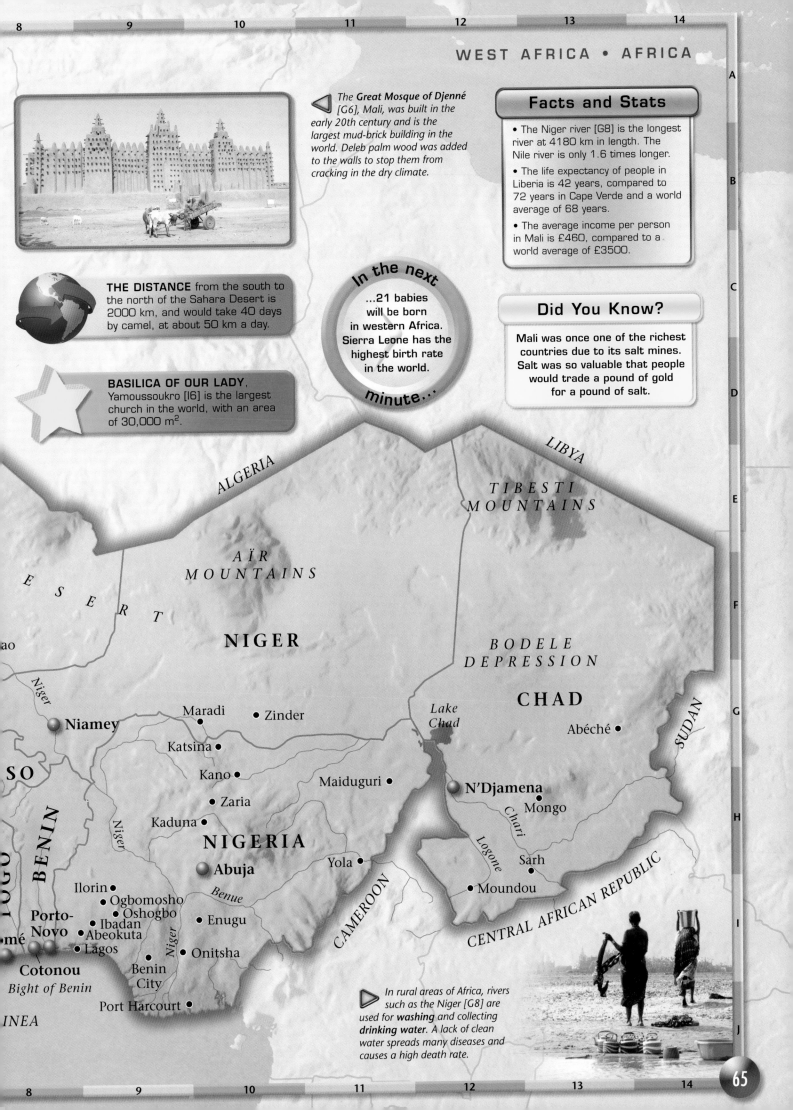

The **Great Mosque of Djenné** [G6], Mali, was built in the early 20th century and is the largest mud-brick building in the world. Deleb palm wood was added to the walls to stop them from cracking in the dry climate.

Facts and Stats

• The Niger river [G8] is the longest river at 4180 km in length. The Nile river is only 1.6 times longer.

• The life expectancy of people in Liberia is 42 years, compared to 72 years in Cape Verde and a world average of 68 years.

• The average income per person in Mali is £460, compared to a world average of £3500.

THE DISTANCE from the south to the north of the Sahara Desert is 2000 km, and would take 40 days by camel, at about 50 km a day.

...21 babies will be born in western Africa. Sierra Leone has the highest birth rate in the world.

In the next minute...

Did You Know?

Mali was once one of the richest countries due to its salt mines. Salt was so valuable that people would trade a pound of gold for a pound of salt.

BASILICA OF OUR LADY, Yamoussoukro [I6] is the largest church in the world, with an area of 30,000 m².

ALGERIA

LIBYA

TIBESTI
MOUNTAINS

AÏR
MOUNTAINS

ESERT

ao

NIGER

BODELE
DEPRESSION

CHAD

Niger

Maradi   Zinder

Niamey

Lake
Chad

Abéché

Katsina

Kano

Maiduguri

N'Djamena

SO

Zaria

Mongo

Chari

Kaduna

BENIN

Niger

NIGERIA

Ilorin

Abuja

Yola

Sarh

Logone

Ogbomosho
Oshogbo

Benue

Moundou

LOGO

Porto-
Novo

Ibadan
Abeokuta

Enugu

CAMEROON

CENTRAL AFRICAN REPUBLIC

mé

Lagos

Niger

Onitsha

Cotonou

Benin
City

Bight of Benin

INEA

Port Harcourt

In rural areas of Africa, rivers such as the Niger [G8] are used for **washing** and collecting **drinking water**. A lack of clean water spreads many diseases and causes a high death rate.

East Africa

Due to the high altitude of Kenya, Tanzania and Uganda, the climate is suited to growing crops. These countries have strong economies based on exporting crops, such as tea and coffee, which are grown on large plantations run by European companies. Kenya also has a strong tourist industry as people visit to see animals in their natural habitat. The countries of Ethiopia, Somalia and Sudan are poorer as they have harsher climates and a history of civil war. The droughts that have repeatedly affected this southern fringe of the Sahara Desert have caused millions of deaths as well as the destruction of crops and animals.

> *Lesser flamingos* are the smallest of the flamingo family. They are numerous throughout Africa and are always found in large groups called 'pats'. The colour of flamingos comes from their food – unhealthy birds are pale in colour.

Facts and Stats

- Mount Kilimanjaro [H9] is the highest mountain at 5895 m. It is 18 times higher than the Eiffel Tower.
- Sudan's area is 2.5 million km². This is 24 times the area of Iceland.
- The population of Tanzania is 37.8 million. This would fill 378 Olympic stadiums. Somalia's population is 8.6 million and would only fill 86 Olympic stadiums.

Extreme Weather

The Danakil Valley [D10], Ethiopia, has the hottest average daily temperature of 55°C.

Did You Know?

The berries of Kaffa trees were used to make coffee 1000 years ago in Ethiopia. Coffee is now the second most popular non-alcoholic beverage in the world.

Map labels:

EGYPT

LIBYA

LIBYAN DESERT   Wadi Ha

CHAD

Japal Marrah 3089 m

El Fasher

El Obeid

Nyala

DARFUR   SUDAN

BAHR AL-GHAZAL

CENTRAL AFRICAN REPUBLIC

Wau

SOUTH SUDA

DEMOCRATIC REPUBLIC OF THE CONGO

Ar

Lake Albe

Lake Edward

RWANDA
Kigali

Lake Kivu

BURUND
Bujumbura

Kigoma

Lake Tanganyik

```
0    100   200   300   400   500 mi
0       200     400     600    800 km
```

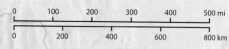

> *The Maasai people* of Kenya and Tanzania wear toga-like garments called shukkas, which can be bought at roadside shops. The official colour of the Maasai tribe is red, and is always worn as clothing or jewellery.

EAST AFRICA • AFRICA

Seaweed is farmed in coastal areas throughout Africa and Asia. It can be used as food or fertilizer and also in medicines.

NUBIAN DESERT

RED SEA

Port Sudan

owe

ara

Kassala

mdurman

Keren   Massawa

Asmara   DAHLAK ISLANDS

Khartoum   **ERITREA**

Wad Medani   Aksum   Ras Dashen 4533 m

Kosti   Asseb

Gonder   **DJIBOUTI**

Lake Tana   **Djibouti**

Debre Markos   Berbera

akal   Dire Dawa   Hargeisa

Addis Ababa   Harer   SOMALILAND

Gore   Nazret

Jima   OGADEN PLATEAU   Eyl

ETHIOPIA

Shebele

DANAKIL VALLEY

Blue Nile

Athara

Blue Nile

GULF OF ADEN

Cape Caseyr

In the next
...625 kg of tea will be produced in Kenya – enough for 500,000 teabags.
minute...

ANDA

Mount Elgon 4322 m

GREAT RIFT VALLEY

Lake Turkana

KENYA

SOMALIA

Jubba

Baidoa

Mogadishu

Marka

Baraawe

MOUNT KILIMANJARO [H9] is only 350 km south of the Equator, yet its summit is covered in snow and ice all year.

Kampala

Kisumu

aka

Nakuru

Nanyuki

Mount Kenya 5200 m

Garissa   Kismaayo

Thika

Nairobi

Tana

toria

Lake Natron

anza

Arusha   Galana   Malindi

Lake Eyasi

Mount Kilimanjaro 5895 m   Mombasa

nyanga

Tabora

TANZANIA

Dodoma

Rungwa

Bagamoyo

Kilosa

Tanga   Pemba Island

Zanzibar   Zanzibar Island

Dar es Salaam

Iringa   Mafia Island

Mbeya

Lake Malawi

Kilwa

MALAWI

Songea   Lindi   Mtwara

Rufiji

Ruvuma

MOZAMBIQUE

INDIAN OCEAN

THE DISTANCE from the far south to the far north of Africa is 7750 km – the same as from Mexico to the North Pole.

Search and Find

Central and southern Africa

This region stretches from the tropical rainforests of Cameroon to the rich agricultural lands of **South Africa.** Only those countries with mineral wealth have prospered. Political unrest is widespread, bringing great poverty to Mozambique, the Central African Republic and Zimbabwe. Once an exporter of food and tobacco, Zimbabwe is now reliant on international aid. Farming, commerce, and gold and diamond mining have brought prosperity to many South Africans.

▷ *Victoria Falls [G8] on the Zambezi river tumbles more than 128 m into the gorge below, creating the largest sheet of falling water in the world. The local people called the waterfall 'the smoke that thunders'.*

Facts and Stats

- The longest river is the Congo [C7]. At 4700 km in length, the Nile river is only 1.5 times longer.

- Mont Ngaliema (Mount Stanley) [C9] is the highest mountain at 5109 m in height – 16 times higher than the Eiffel Tower.

- The life expectancy of people in Swaziland is 32 years, compared to 74 years in Mauritius and a world average of 68 years.

Did You Know?

The Namib Desert [H6] is the oldest desert in the world. It covers 270,000 km^2 – more than twice the area of Iceland. Some parts have less than 2 cm of rain a year.

▷ *The **quiver tree** is a species of aloe found in southern Africa, especially throughout Namibia. Native people use the branches and bark of the tree to make containers, or quivers, for their arrows.*

NIGERIA
Garoua
Garba
CH

CEN
AFRICAN

Mount Cameroon
4071 m
Bamenda
Bouar   Bambar
CAMEROON
Berbérati
Malabo
Douala
Bangui
Bioko Island
Yaoundé
EQUATORIAL GUINEA
SÃO TOMÉ   *Príncipe*
AND PRÍNCIPE
São   *São*
Tomé   *Tomé*
Libreville
Mbanc

Port-Gentil   GABON
REPUBLIC OF THE CONGO
DEMOCR
OF T
*Lake
Mai-Ndombe*
Loubomo
Brazzaville
Bandundu
Kasai
Pointe-Noire
Kinshasa   Kikw
Matadi
Kwilu
Kwango
Tsh

Cuanza
Luanda
Saurimo
Lue

Lobito
ANGOLA
Benguela
Huambo

Namibe
Lubango
Cunene   *Cubango*   *Cuito*

*ETOSHA
PAN*
Cape Fria
Grootfontein
NAMIBIA
NAMIB DESERT
Windhoek
Swakopmund
*KALAH
DESE*
Walvis Bay
Rehoboth

Lüderitz
Keetmanshoo

Alexander Bay
SO
Kenhardt

Carnarvor
Calvinia
Beaufort V
Great Karoo
Cape Town   Worc
Cape of Good Hope   Mossel
False Bay

THE DISTANCE to the bottom of South Africa's deepest gold mine is 3777 m – this would take four minutes in a high-speed lift.

In the next minute... ...South Africa's diamond mines will produce enough gems for 21 pairs of earrings.

Search and Find

Angola
- Luanda E6

Botswana
- Gaborone H8

Cameroon
- Yaoundé C5

Central African Republic
- Bangui B7

Comoros
- Moroni F12

Democratic Republic of the Congo
- Kinshasa D6

Equatorial Guinea
- Malabo C5

Gabon
- Libreville C5

Lesotho
- Maseru I8

Madagascar
- Antananarivo . G12

Malawi
- Lilongwe F10

Mauritius
- Port Louis . . . H14

Mozambique
- Maputo I9

Namibia
- Windhoek H7

Republic of the Congo
- Brazzaville D6

São Tomé and Príncipe
- São Tomé C4

Seychelles
- Victoria D14

South Africa
- Cape Town J7
- Pretoria H9

Swaziland
- Lombamba . . . I9
- Mbabane I9

Zambia
- Lusaka F9

Zimbabwe
- Harare G9

SUDAN

BLIC

kouma

Bondo

Uele

Watsa

Mount Ngaliema 5109 m

Basoko

Kisangani

UGANDA

C REPUBLIC

NGO

Lake Edward

RWANDA

Lake Kivu

Bukavu

BURUNDI

TANZANIA

Lake Tanganyika

Congo

Lomani

Kalemie

Mbuji-Mayi

Kamina

Lake Mweru

Mbala

Kasama

vezi

Likasi

Lake Bangweulu

Lubumbashi

Mufulira

MALAWI

Lake Malawi

Kitwe

Ndola

Kafue

Kabwe

Chipata

Lilongwe

AMBIA

Lusaka

Lake Cahora Bassa

Zomba

Tete

Zambezi

Blantyre

Livingstone

Lake Kariba

Harare

ngo

Victoria Falls

Chitungwiza

Chimoio

MOZAMBIQUE

Maun

ZIMBABWE

Beira

WANA

Bulawayo

Save

ncistown

ebi-Phikwe

Messina

Limpopo

Inhambane

olepolole

Pietersburg

tse

Gaborone

Pretoria

hannesburg

Mbabane

Maputo

Soweto

Vaal

Vereeniging

SWAZILAND

AFRICA

Lobamba

Kimberley

Maseru

mfontein

Pietermaritzburg

LESOTHO

Durban

nge

Port Shepstone

DRAKENSBERG MOUNTAINS

delburg

Umtata

East London

Port Elizabeth

Lúrio

Nacala

Nampula

Moçambique

Quelimane

Cape Delgado

COMOROS

Moroni

MAYOTTE (FRANCE)

SEYCHELLES

Victoria

INDIAN OCEAN

Antsiranana

Mahajanga

MADAGASCAR

Antananarivo

Fianarantsoa

MAURITIUS

RÉUNION (FRANCE)

Port Louis

MOZAMBIQUE CHANNEL

| 0 | 100 | 200 | 300 | 400 | 500 mi |

| 0 | 200 | 400 | 600 | 800 km |

African elephants live in herds of females, led by a matriarch – normally the oldest female. They work together to keep the herd safe. When they walk in file, the youngsters stay close to the adults so they are protected from predators.

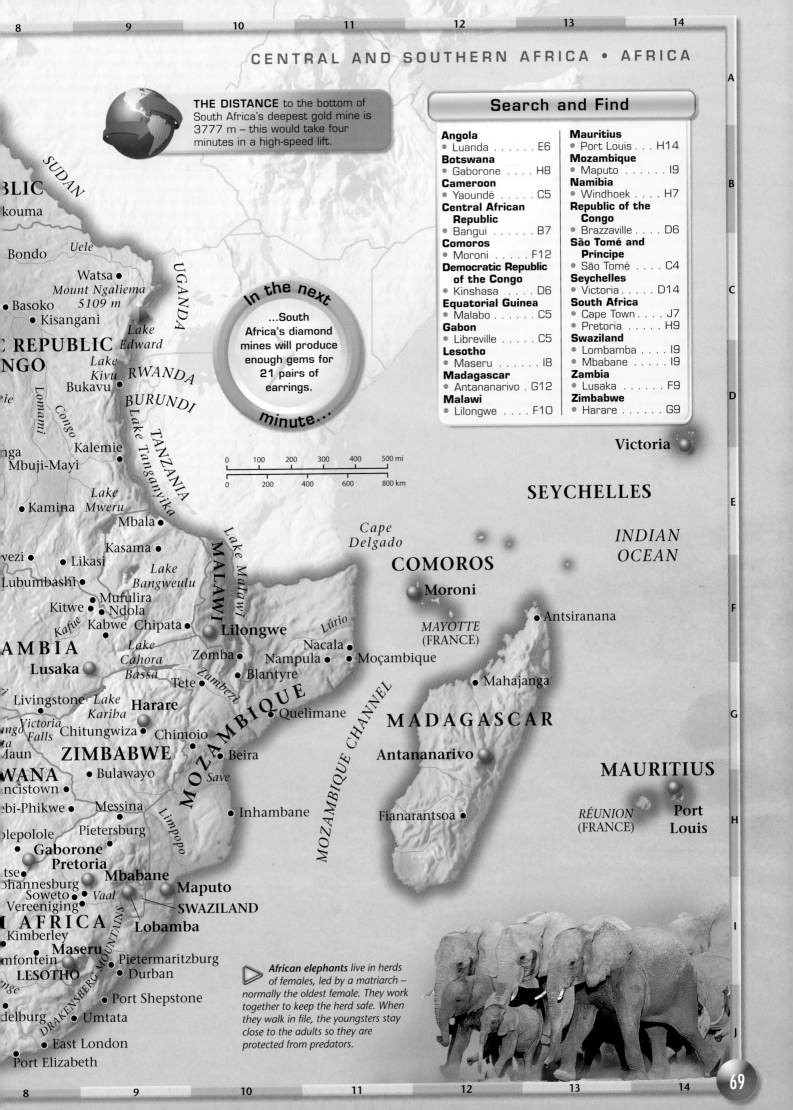

Asia

ARCTIC OCEAN

RUSSIAN FEDERATION

KAZAKHSTAN

MONGOLIA

UZBEKISTAN

KYRGYZSTAN

NORTH
KOREA

TURKEY

TURKMENISTAN

TAJIKISTAN

JAPAN

1
SYRIA
2
IRAQ
3 4

AFGHANISTAN

C H I N A

SOUTH
KOREA

IRAN
5

PAKISTAN

NEPAL
9

TAIWAN

6
7
8

BANGLADESH

SAUDI
ARABIA

*PACIFIC
OCEAN*

OMAN

INDIA

MYANMAR
(BURMA)

LAOS

YEMEN

THAILAND

VIETNAM

CAMBODIA

PHILIPPINES

SRI
LANKA

10

12

MALAYSIA

11

I N D O N E S I A

*INDIAN
OCEAN*

EAST
TIMOR

KEY
1 CYPRUS
2 LEBANON
3 ISRAEL
4 JORDAN
5 KUWAIT
6 BAHRAIN
7 QATAR
8 UNITED ARAB EMIRATES
9 BHUTAN
10 BRUNEI
11 SINGAPORE
12 MALDIVES

COUNTRY FACTFILE

Country	Life expectancy	Population in thousands	Population growth %	Population as urban %	Literacy %	Area km²	Population density per km²	Capital city	Currency	Languages
Afghanistan	45	22,576	2.6	22	28.1	645,807	35	Kabul	Afghani	Dari, Pashto
Bahrain	75	725	1.3	91	86.5	716	1012.6	Manama	Bahraini Dinar	Arabic
Bangladesh	60	129,247	1.3	27	47.9	147,570	875.8	Dhaka	Taka	Bangla, English
Bhutan	66	672	1.3	36	47	46,500	14.5	Thimphu	Ngultrum	Dzongkha, Nepali
Brunei	76	383	1.8	75	92.7	5765	66.4	Bandar Seri Begawan	Bruneian Dollar	Malay
Cambodia	62	13,389	1.8	22	73.6	181,035	74	Phnom Penh	Riel	Khmer
China	73	1,240,000	0.7	43	90.9	9,559,686	134.4	Beijing	Yuan	Chinese (Guoyo)
Cyprus	78	1023	0.5	69.5	97.6	9251	110.6	Nicosia	Euro	Greek, Turkish, English
East Timor	67	923	2	27	58.6	14,874	62.1	Dili	US Dollar	Tetum, Portuguese
India	70	1,148,000	1.5	29	61	3,287,263	362.6	New Delhi	Indian Rupee	Hindi, English, Telegu, Bengali
Indonesia	71	222,192	1.1	52	90.4	1,904,413	116.7	Jakarta	Indonesian Rupiah	Bhasa Indonesia, Javanese, Sudanese
Iran	71	70,496	0.9	68	77	1,641,918	42.9	Tehran	Iranian Rial	Farsi (Persian), Azeri
Iraq	70	27,475	2.5	76	74	434,128	63.3	Baghdad	New Iraqi Dinar	Arabic, Kurdish
Israel	81	7338	1.7	91	97.1	20,400	359.7	Jerusalem	Israeli Shekel	Hebrew, Arabic
Japan	82	127,931	-0.2	78	99	377,819	338.6	Tokyo	Yen	Japanese
Jordan	79	5103	2.3	79	89.9	89,342	57.1	Amman	Jordanian Dinar	Arabic
Kazakhstan	68	15,572	0.4	56	99.5	2,717,300	5.7	Astana	Tenge	Kazakh, Russian
Korea, North	64	24,051	0.4	61	99	122,762	195.9	Pyongyang	North Korean Won	Korean
Korea, South	79	50,034	0.3	81	97.9	99,461	503.1	Seoul	South Korean Won	Korean
Kuwait	78	2213	3.5	97	93.3	17,818	124.2	Kuwait City	Kuwaiti Dinar	Arabic
Kyrgyzstan	69	5252	1.4	35	98.7	198,500	26.5	Bishkek	Som	Kyrgyz, Russian
Laos	57	5622	2.3	31	68.7	236,800	23.7	Vientiane	Kip	Lao
Lebanon	74	3754	1.1	90	87.4	10,201	368	Beirut	Lebanese Pound	Arabic
Malaysia	73	26,128	1.7	70	88.7	329,847	79.2	Kuala Lumpur, Putrajaya	Ringgit	Bahasa Melayu (Malay), Chinese, English
Maldives	74	299	-0.2	38	96.3	298	1003.4	Male	Rufiyaa	Dhivehi (Maldivian)
Mongolia	68	2635	1.5	62	97.8	1,564,100	1.7	Ulaanbaatar	Tugrik	Khalkha Mongol
Myanmar (Burma)	63	49,008	0.8	33	89.9	676,577	72.4	Naypyidaw	Kyat	Burmese, Shan
Nepal	63	23,078	1.3	17	48.6	147,181	156.8	Kathmandu	Nepalese Rupee	Nepali, Maithali
Oman	74	2744	3.1	81	81.4	309,500	8.9	Muscat	Omani Rial	Arabic, Baluchi
Pakistan	64	162,508	1.9	38	49.9	796,095	204.1	Islamabad	Pakistani Rupee	Urdu, Punjabi, Sindhi
Philippines	71	88,575	2	65	92.6	300,076	295.2	Manila	Philippine Peso	Filipino (Tagalog), Cebuano, English
Qatar	75	838	1	96	89	11,427	73.3	Doha	Qatari Rial	Arabic
Russian Federation	66	142,754	-0.5	78	99.4	17,075,400	8.4	Moscow	Rouble	Russian, Tatar, Ukrainian
Saudi Arabia	76	23,980	1.8	85	78.8	2,149,690	11.2	Riyadh	Saudi Riyal	Arabic
Singapore	82	4484	1	100	92.5	697	6433.3	Singapore	Singapore Dollar	Chinese, Malay, English
Sri Lanka	75	20,010	0.9	23	90.7	65,610	305	Colombo, Kotte	Sri Lankan Rupee	Sinhala, Tamil
Syria	71	19,880	2.1	52	80	185,180	107.4	Damascus	Syrian Pound	Arabic
Taiwan	78	22,790	0.2	75	96.1	36,179	629.9	Taipei	Taiwan dollar	Chinese (Mandarin), Min
Tajikistan	65	7216	1.9	28	99.5	143,100	40.4	Dushanbe	Somoni	Tajik, Uzbek
Thailand	73	66,148	0.6	35	92.6	514,000	128.9	Bangkok	Baht	Thai
Turkey	72	70,586	1.3	75	87.4	780,580	90.6	Ankara	Turkish Lira	Turkish, Kurdish
Turkmenistan	68	5673	1.1	49	98.8	488,100	11.6	Ashgabat	Turkmen Manat	Turkmen, Uzbek
United Arab Emirates	76	4765	3.7	57	77.9	83,600	45.1	Abu Dhabi	Emirati Dirham	Arabic, Hindu, Urdu
Uzbekistan	72	27,314	0.9	39	99.3	447,400	61.1	Tashkent	Uzbek Soum	Uzbek, Russian
Vietnam	72	85,155	1	28	90.3	329,315	258.6	Hanoi	Dong	Vietnamese
Yemen	63	20,901	3.5	31	50.2	527,970	39.6	Sanaa	Yemeni Rial	Arabic

The Near East

A poor, mountainous region, Turkey has a beautiful coastline and thriving tourist industry. The country is currently being transformed by the Great Anatolian project – reservoirs will be built along the Tigris and Euphrates rivers, to irrigate 16,000 km² of land. Although geographically closer to Asia, Turkey is internationally recognized as part of Europe. Israel was created in 1948. Land was taken from the Palestinians resulting in conflict with Syria, Jordan and Lebanon. Sheep and goats are the main livestock. Where irrigation is possible, vegetables and fruit are grown, much of which is exported to Europe.

BULGARIA

GREECE

Edirne

Bosporus Strait

Tekirdag

Istanbul

Sea of Marmara

Izmi

Bursa

Sak

Balikesir

Eskisehir

Kütahy

A N A T

Manisa

P L A

Izmir

Usak

Ephesus

Aydin

Nazilli

Denizli

Isp

Bodrum

T A

Antalya

The **Temple Mount** in Jerusalem [I9] is an important religious site. The Dome of the Rock is a Muslim shrine. The Western Wall dates back to 500 BC and is used by Jews for prayer.

THE DISTANCE from Europe to Asia across the Bosporus Strait [B6] is only 700 m and takes one minute by car across a bridge.

Search and Find

Cyprus
- Nicosia F8

Israel
- Jerusalem I9

Jordan
- Amman H10

Lebanon
- Beirut G9

Syria
- Damascus . . . H10

Turkey
- Ankara C8

Did You Know?

Cyprus is the third largest island in the Mediterranean. The northern area of the island is Turkish Cypriot and the southern area is Greek Cypriot. Although geographically closer to Asia, Cyprus joined the EU in 2004.

Facts and Stats

- Turkey's area of 780,580 km² is 7.5 times the area of Iceland.
- Mount Ararat [D14] is the highest mountain at 5137 m –16 times higher than the Eiffel Tower.
- The life expectancy of people in Israel is 81 years, compared to 71 years in Syria and a world average of 68 years.

Pamukkale, which means 'cotton castle' in Turkish, was formed from the water of a very hot spring. The water contains a lot of chalk, which results in the limestone cliffs that can be seen today.

0 50 100 150 200 mi
0 100 200 300 km

The **Dead Sea** [I9] is the second saltiest body of water in the world and is called 'dead' because fish and other organisms cannot survive in it. Salty deposits cover the beaches and cliffs, and it is almost impossible to sink in the water because of the high salt content.

BLACK SEA

GEORGIA

ARMENIA

Zonguldak
• Karabük

• Samsun

Ordu •   Trabzon •

• Çorum

PONTIC MOUNTAINS

Kars •

Ankara
• Kirikkale

Kelkit

Erzurum •

Mount Ararat 5137 m

• Sivas

• Erzincan

I A N
A U

TURKEY

Kizilirmak

Murat

Lake Tuz

• Kayseri

Elazig •

Lake Van • Van

• Konya

Malatya •

Adiyaman •

Diyarbakir •

• Batman

U S   M O U N T A I N S

Firat

Khabur

• Al Qamishli

Tarsus •   Adana
•   •

• Osmaniye

• Gaziantep

Al Hasakah •

Mersin •

• Al Bab

Aleppo •

Ar Raqqah •

Euphrates

CYPRUS

Antakya •

Lake Assad

• Latakia

Nicosia

Dayr az Zawr •

SYRIA

aphos

Baniyas •

• Hamah

• Limassol

Tartus •

• Hims

Abu Kamal •

Tripoli •

LEBANON

SYRIAN DESERT

IRAQ

Beirut

EDITERRANEAN SEA

Sidon •

LEBANON MOUNTAINS

Damascus

Tyre •

• Al Kiswah

Acre •

GOLAN HEIGHTS

• Al Qunaytirah

Haifa •

Nazareth •

Sea of Galilee

• Dar'a

Hadera •

WEST

• Irbid

Netanya •

BANK

Jordan

Ramallah •

• Az-Zarqa

Tel Aviv •

Amman

Jerusalem

Dead Sea

Gaza •

Bethlehem •

• Ma'daba

GAZA STRIP

Beersheba •

• Al-Karak

ISRAEL

Wadi al Hasa

NEGEV DESERT

• Ma'an

EGYPT

JORDAN

Elat •   • Aqaba

Gulf of Aqaba

SAUDI ARABIA

In the next
...Turkey will produce enough Turkish delight confectionery to create a pillar 305 m in height.
minute...

The ruins of Ephesus [D5] are a major tourist attraction. Built in 135 AD, the restored **Library of Celsus** is a monumental tomb for Celsus Polemaeanus, the governor of Asia. His grave is across the entrance, under the ground floor.

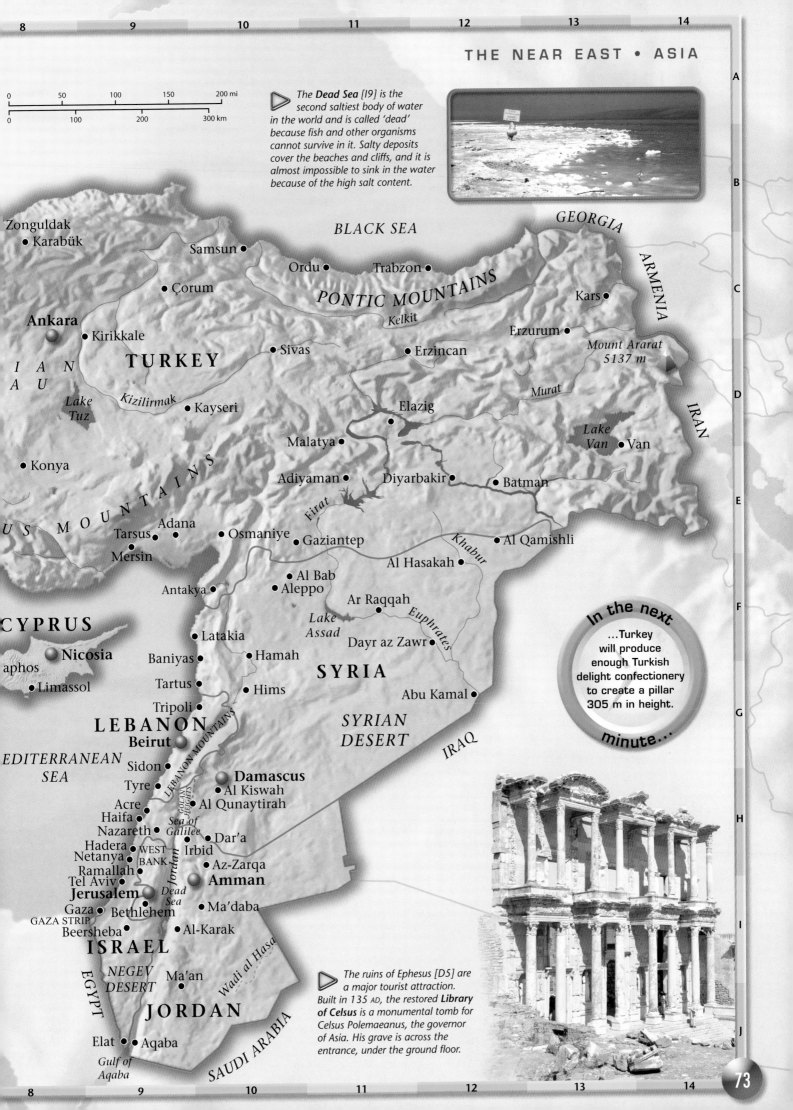

The Middle East

Vast oil and gas reserves have made several countries in the Middle East some of the wealthiest in the world. However, before oil was discovered, this was a poor region of desert tribes and coastal fishing. The area between the Euphrates and Tigris rivers was once home to the great civilization of Mesopotamia. Recent wars have damaged the economies of Iran and Iraq, but other countries such as Bahrain are investing in tourism and other forms of industry. The city of Dubai now has the largest indoor ski slope in the world.

*For thousands of years, Iran has been the centre of the hand-woven **Persian carpet** industry. Although machinery is widely used today, traditional methods are still used in some areas. A medium-sized rug can take a skilled worker up to a year to complete.*

Extreme Weather

Midday temperatures can reach 50°C in the desert areas, but snow is common in the mountains of Iran and Iraq.

Did You Know?

The United Arab Emirates obtains more than 80 percent of its water supply by desalinating sea water.

*Millions of Muslims have made a pilgrimage, or Hajj, to Mecca [G5]. The holiest place in Islam is the **Kaaba**. Non-Muslims cannot enter Mecca.*

ARMEN

TURKEY

T

Mosul • • Arbil

Kirkuk •

SYRIA

IRAQ

Bakht..

Baghdad

S Y R I A N
D E S E R T

Tigris

JORDAN

Karbala •

Najaf •

Euphrates

An Nasiriyah

EGYPT

Al Jawf • • Sakakah

N A F U D
D E S E R T

Buraydah •

Shaqra •

Riyadh

H I J A Z

Medina •

• Yanbu

S A U I

RED SEA

Jiddah
• • Mecca
• Taif

As-Sulayyil •

A S I R

• Abha

• Jizan
• Harad

Sanaa
• Al-Hudaydah

• Ta'izz

Shad..

• Aden

GU..

Grid coordinates (top)
8   9   10   11   12   13   14

Map labels

CASPIAN SEA
TURKMENISTAN
RBAIJAN
asht
Babol
Gorgan
Mashhad
ELBURZ MOUNTAINS
Karaj
Tehran
Qom
Hamadan
Kashan
IRAN
AFGHANISTAN
AGROS MOUNTAINS
Esfahan
Yazd
Ahvaz
Kerman
Zahedan
sra
Abadan
PAKISTAN
WAIT
Kuwait City
Shiraz
Bushehr
PERSIAN GULF
Bandar-e Lengeh
Bandar 'Abbas
Strait of Hormuz
Al Qatif
BAHRAIN
Dammam
Manama
Jask
QATAR
Sharjah
GULF OF OMAN
Al-Hufuf
Doha
Dubai
Suhar
Abu Dhabi
UNITED ARAB EMIRATES
Jabal ash Sham 3035 m
Matrah
Muscat
ARABIA
Nizwa
Sur
ARABIAN SEA
EMPTY QUARTER
OMAN
Khaluf
YEMEN
Salalah
Al Mukalla
SOCOTRA (YEMEN)
ADEN

Search and Find

Bahrain		Qatar	
• Manama	E8	• Doha	F9
Iran		Saudi Arabia	
• Tehran	B9	• Riyadh	F7
Iraq		United Arab Emirates	
• Baghdad	C7	• Abu Dhabi	F10
Kuwait		Yemen	
• Kuwait City	D8	• Sanaa	I7
Oman			
• Muscat	F11		

THE DISTANCE from Yemen to Africa is only 30 km across the Red Sea and takes four hours by canoe.

Facts and Stats

• The average income per person in Bahrain is £11,000, compared to a world average of £3500.

• Saudi Arabia has an area of 2.2 million km² and is 21 times the area of Iceland.

• The longest river is the Euphrates [C7]. At 2800 km in length, it is nearly 2.5 times shorter than the Nile river.

In the next minute... ...Saudi Arabia will produce 850,000 litres of oil – enough for a car to travel 10 million km.

Scale
0   100   200   300   400 mi
0   200   400   600 km

Built in the 1970s, **Kuwait's water towers** [D8] are more than 145 m in height. One tower provides electricity, and the other two towers store water – the middle tower holds more than 4 million litres of water. The main tower also has a viewing platform and revolving restaurant.

Indian subcontinent

With ice-covered mountains, tropical lowlands and hot deserts, this region is one of contrasts. Afghanistan is a war-torn, semi-desert nation that is in the process of rebuilding after recent conflicts. India has one of the most rapidly growing economies in the world. A highly educated, English-speaking workforce has resulted in many European and American companies establishing various support operations in India. The 'Bollywood' film studios are a worldwide success and cities are rapidly expanding. However, out of India's 1.1 billion population, two-thirds remain poor, rural farmers. Pakistan, Bangladesh and the Himalayan states of Nepal and Bhutan remain relatively undeveloped.

The **Taj Mahal** in Agra [D9], India, was built for Mumtaz Mahal, the wife of Emperor Shah Jahan. When she died in 1629, the Emperor ordered the most beautiful tomb in the world to be built. It took 20,000 workers about 20 years to build. The Emperor and his wife are buried beneath the 60-m-high white dome.

Search and Find

Afghanistan
- Kabul B7

Bangladesh
- Dhaka E11

Bhutan
- Thimphu D11

India
- New Delhi D9

Nepal
- Kathmandu . . D10

Pakistan
- Islamabad B8

Sri Lanka
- Colombo J9
- Kotte J9

Did You Know?

Great Britain ruled India until 1947. This is why English is widely spoken and cricket is the national sport.

THE DISTANCE from the Everest base camp to the summit is 10 km. In 2000, it was climbed in less than 17 hours.

World Record

In July 1861, Cherrapunji [E12] recorded the world's highest rainfall in a month – 93 cm.

Many Hindus go to a 'mandir', or **temple**, to say prayers and to make offerings of food to the gods. The temples are beautifully decorated with carvings of gods and spirits.

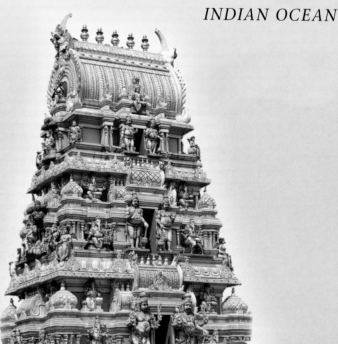

TURKMENISTAN

Sheberghan •

Mazar-e Sh

• Herat

Kab

AFGHANISTA

IRAN

• Farah

Helmand

• Qandaha

RIGESTAN
DESERT

Quetta •

PAKISTA

Larkana •   • Suk

• Gwadar

Indus

Hyderabad •   •
Karachi •   • Mirpur K

Gulf of
Kachchh

RANN O
KACHCH

Ahmadal

Jamnagar •

ARABIAN
SEA

Bhavnagar
Su

Gulf of
Khambhat

Mumba
(Bombay

INDIAN OCEAN

SIGIRIYA, or Lion's Mouth, was the fortress of Sri Lankan King Kashyapa (AD 477–495). Only the two giant paws of the lion remain.

Facts and Stats

• The longest river in the region is the Brahmaputra [D12]. At 2900 km in length, it is almost half the length of the Nile river.

• The highest mountain in the world is Mount Everest [D11] at 8850 m in height – 28 times higher than the Eiffel Tower.

• The life expectancy of people in Afghanistan is 45 years, compared to 75 years in Sri Lanka and a world average of 68 years.

Extreme Weather

The heaviest recorded hailstones, weighing up to one kg killed 92 people in Bangladesh on 14 April 1986.

TAJIKISTAN

K2
8611 m

Mardan
Islamabad
awar
valpindi · Srinagar
alabad · Gujranwala
Lahore · Amritsar
tan · Sahiwel
Sutlej · Ludhiana
awalpur · Chandigarh

CHINA

HIMALAYAS

Meerut
Delhi
New Delhi

Ganges

NEPAL

Kathmandu
Mount Everest
8850 m
Thimphu
BHUTAN

Jaipur · Agra
hpur · Ajmer
Yamuna
Lucknow
Biratnagar
Brahmaputra
Jorhat
Kanpur
Guwahati
Udaipur
Allahabad
Varanasi
Rangpur
NAGA HILLS
Lalitpur
Patna
Cherrapunji
Rajshahi
Sylhet · Imphal

Bhopal
Narmada
Dhanbad
BANGLADESH
Agartala
odara
Indore
Dhaka

INDIA
Jamshedpur
Khulna
Chittagong

Nagpur · Raipur
Kolkata
(Calcutta)

MYANMAR (BURMA)

Cuttack

BAY OF
BENGAL

Godavari
ne
na)
EASTERN GHATS
Solapur
Hyderabad
hapur
Krishna
Vishakhapatnam
Vijayawada
Kurnool
bli-Dhawar

Nellore

galore
Bengaluru
(Bangalore)
Chennai
(Madras)
Mysore
Puducherry
ozhikode (Calicut)
Coimbatore
Tiruchchirappalli

ANDAMAN
ISLANDS
(INDIA)

Kochi
Madurai
Cochin)
Palk Strait
Jaffna
iruvananthapuram
vandrum)
Trincomalee

SRI LANKA

Colombo
Kandy
Kotte
Galle

NICOBAR
ISLANDS
(INDIA)

The **Ganges river** flows through the city of Varanasi [E10] and is believed to be sacred. Many Hindus make pilgrimages to pray and bathe in the holy water.

In the next
...more than 50 babies will be born in India – that's 66,000 every day.
minute...

0   100   200   300   400 mi
0   200   400   600 km

Vietnam and the Philippines

Lush tropical rainforests lead to wonderful sandy beaches and warm seas. Rice fields and remote villages give way to sprawling cities. Despite the rapid growth of tourism in Thailand and Vietnam, most of this area is poor. Many people live near the coast and they are still mainly dependent on fishing and farming. Rice is the main crop, grown in the river valleys in wet paddy fields. Wars in Vietnam and Cambodia have devastated many cities, leaving Cambodia with the highest number of widows and orphans in the world.

| 0 | 100 | 200 | 300 | 400 mi |
| 0 | 200 | 400 | | 600 km |

INDIA

CHINA

Thai Nguyen

Mandalay

MYANMAR (BURMA)

Hanoi · Haiphong
Nam Dinh

Thanh Hoa

Gulf of Tonkin

BANGLADESH

Luang Prabang

Vinh

Sittwe

Naypyidaw

LAOS

ARAKAN RANGE

Irrawaddy

Chiang Mai

Prome

PEGU RANGE

Vientiane

Udon Thani

Hué

Da Nang

Henzada

THAILAND

Savannakhet

Khon Kaen

Pegu

Bassein

Yangon (Rangoon)

Moulmein

Pakxe
Champassak

Ubon Ratchathani

Gulf of Martaban

Nakhon Sawan

VIETNAM

Qui Nhon

Tavoy

Nakhon Ratchasima

Angkor Wat

Mekong

BILAUKTAUNG RANGE

ANDAMAN SEA

Bangkok · Batdâmbang

Nha Trang

Chon Buri

CAMBODIA

Da Lat

Mergui

Kampong Cham

Phnom Penh

Ho Chi Minh City

GULF OF THAILAND

Can Tho

Facts and Stats

• The life expectancy of people in Cambodia is 62 years, compared to 72 years in Vietnam and a world average of 68 years.

• There are only 1.6 doctors per 10,000 people in Cambodia, compared to a world average of 17.

• The average income per person in Cambodia is £1000, compared to a world average of £3500.

Nakhon Si Thammarat

SPRATLY ISLANDS

In the next ...the Mekong river [G5] will deposit enough silt to fill 50 bathtubs – 30 million tonnes a year. **minute...**

Phuket

Hat Yai · Songkhla

MALAYSIA

A

▷ Many young men in Thailand become **Buddhist monks** to learn more about their faith. They shave their heads and beards and wear robes to show commitment to the holy life.

Search and Find

Cambodia	Philippines
● Phnom Penh . . H5	● Manila F10
Laos	**Thailand**
● Vientiane F4	● Bangkok H4
Myanmar (Burma)	**Vietnam**
● Naypyidaw F2	● Hanoi E5

B

THE DISTANCE from Yangon [G2] to Bangkok [H4] is 640 km and would take an elephant three days of non-stop walking.

C

▷ The canals in Bangkok [H4] are used for **floating markets** where fresh produce, such as fruit, vegetables and flowers, is sold from boats.

D

Luzon Strait

BABUYAN ISLANDS

Laoag ●

● Tuguegarao

Luzon

E

PHILIPPINES

PACIFIC OCEAN

● Cabanatuan

Angeles ●

● Quezon City

Manila ●

Batangas ●

F

● Calbayog
Samar

Mindoro

● Ormoc
Leyte

SOUTH CHINA SEA

Mindoro Strait

Panay ● Bacolod

Iloilo ●

● Cebu

Did You Know?

The ruins of the ancient city of Angkor Wat [G5], complete with Hindu temples and royal palaces, were discovered in the Cambodian rainforest 150 years ago.

G

Negros

● Butuan

Cagayan de Oro ●

Palawan Passage

● Puerto Princesa

Palawan

Mindanao

Extreme Weather

In July, the monsoon rains bring the city of Yangon [G2] as much rain as London gets in a year.

H

Pagadian ●

● Davao

SULU SEA

Moro Gulf

General Santos

Zamboanga

CELEBES SEA

Balabac Strait

I

SULU ARCHIPELAGO

▷ Many tropical countries suffer from rainy seasons called monsoons, which result in serious flooding. In some parts of Asia, **houses are built on stilts** over bodies of water to protect them against water damage.

J

Indonesia, Malaysia and Singapore

Situated on the Equator, this region has a hot, wet climate. Malaysia is part of the Asian mainland and the large island of Borneo. It is developing rapidly with car and shipbuilding industries. Singapore is the richest country in this region, based on its technology industry, banking and high educational standards. A safe, law-abiding nation, laws against all types of crime, even dropping litter, are strictly enforced. Indonesia consists of over 13,000 islands. Natural disasters, poor communications and corruption have restricted economic growth. Although East Timor became independent from Indonesia in 2002, it remains impoverished.

THAILAND

George Town
Ipoh • MALAY
Kuala Terengganu
PENINSULA
Medan •
Kelang • **Kuala Lumpur** Natuna Island
Putrajaya M A L A Y S I A
Johor Baharu
Singapore
Pekanbaru • SINGAPORE
Strait of Malacca
Sumatra
Padang •
Bangka
Jambi •
Belitung
Palembang •

Kota Kinabalu
Bandar Seri Begawan • Sandakan
BRUNEI SABAH
CELEBES SEA
SARAWAK
• Kuching Manado •
Pontianak • Kapuas
KALIMANTAN MOLU SE
• Palu
Balikpapan Sulawesi
Borneo Barito
Banjarmasin • Makassar Strait

INDONESIA

Tanjungkarang •
Telukbetung • Makasar
Jakarta JAVA SEA
Bandung • Java • Semarang FLORES SEA
Surakarta • • Surabaya
Malang • Komodo Flores
Bali • Mataram • Ende
Lombok Sumbawa
Sumba Kupang • Th

More than 450 m in height, the **Petronas Towers** in Kuala Lumpur [E2] contain 88 floors of offices, a shopping mall, a concert hall and parking for 4500 cars.

Extreme Weather

At the Equator, the climate is the same throughout the year – hot and very wet. Singapore's temperature averages at 27°C.

A

In the next

...five new cars will be made in this region – that's 2.6 million a year.

minute...

▷ **Tea** has been grown throughout Indonesia for more than 200 years, especially in Java and Sumatra. These small islands now produce 7 percent of the world's tea exports. The shoots are picked by hand, packed and exported.

B

C

Did You Know?

The 2004 tsunami in southeast Asia was caused by an undersea earthquake. The waves travelled at speeds of up to 800 km/h – 190,000 people were killed and five million were made homeless.

Search and Find

Brunei
- Bandar Seri Begawan E5

East Timor
- Dili H7

Indonesia
- Jakarta H3

Malaysia
- Kuala Lumpur . . E2
- Putrajaya E2

Singapore
- Singapore F2

D

THE DISTANCE from Singapore to Malaysia is only 1056 m and the Joho–Singapore Causeway can be crossed by car in one minute.

E

hera

• Sorong

Jayapura •

ERAM SEA

Seram

Ambon

F

New Guinea

G

SEA

ARU ISLANDS

Tanimbar Island

ARAFURA SEA

H

TIMOR

◁ The **Batak people** live in Sumatra, Indonesia. Easily recognizable, their houses are built on stilts and have high, thatched roofs. Often ornaments and paintings are placed on the outside to ward away evil spirits.

Facts and Stats

- The average income per person in Singapore is £15,000, compared to £430 in East Timor and a world average of £3500.

- The life expectancy of people in Singapore is 82 years, compared to 73 years in Malaysia and a world average of 68 years.

- Indonesia's area of 1.9 million km^2 is 18 times the area of Iceland.

I

J

Japan

Japan consists of four main islands – Kyushu, Hokkaido, Honshu and Shikoku. More than 70 percent of the country is covered with forested volcanic mountains such as Mount Fuji. Most of Japan's population lives on the flatlands along the coast, resulting in a very high population density. People live in high-rise flats or small houses, but frequent earthquakes can cause immense damage. Agriculture, industry, and urban development are concentrated on the main island of Honshu in the area between Osaka and Tokyo. Japan is one of the richest nations in the world, with well-known brands such as Toyota, Honda, Nissan, Sony, Panasonic and JVC.

◁ **The Golden Pavilion,** Kyoto [G8], was originally built in the 14th century for a samurai general. The temple has been destroyed many times, and was most recently rebuilt in the 1950s. The pavilion, except the basement floor, is covered in pure gold leaf.

World Record
The Seikan railway tunnel is the longest tunnel in the world at 54 km in length.

MOUNT FUJI [G9] is an active volcano, but last erupted in 1707. More than 200,000 people walk to its snow-capped summit each year.

THE DISTANCE from Tokyo [G10] to Osaka [H8] is 515 km. It only takes 2.5 hours by high-speed train, travelling at 206 km/h.

SEA OF JAPAN

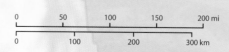
| 0 | 50 | 100 | 150 | 200 mi |
| 0 | 100 | 200 | 300 km |

Oki Island

Matsue • Yonago • • Tott...

Korea Strait

Tsushima

Hiroshima Okayama • Ko...

Shimonoseki • Kure • Takamatsu • Wakay...

Kitakyushu • Hofu Tokushima

Fukuoka • Matsuyama • Kochi

Sasebo • Oita • *Shikoku*

Kumamoto Saiki • *Bungo Channel*

Nagasaki •

Amakusa Island Nobeoka •

Koshiki Island *Kyushu*

• Miyazaki
• Miyakonojo

Kagoshima •

◁ **Sumo wrestling** is a popular sport in Japan. Competitors have a body weight of up to 270 kg and their aim is to push their opponent out of the ring. Sumo is more than 2000 years old, and has strict rules and ceremonies.

Tanega Island

Yaku Island

8   9   10   11   12   13   14

A
B
C
D
E
F
G
H
I
J

Soya Strait

Rebun Island • Wakkanai

Rishiri Island

• Abashiri

Ishikari • Asahikawa

Hokkaido

Otaru • • Ebetsu
Sapporo • • Obihiro • Kushiro
• Chitose
Tomakomai •

• Muroran

Uchiura Bay   *Cape Erimo*

Hakodate •

Tsugaru Strait

Aomori • • Hachinohe
Hirosaki •

Akita •   • Miyako
Hanamaki •   • Kamaishi

Sakata •   • Kesennuma

• Ishinomaki
Yamagata • • Sendai

Sado
Island   • Niigata
• Fukushima
Nagaoka • Aizu • • Koriyama

Shinano *Honshu*

Toyama   • Iwaki
...azawa • Utsunomiya • • Hitachi
• Komatsu • Nagano   • Mito
• Takasaki

Matsumoto • • Saitama

JAPAN Kofu • **Tokyo**

Mount Fuji   • Chiba
3776 m   • Kawasaki
Gifu • • Fuji Yokohama
...oto   • Shizuoka
Nagoya • • Toyota
...ka Hamamatsu
Toyohashi

*PACIFIC
OCEAN*

*Miyake
Island*

*Hachijo
Island*

Geisha are female Japanese entertainers who are skilled in many traditional arts, such as music, singing and dancing. Although the make-up and clothing of geisha change throughout their career, they generally wear a white base, red lipstick and black outlines to their eyes.

In the next
...Japan will manufacture 15 cars and 50 computer consoles.
minute...

Did You Know?

People in Japan often wear face masks to protect themselves from fumes, pollution and germs.

Extreme Weather

The mountains of the northern island of Hokkaido have some of the heaviest snowfall in the world. The 1972 Winter Olympics were held there.

With so many people, cars and businesses crammed into a small area, **Tokyo** [G10] is one of the most congested cities in the world. Tokyo Tower is based on the Eiffel Tower, Paris, although it is actually more than 8 m taller.

Facts and Stats

• The highest mountain is Mount Fuji [G9] at 3776 m. It is 12 times higher than the Eiffel Tower.

• The life expectancy of people in Japan is 82 years, compared to a world average of 68 years.

• The average income per person in Japan is £16,000, compared to a world average of £3500.

China and Korea

One-fifth of the world's population lives in China, despite each family being limited to just one child. Once a poor, rural nation, China has the fastest-growing economy in the world. Each year, millions of farm workers move to the cities to work in factories. A new power station has to be built every week, making China the biggest user of coal and oil in the world. In contrast, Mongolia has a small, mainly rural population. North Korea is a Communist state with a low standard of living, but South Korea is much richer due to its shipbuilding, electronic and car industries.

In 210–209 BC, thousands of **terracotta soldiers** were buried with the first emperor of China, Qin Shi Huangdi, as it was believed to make him powerful in heaven. The tomb was discovered in 1974 near Xi'an [F10].

Search and Find

China	South Korea
• Beijing E11	• Seoul E13
Mongolia	**Taiwan**
• Ulaanbaatar . . . C9	• Tapai H13
North Korea	
• Pyongyang . . . D12	

LHASA [H7] in the Himalayas is the capital of Tibet and home to many Buddhist monasteries and ancient palaces.

THE DISTANCE from one end of The Great Wall of China to the other is 3460 km – nearly half the length of the Nile river.

Facts and Stats

• China has a population of 1240 million, which would fill 12,400 Olympic stadiums. Mongolia's population of 2.6 million would only fill 26 stadiums.

• China's area of 9.6 million km² is 93 times the area of Iceland.

• The Yangtze [G10] is the longest river at 6300 km in length. The Nile river is nearly twice as long.

One of China's largest cities, **Shanghai** [F12] has a population of 9.8 million. The skyline is dominated by high-rise office buildings and the city is rapidly becoming one of the most important financial centres in the world. The Oriental Pearl Tower is the third highest tower in the world at 468 m.

Map labels

• Ula
ALTAI MOUN
KAZAKHSTAN
• Tacheng
U
• Yining
• Urumqi
• Turpan
Bosten Hu
KYRGYZSTAN
Korla •
TARIM BASIN
• Kashi
SINKIANG
TAJIKISTAN
• Shache
TAKLIMAKAN
DESERT
ALTUN SHAN
AFGHANISTAN
• Hotan
Goln
PAKISTAN
KUNLUN SHAN
TIBET
INDIA
• Gar
Amdo •
HIMALAYAS
PLATEAU
NEPAL
• Lhas
• Gyangzê
Mount Everest 8850 m
BHUTAN

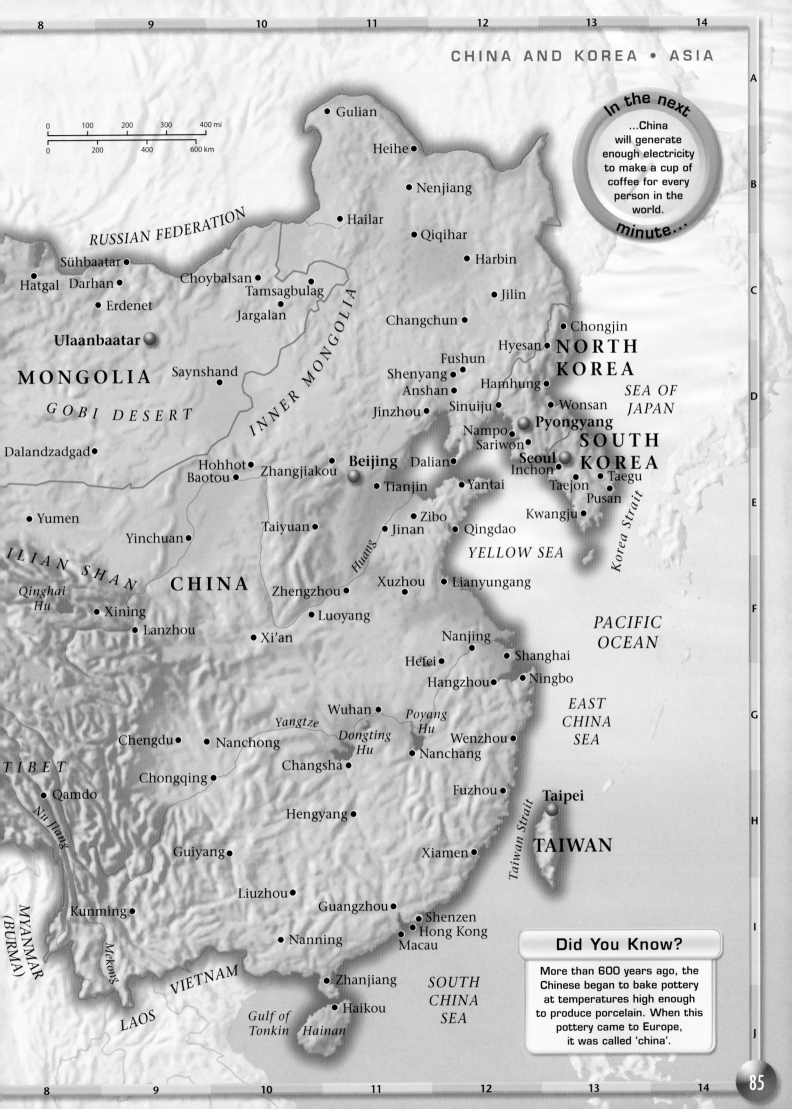

In the next minute...

...China will generate enough electricity to make a cup of coffee for every person in the world.

0 100 200 300 400 mi
0 200 400 600 km

Gulian

Heihe

Nenjiang

Hailar

RUSSIAN FEDERATION

Qiqihar

Harbin

Sühbaatar

Hatgal Darhan

Choybalsan

Tamsagbulag

Jilin

Erdenet

Jargalan

Changchun

Chongjin

Ulaanbaatar

Hyesan

NORTH KOREA

Fushun

Shenyang

Hamhung

SEA OF JAPAN

MONGOLIA

Saynshand

Anshan

GOBI DESERT

Wonsan

Sinuiju

Jinzhou

Nampo

Pyongyang

SOUTH KOREA

Dalandzadgad

Sariwon

Seoul

Hohhot

Zhangjiakou

Beijing

Dalian

Inchon

Taegu

Baotou

Tianjin

Yantai

Taejon

Pusan

Yumen

Zibo

Kwangju

Korea Strait

Yinchuan

Taiyuan

Jinan

Qingdao

YELLOW SEA

ILIAN SHAN

Qinghai Hu

CHINA

Huang

Xining

Zhengzhou

Xuzhou

Lianyungang

Lanzhou

Luoyang

PACIFIC OCEAN

Xi'an

Nanjing

Hefei

Shanghai

Hangzhou

Ningbo

EAST CHINA SEA

Yangtze

Wuhan

Poyang Hu

Chengdu

Nanchong

Dongting Hu

Wenzhou

TIBET

Chongqing

Changsha

Nanchang

Qamdo

Fuzhou

Taipei

Nu Jiang

Hengyang

TAIWAN

Guiyang

Xiamen

Taiwan Strait

MYANMAR (BURMA)

Liuzhou

Mekong

Kunming

Guangzhou

Shenzen

Nanning

Hong Kong

Macau

VIETNAM

Zhanjiang

SOUTH CHINA SEA

LAOS

Haikou

Gulf of Tonkin

Hainan

Did You Know?

More than 600 years ago, the Chinese began to bake pottery at temperatures high enough to produce porcelain. When this pottery came to Europe, it was called 'china'.

East Russia

The Russian Federation is the largest country in the world. However, eastern Russia contains large areas that are unpopulated. Vast areas north of the Arctic Circle suffer freezing conditions that make farming impossible. To the south, much is covered by forest or grassland. Towns are found only where there are natural resources, such as coal, oil, gas, iron and uranium. Kazakhstan is rapidly becoming wealthy due to selling oil, gas and metals to Europe and China, but Turkmenistan, Uzbekistan, Tajikistan and Kyrgyzstan remain underdeveloped.

Extreme Weather

In January 1926, Oymyakon [F10] recorded the lowest temperature for any permanently inhabited location on Earth at –71.2°C.

In the next ...11,000 Russians will be playing chess, making it the nation's most popular sport. minute...

SEVERNAYA ZEMLYA

ARCT OCEA

KARA SEA

SIBERI

Vorkuta

Noril'sk

Yenisey

Tunguska

RUSSIA

Serov

Surgut

Nizhnevartovsk

Ob

Angara

Lena

Ust'Ilimsk

U
R
A
L

M
O
U
N
T
A
I
N
S

Yekaterinburg

Kurgan

Chelyabinsk

Omsk

Tomsk

Krasnoyarsk

Kansk

Bratsk

Y A B
M O

Kemerovo

Novosibirsk

Novokuznetsk

Abakan

Usol'ye-Sibirskoye

Lake Baikal

Semey

Kokshetau

Barnaul

Angarsk

Chita

Orenburg

Pavlodar

Irkutsk

Ulan-U

Ural

Astana

Oskemen

MONGOLIA

Aqtobe

Qaraghandy

Lake Balkhash

Atyrau

Zhezkazgan

KAZAKHSTAN

CHINA

Ustyurt Plateau

Aral Sea

Qyzylorda

Taldyqorgan

Aktau

UZBEKISTAN

Almaty

Tashkent

Bishkek

Urganch

KYRGYZSTAN

Samarkand

TURKMENISTAN

Amu-Dar'ya

Nebitdag

Dushanbe

Ashgabat

TAJIKISTAN

IRAN

AFGHANISTAN

PAKISTAN

CASPIAN SEA

Search and Find

Kazakhstan	Tajikistan
● Astana H3	● Dushanbe J3
Kyrgyzstan	**Turkmenistan**
● Bishkek I4	● Ashgabat. J3
Russian Federation	**Uzbekistan**
● Moscow (see page 45)	● Tashkent. I3

Lake Baikal [H7] is the oldest and deepest lake in the world at 1637 m in depth. It holds more than 20 percent of the world's fresh water.

Facts and Stats

- Turkmenistan's population of 5.7 million would fill 57 stadiums.

- The life expectancy in Russia is 66 years, compared to a world average of 68 years.

- The average income per person in Russia is £5500, compared to £1800 in Tajikistan and a world average of £3500.

THE DISTANCE from Moscow in European Russia to the far east of Russia takes six days and four hours to travel by train at 62 km/h.

Did You Know?

Russia has 11 time zones. When it is 12 p.m. in Moscow, it is 4 p.m. in Novosibirsk [H5] and 7 p.m. in Vladivostok [I9].

LAPTEV SEA

EAST SIBERIAN SEA

CHUKCHI SEA

Lena

VERKHOYANSKIY MOUNTAINS

CHERSKIY MOUNTAINS

Kolyma

Yakutsk •

Oymyakon •

DERATION

Magadan •

BERING SEA

0	250	500	750	1000 mi
0	400	800	1200	1600 km

SEA OF OKHOTSK

VLADIVOSTOK [I9] is home to the Russian navy's Pacific fleet. Until 1991, foreigners were not allowed into the city in case they were spies.

VYY INS

Amur

Petropavlovsk-Kamchatskiy •

HINA

Blagoveshchensk •

Komsomol'sk-na-Amure •

PACIFIC OCEAN

Khabarovsk •

SIKHOTE-ALIN MOUNTAINS

• Yuzhno-Sakhalinsk

Vladivostok •

The *Aral Sea* [I3] has shrunk by 80 percent since 1960. The remaining water has become very salty, killing off so many fish that the commercial fishing industry stopped and many boats have been abandoned.

NORTH KOREA

Oceania

PACIFIC
OCEAN

MARSHALL
ISLANDS

PALAU

MICRONESIA

NAURU

PAPUA
NEW GUINEA

SOLOMON
ISLANDS

TUVALU

KIRIBATI

SAMOA

VANUATU

TONGA

FIJI

INDIAN
OCEAN

PACIFIC
OCEAN

AUSTRALIA

NEW
ZEALAND

SOUTHERN OCEAN

COUNTRY FACTFILE

Country	Life expectancy	Population in thousands	Population growth %	Population as urban %	Literacy %	Area km²	Population density per km²	Capital city	Currency	Languages
Australia	82	19,855	1.2	90	99	7,703,429	2.6	Canberra	Australian Dollar	English
Fiji	71	837	1.4	52	93.7	18,272	45.8	Suva	Fijian Dollar	English, Fijian
Kiribati	63	93	2.2	44	90	717	129.7	Bairiki	Australian Dollar	I-Kiribati, English
Marshall Islands	71	51	2.1	71	93.7	181	281.8	Majuro	US Dollar	Marshallese, English
Micronesia	71	108	−0.2	26	89	701	154.1	Palikir	US Dollar	English, Chuukese, Pohnpeain
Nauru	64	10	1.7	N/A	90	21	481	Yaren	Australian Dollar	Nauruan
New Zealand	80	4269	0.9	87	99	270,534	15.8	Wellington	New Zealand Dollar	English, Maori
Palau	71	20	0.4	81	92	458	43.4	Melekeok	US Dollar	Palauan, English
Papua New Guinea	66	5191	2.1	17	57.3	462,840	11.2	Port Moresby	Kina	Tok Pisin (Pidgin English), English
Samoa	72	179	1.3	23	99.7	2831	63.2	Apia	Tala	Samoan
Solomon Islands	74	495	2.4	18	54	28,370	17.4	Honiara	Solomon Islands Dollar	Melanesian languages
Tonga	71	102	1.5	43	98.9	748	136.4	Nuku'Alofa	Pa'anga	Tongan
Tuvalu	69	9.6	1.6	46	95	24	400	Vaiaku (Funafuti)	Australian Dollar	Melanesian languages
Vanuatu	64	195	1.4	25	74	12,190	16	Port-Vila	Vatu	Bislama, English, French

Australia

Much of Australia's inland is desert, known as the outback. Most people live in the eastern fertile land between Adelaide and Brisbane, and the capital, Canberra, is in the mountains of the Great Dividing Range. Many lakes in Australia vary in extent and some dry out in drought. Aboriginal people have lived in Australia for more than 40,000 years, but in 1787, British settlers began to arrive and immigration has continued ever since. Aboriginals now make up just 2 percent of the population. Rich in gold, iron ore and coal, Australia is one of the wealthiest nations in the world.

Extreme Weather

To fight the effects of long periods of drought, Toowoomba [F13] may use recycled sewage in the water supply.

Did You Know?

The Great Barrier Reef [D12] stretches for more than 2000 km off the coast of Queensland.

SYDNEY [H12] is the largest city and has two of the most famous sights in the world – the Opera House and Sydney Harbour Bridge.

THE DISTANCE from the east coast to the west coast is 3000 km – the same as from London to Boston, USA.

Facts and Stats

- Australia's area of 7.7 million km^2 is 75 times the area of Iceland.
- The Murray–Darling [H11] is the longest river. At 3750 km, it is more than half the length of the Nile river.
- Mount Kosciuszko [H11] is the highest mountain at 2229 m in height – seven times higher than the Eiffel Tower.

*The widest bridge in the world, **Sydney Harbour Bridge** [H12] is almost 50 m in width. At 503 m in length, the bridge has two railway tracks, eight lanes for cars, a bicycle path and a pedestrian path. About 160,000 vehicles cross the bridge each day.*

INDIAN OCEAN

Me
Is

Bathurst
Island

Darwi

*Joseph
Bonaparte
Gulf*

Drysdale

Wyndham

KIMBERLEY
PLATEAU

Broome

Derby
Fitzroy

Halls Creek

N

Port Hedland

Dampier

GREAT SANDY
DESERT

De Grey

Onslow

Exmouth

Ashburton

WESTERN AUSTRALIA

Carnarvon

GIBSON DESERT

Denham

Murchison

Ay
Ro
(Ult

Meekatharra

Laverton

Geraldton

GREAT VICTORIA DESERT

Kalgoorlie

Perth
Freemantle
Mandurah

Balladonia

Norseman

Great Austral

Bunbury

Wagin

Esperance

Augusta

Albany

SOUTHERN OCEAN

8 9 10 11 12 13 14

Kangaroos can reach speeds of up to 50 km/h. They can be a danger on the roads, causing damage to vehicles in accidents as they weigh up to 90 kg. Therefore 'kangaroo crossing' signs are found throughout Australia.

HEM LAND

Groote Eylandt

Gulf of Carpentaria

Roper

erine

WELLESLEY ISLANDS

Cape York Peninsula

Mitchell

● Cooktown

● Port Doulgas

Cairns ●
Atherton ●   ● Innisfail

GREAT BARRIER REEF

PACIFIC OCEAN

Normanton ●

Burketown ●

Flinders

● Tennant Creek

Norman

● Townsville
Bowen ●

● Mackay

● Mount Isa

AMI
ERT

ERN TERRITORY

Georgina

QUEENSLAND

● Rockhampton
  ● Gladstone

● Alice Springs

NNELL RANGES

Diamantina

Thomson

Barcoo

Bundaberg ●

Fraser Island

AUSTRALIA

Charleville ●

Warrego

Marla ●

● Sunshine Coast
  ● Brisbane
  ● Gold Coast

Toowoomba ●

ober Pedy ●

● Marree

SOUTH AUSTRALIA

Bourke ●

Darling

Tarcoola ●

Ceduna ●

Port Augusta ●
Whyalla ●   ● Port Pirie

NEW SOUTH WALES

● Grafton

● Coffs Harbour

● Port Macquarie

Tamworth ●

GREAT DIVIDING RANGE

Dubbo ●

● Newcastle
  ● Gosford
  ● Sydney
  ● Wollongong

● Mildura

Murray

Wagga Wagga ●

Port Lincoln ●   ● Adelaide

● Canberra
AUSTRALIAN
CAPITAL
TERRITORY

Mount Kosciuszko 2229 m

VICTORIA

Bendigo ●

Kangaroo Island

Ballarat ●
Geelong ●

● Melbourne
Sale ●

TASMAN SEA

Mount Gambier ●

King Island

Bass Strait

Flinders Island

Cape Barren Island

Burnie ●   ● Devonport
  ● Launceston

Queenstown ●

TASMANIA

● Hobart

South East Cape

100 200 300 400 500 mi

200 400 600 800 km

In the next ...38 kangaroos will be born in Australia. There are three times more kangaroos than humans. minute...

New Zealand and the Pacific Islands

New Zealand consists of two main islands and has a population of four million. The country generates a wealthy economy, mainly by selling its farm produce worldwide. English is the national language due to the many immigrants who started commercial farms and industries. The area of the Pacific Ocean east of Australia contains thousands of tropical islands including the Solomon Islands, Fiji, Vanuatu, Samoa, Kiribati, Tonga, Micronesia, Palau, the Marshall Islands, Papua New Guinea, Nauru and Tuvalu. Many people are leaving the Pacific Islands for education and work in Australia, New Zealand and the USA.

Bora-Bora is a small island in French Polynesia [I14] with a population of only 8000 people. The biggest industry is tourism as people are attracted to the stunning clear waters and tranquil atmosphere. Resorts with bungalows on stilts are a common feature.

In the next ...New Zealand's wine growers will make more than 230 bottles of wine for export. **minute...**

THE DISTANCE from the top to the bottom of the Nevis Highwire, New Zealand's highest bungee jump, is 135 m.

OTAGO PENINSULA [I7] is home to albatrosses, penguins, seals, whales and dolphins.

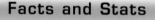

Facts and Stats

- The life expectancy of people in New Zealand is 80 years, compared to a world average of 68 years.
- There are 24 doctors per 10,000 people compared to a world average of 17 doctors.
- Mount Cook [H7] is the highest mountain at 3754 m – 12 times higher than the Eiffel Tower.

TASMAN SEA

Cape Foulwin
Westpo

Greymouth

Soi

Mount Cook 3754 m

SOUTHERN ALPS

Timaru
Waitaki

Oam

Otag Penins

Clutha

Dunedin

The Maori were the first settlers in New Zealand, as they sailed from Polynesia 1000 years ago. Maori tikis are large carvings that are believed to protect sacred sites against evil.

Cape Providence

Invercargill

Foveaux Strait Ruapuke Island

Codfish Island
Stewart Island

NEW ZEALAND AND THE PACIFIC ISLANDS • OCEANIA

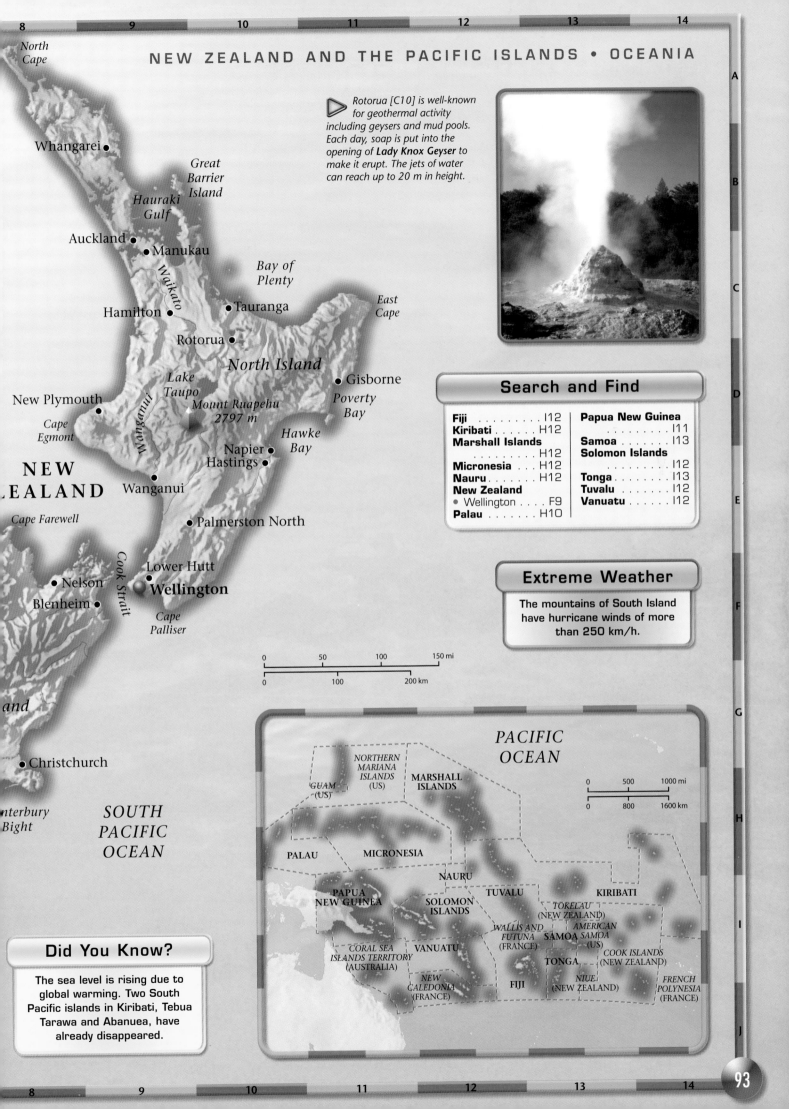

North Cape

Whangarei

Great Barrier Island

Hauraki Gulf

Auckland

Manukau

Waikato

Bay of Plenty

Hamilton

Tauranga

East Cape

Rotorua

North Island

Lake Taupo

New Plymouth

Mount Ruapehu 2797 m

Gisborne

Poverty Bay

Cape Egmont

Hawke Bay

NEW ZEALAND

Napier

Hastings

Wanganui

Cape Farewell

Palmerston North

Lower Hutt

Wellington

Nelson

Cook Strait

Cape Palliser

Blenheim

Christchurch

SOUTH PACIFIC OCEAN

Canterbury Bight

Rotorua [C10] is well-known for geothermal activity including geysers and mud pools. Each day, soap is put into the opening of **Lady Knox Geyser** to make it erupt. The jets of water can reach up to 20 m in height.

Search and Find

Fiji I12		**Papua New Guinea**
Kiribati H12		. . . . I11
Marshall Islands		**Samoa** I13
. . . . H12		**Solomon Islands**
Micronesia . . . H12		. . . . I12
Nauru H12		**Tonga** I13
New Zealand		**Tuvalu** I12
● Wellington F9		**Vanuatu** I12
Palau H10		

Extreme Weather

The mountains of South Island have hurricane winds of more than 250 km/h.

0   50   100   150 mi

0   100   200 km

PACIFIC OCEAN

NORTHERN MARIANA ISLANDS (US)

GUAM (US)

MARSHALL ISLANDS

PALAU

MICRONESIA

NAURU

0   500   1000 mi

0   800   1600 km

PAPUA NEW GUINEA

SOLOMON ISLANDS

TUVALU

KIRIBATI

TOKELAU (NEW ZEALAND)

WALLIS AND FUTUNA (FRANCE)

SAMOA

AMERICAN SAMOA (US)

COOK ISLANDS (NEW ZEALAND)

VANUATU

CORAL SEA ISLANDS TERRITORY (AUSTRALIA)

TONGA

NEW CALEDONIA (FRANCE)

FIJI

NIUE (NEW ZEALAND)

FRENCH POLYNESIA (FRANCE)

Did You Know?

The sea level is rising due to global warming. Two South Pacific islands in Kiribati, Tebua Tarawa and Abanuea, have already disappeared.

A

B

C

D

E

F

G

H

I

J

Countries of the world

Gazetteer

The gazetteer helps you to find towns and features on the maps. For example,
New York City *Town* New York, USA 21 F12 shows that New York City is a town in the state
of New York, USA. The town is on page 21 and can be found in square F12 by using
the grid, or graticule. The letters run on the left and right, and the numbers run
along the top and bottom. Trace where F and 21 meet to find New York City.

KEY – DRC – Democratic Republic of the Congo, UAE – United Arab Emirates, CAR – Central African Republic, RS – Research station

Aachen *Town* Germany 50 F6
Aalst *Town* Belgium 50 E5
Abadan *Town* Iran 75 D8
Abakan *Town* Russian Fed. 86 H5
Abéché *Town* Chad 65 G13
Aberdeen *Town* Scotland, UK 41 D9
Aberdeen *Town* S Dakota, USA 25 F13
Aberystwyth *Town* Wales, UK 41 H8
Abha *Town* Saudi Arabia 74 H6
Abidjan *Capital* Côte d'Ivoire 64 I6
Abilene *Town* Texas, USA 27 G12
Abu Dhabi *Capital* UAE 75 F10
Abuja *Capital* Nigeria 65 H10
Abu Kamal *Town* Syria 73 G12
Acapulco *Town* Mexico 31 I9
Acarigua *Town* Venezuela 35 F9
Accra *Capital* Ghana 64 I7
Aconcagua, Cerro *Mountain* Argentina 36 G7
Adana *Town* Turkey 73 E9
Ad-Dammam *Town* Saudi Arabia 75 E8
Addis Ababa *Capital* Ethiopia 67 E9
Adelaide *Town* Australia 91 H9
Aden, Gulf of 67 C12, 74 J7
Aden *Town* Yemen 74 J7
Adirondack Mountains USA 21 E11
Adiyaman *Town* Turkey 73 E11
Adrar *Town* Algeria 62 F4
Adriatic Sea 49 E8
Afghanistan *Country* 76
Agadir *Town* Morocco 62 E2
Agen *Town* France 46 G7
Agra *Town* India 77 D9
Agrigento *Town* Sicily, Italy 48 H6
Aguascalientes *Town* Mexico 31 G8
Ahaggar *Mountain range* Algeria 62 G6
Ahmadabad *Town* India 76 E7
Ahvaz *Town* Iran 75 D8
Aïr Mountains Niger 65 F10
Aix-en-Provence *Town* France 47 H10
Aizu *Town* Japan 83 F10
Ajaccio *Town* France 47 J12
Akita *Town* Japan 83 D10
Akron *Town* Ohio, USA 21 G8
Aktau *Town* Kazakhstan 86 I2
Alabama *River* Alabama, USA 23 F8
Alabama *State* USA 23
Åland Island Finland 43 G9
Alaska, Gulf of 25 C11, 28 F4
Alaska *State* USA 25
Albacete *Town* Spain 45 F10
Alba Iulia *Town* Romania 55 E9
Albania *Country* 49
Albany *River* Ontario, Canada 29 H10
Albany *State capital* New York, USA 21 E11
Albany *Town* Australia 90 H5
Albany *Town* Georgia, USA 23 F9
Albert, Lake DRC/Uganda 66 F7
Alberta *Province* Canada 28
Albuquerque *Town* New Mexico, USA 27 F9

Alcoy *Town* Spain 45 G11
Aleppo *Town* Syria 73 F10
Alessandria *Town* Italy 48 C5
Aleutian Islands Alaska, USA 25 C9
Alexandria *Town* Egypt 63 E12
Alexandria *Town* Louisiana, USA 22 G5
Alexandroúpolis *Town* Greece 49 F13
Algeciras *Town* Spain 44 I7
Algeria *Country* 62
Algiers *Capital* Algeria 62 C6
Al Hasakah *Town* Syria 73 F12
Al-Hudaydah *Town* Yemen 74 I6
Al-Hufuf *Town* Saudi Arabia 75 F8
Alicante *Town* Spain 45 G11
Alice Springs *Town* Australia 91 E8
Al Jawf *Town* Saudi Arabia 74 D5
Al-Karak *Town* Jordan 73 I9
Alkmaar *Town* Netherlands 50 C6
Allahabad *Town* India 77 E9
Allegheny *River* Pennsylvania, USA 21 G9
Allentown *Town* Pennsylvania, USA 21 G11
Almaty *Town* Kazakhstan 86 I4
Almería *Town* Spain 45 H9
Al Mukalla *Town* Yemen 75 I8
Alps *Mountain range* France/Italy/Switzerland 47 G10
Al Qamishli *Town* Syria 73 E12
Al Qunaytirah *Town* Syria 73 H9
Altai Mountains Mongolia/Russian Fed. 84 D7
Altamaha *River* Georgia, USA 23 F10
Altamira *Town* Brazil 37 B9
Altun Shan *Mountain range* China 84 F6
Amarillo *Town* Texas, USA 27 F11
Amazon *River* Brazil 36 B7, 37 B9
Amazon Basin Brazil 36 B7
Ambato *Town* Ecuador 36 B5
Ambon *Town* Indonesia 81 G8
American Samoa *Dep. territory* USA 93 I13
Amiens *Town* France 47 B9
Amman *Capital* Jordan 73 H10
Amritsar *Town* India 77 C8
Amsterdam *Capital* Netherlands 50 D6
Amu Dar'ya *River* Uzbekistan 86 J3
Amundsen Gulf 17 D9
Amundsen-Scott (US) *RS* Antarctica 16 F4
Amundsen Sea 16 F1
Amur *River* China/Russian Fed. 87 H8
Anaheim *Town* California, USA 26 F5
Anápolis *Town* Brazil 37 D9
Anatolian Plateau Turkey 72 D7
Anchorage *Town* Alaska, USA 25 C11
Ancona *Town* Italy 48 D7
Andaman Islands India 77 H12
Andaman Sea 78 H2
Anderson *Town* Indiana, USA 20 H7
Andes *Mountain range* 36 F7
Andorra *Country* 45
Andorra la Vella *Capital* Andorra 45 C12

Andreanof Islands Alaska, USA 25 C9
Angarsk *Town* Russian Fed. 86 H6
Angeles *Town* Philippines 79 F10
Angers *Town* France 46 C7
Angola *Country* 68
Angoulême *Town* France 46 E7
Anguilla *Dep. territory* UK 35 D12
Ankara *Capital* Turkey 73 C8
Annaba *Town* Algeria 62 D7
Annapolis *State capital* Maryland, USA 21 H11
Ann Arbor *Town* Michigan, USA 20 F7
An Nasiriyah *Town* Iraq 74 D7
Anshan *Town* China 85 D12
Antakya *Town* Turkey 73 F10
Antalya *Town* Turkey 72 E7
Antananarivo *Capital* Madagascar 69 G12
Antarctica 16
Antarctic Peninsula Antarctica 16 E2
Antibes *Town* France 47 H11
Anticosti Island Quebec, Canada 29 H13
Antigua and Barbuda *Country* 35
Antofagasta *Town* Chile 36 E6
Antsiranana *Town* Madagascar 69 F13
Antwerp *Town* Belgium 50 E5
Aomori *Town* Japan 83 D10
Aosta *Town* Italy 48 B4
Apeldoorn *Town* Netherlands 50 D7
Appalachian Mountains USA 21 H10, 23 C10
Appleton *Town* Wisconsin, USA 20 F5
Aqaba *Town* Jordan 73 J9
Aqtobe *Town* Russian Fed. 86 H2
Arabian Sea 75 F12, 76 E6
Aracaju *Town* Brazil 37 C11
Arad *Town* Romania 54 D7
Arafura Sea 81 H9
Araguaína *Town* Brazil 37 C10
Arakan Range *Mountain range* Myanmar (Burma) 78 F2
Aral Sea Kazakhstan/Uzbekistan 86 I3
Ararat, Mount Turkey 73 D14
Arbil *Town* Iraq 74 B7
Arctic Ocean 17, 28, 43, 59, 86
Arequipa *Town* Peru 36 D6
Arezzo *Town* Italy 48 D6
Argentina *Country* 36
Århus *Town* Denmark 42 I6
Arica *Town* Chile 36 D6
Arizona *State* USA 26
Arkansas *State* USA 22
Arkhangelsk *Town* Russian Fed. 59 D8
Arles *Town* France 47 H9
Arlington *Town* Texas, USA 27 G13
Armenia *Country* 59
Armenia *Town* Colombia 35 H8
Arnhem *Town* Netherlands 50 D6
Arnhem Land Australia 91 B8
Ar Raqqah *Town* Syria 73 F11
Arua *Town* Uganda 66 F7
Aruba *Dep. territory* Netherlands 35 E9
Aru Islands Indonesia 81 G9

Arusha *Town* Tanzania 67 H9
Asahikawa *Town* Japan 83 B10
Ashgabat *Capital* Turkmenistan 86 J3
Asmara *Capital* Eritrea 67 C9
Assad, Lake Syria 73 F11
Assen *Town* Netherlands 50 C7
As-Sulayyil *Town* Saudi Arabia 74 G7
Astana *Capital* Kazakhstan 86 H3
Astrakhan *Town* Russian Fed. 59 H8
Asunción *Capital* Paraguay 37 E8
Aswan *Town* Egypt 63 H13
Asyut *Town* Egypt 63 G13
Atacama Desert Chile 36 E7
Atbara *Town* Sudan 67 B8
Athens *Capital* Greece 49 H12
Atlanta *State capital* Georgia, USA 23 E9
Atlantic City *Town* New Jersey, USA 21 G12
Atlantic Ocean 21, 23, 29, 37, 40, 42, 43, 44, 62, 64
Atlas Mountains Morocco 62 E3
Atyrau *Town* Kazakhstan 86 I2
Auckland *Town* New Zealand 93 C9
Augsburg *Town* Germany 51 I9
Augusta *Town* Georgia, USA 23 E10
Augusta *State capital* Maine, USA 21 D13
Aurora *Town* Illinois, USA 20 G6
Austin *State capital* Texas, USA 27 H13
Australia *Country* 90
Australian Capital Territory *State* Australia 91
Austria *Country* 40
Auxerre *Town* France 47 D9
Aveiro *Town* Portugal 44 E5
Avignon *Town* France 47 G9
Ávila *Town* Spain 45 E8
Axel Heiberg Island Nunavut, Canada 29 C9
Ayacucho *Town* Peru 36 D6
Aydin *Town* Turkey 72 D6
Azerbaijan *Country* 59
Azov, Sea of 58 I7
Az-Zarqa *Town* Jordan 73 H10
Az-Zawiyah *Town* Libya 73 H10

Bacău *Town* Romania 55 D12
Bacolod *Town* Philippines 79 G11
Badajoz *Town* Spain 44 F6
Baden-Baden *Town* Germany 50 H7
Baffin Bay Canada 17 G9, 29 D10
Baffin Island Canada 17 G8, 29 E10
Baghdad *Capital* Iraq 74 C7
Bahamas *Country* 35
Bahawalpur *Town* Pakistan 77 C8
Bahía Blanca *Town* Argentina 37 G8
Bahrain *Country* 75
Baikal, Lake Russian Fed. 86 H7
Bakersfield *Town* California, USA 26 E5
Bakhtaran *Town* Iran 74 C7
Baku *Capital* Azerbaijan 59 J9
Balaton, Lake Hungary 54 D5
Balearic Islands Spain 45
Bali *Island* Indonesia 80 H5

Balikesir *Town* Turkey 72 C6
Balikpapan *Town* Indonesia 80 F5
Balkan Mountains Bulgaria 55 H10
Balkhash, Lake Kazakhstan 86 I4
Ballarat *Town* Australia 91 I10
Baltic Sea 43 H9, 56 B6, 58 F5
Baltimore *Town* Maryland, USA 21 H11
Bamako *Capital* Mali 64 G5
Bambari *Town* CAR 68 B7
Bamberg *Town* Germany 51 G9
Bamenda *Town* Cameroon 68 B5
Bandar 'Abbas *Town* Iran 75 E10
Bandar Seri Begawan *Capital* Brunei 80 E5
Banda Sea 81 G8
Bandundu *Town* DRC 68 D7
Bandung *Town* Indonesia 80 H3
Bangalore *See Bengaluru*
Bangkok *Capital* Thailand 78 H4
Bangladesh *Country* 77
Bangor *Town* Maine, USA 21 C13
Bangui *Capital* CAR 68 B7
Baniyas *Town* Syria 73 F10
Banja Luka *Town* Bosnia and Herz. 49 C8
Banjarmasin *Town* Indonesia 80 G5
Banjul *Capital* Gambia 64 G3
Banská Bystrica *Town* Slovakia 57 I8
Baotou *Town* China 85 E10
Bar *Town* Montenegro 49 E9
Barbados *Country* 35
Barcelona *Town* Spain 45 D13
Barcelona *Town* Venezuela 35 F11
Barents Sea 17 G13, 58 B7
Bari *Town* Italy 49 F8
Barinas *Town* Venezuela 35 F9
Barnaul *Town* Russian Fed. 86 H5
Barquisimeto *Town* Venezuela 35 F9
Barrancabermeja *Town* Colombia 35 G8
Barranquilla *Town* Colombia 35 F8
Basel *Town* Switzerland 52 E3
Basra *Town* Iraq 75 D8
Bassein *Town* Myanmar (Burma) 78 G2
Basseterre *Capital* St. Kitts and Nevis 35 D12
Bass Strait Australia 91 I11
Batangas *Town* Philippines 79 F10
Batdâmbang *Town* Cambodia 78 G5
Batman *Town* Turkey 73 E12
Batna *Town* Algeria 62 D6
Baton Rouge *State capital* Louisiana, USA 22 G6
Bayamo *Town* Cuba 35 C8
Bayreuth *Town* Germany 51 G10
Beaufort Sea 17 C9, 28 D6
Beaumont *Town* Texas, USA 27 H14
Béchar *Town* Algeria 62 E4
Beersheba *Town* Israel 73 I9
Beijing *Capital* China 85 E11
Beira *Town* Mozambique 69 G10
Beirut *Capital* Lebanon 73 G9
Beja *Town* Portugal 44 G5
Belarus *Country* 58
Belém *Town* Brazil 37 B10

Belfast *Capital* Northern Ireland, UK 40 F7
Belgium *Country* 50
Belgrade *Capital* Serbia 49 C10
Belgrano II (Argentina) *RS* Antarctica 16 E3
Belize *Country* 34
Belize City *Town* Belize 34 C5
Bellingham *Town* Washington, USA 24 C4
Belmopan *Capital* Belize 34 C5
Belo Horizonte *Town* Brazil 37 E10
Bendigo *Town* Australia 91 H11
Benevento *Town* Italy 48 F7
Bengal, Bay of 77 F11
Bengaluru (Bangalore) *Town* India 77 H8
Benghazi *Town* Libya 63 E10
Benguela *Town* Angola 68 F6
Benidorm *Town* Spain 45 G11
Benin *Country* 65
Benin City *Town* Nigeria 65 I9
Ben Nevis *Mountain* Scotland, UK 41 D8
Benue *River* Nigeria 65 I10
Berbera *Town* Somalia 67 D11
Bergamo *Town* Italy 48 B5
Bergen *Town* Norway 42 F5
Bergerac *Town* France 46 F7
Bering Sea 25 B9, 87 G13
Berlin *Capital* Germany 51 D11
Bern *Capital* Switzerland 52 F3
Besançon *Town* France 47 E10
Bethlehem *Town* Israel 73 I9
Béziers *Town* France 47 H8
Bhavnagar *Town* India 76 E7
Bhopal *Town* India 77 E8
Bhutan *Country* 77
Bialystok *Town* Poland 57 D11
Biel *Town* Switzerland 52 F3
Bielefeld *Town* Germany 51 D8
Bielsko-Biala *Town* Poland 57 H8
Bighorn Mountains Wyoming, USA 25 G9
Bihac *Town* Bosnia and Herz. 49 C8
Bilauktaung Range Thailand 78 G3
Bilbao *Town* Spain 45 B9
Billings *Town* Montana, USA 25 F9
Biloxi *Town* Mississippi, USA 22 G7
Biratnagar *Town* Nepal 77 D11
Birmingham *Town* Alabama, USA 23 E8
Birmingham *Town* England, UK 41 H9
Biscay, Bay of 45 A9, 46 E5
Bishkek *Capital* Kyrgyzstan 86 I4
Bismarck *State capital* N Dakota, USA 25 F12
Bissau *Capital* Guinea-Bissau 64 G3
Bitola *Town* Macedonia 49 F11
Bizerte *Town* Tunisia 62 C7
Black Forest Germany 50 I7
Blackpool *Town* England, UK 41 F8
Black Sea 55 H14, 58 I6, 73 B11
Blagoevgrad *Town* Bulgaria 55 I9
Blagoveshchensk *Town* Russian Fed. 87 H8
Blantyre *Town* Malawi 69 G10
Blida *Town* Algeria 62 D6
Bloemfontein *Town* South Africa 69 I8
Bloomington *Town* Indiana, USA 20 I6
Bloomington *Town* Minnesota, USA 20 E3
Blue Nile *River* Ethiopia/Sudan 67 D8
Bo *Town* Sierra Leone 64 I4
Boa Vista *Town* Brazil 37 A8
Bobo Dioulasso *Town* Burkina Faso 64 H6
Bodrum *Town* Turkey 72 E5
Bogotá *Capital* Colombia 35 H8

Bohemian Forest Czech Republic/ Germany 51 H11, 56 H4
Boise *State capital* Idaho, USA 24 G5
Bolivia *Country* 36
Bologna *Town* Italy 48 C6
Bolzano *Town* Italy 48 B6
Bombay *See Mumbai*
Bonaire *Dep. territory* Netherlands 35 F10
Bonifacio, Strait of 47 J12
Bonn *Town* Germany 50 F7
Borås *Town* Sweden 42 H7
Bordeaux *Town* France 46 F6
Borgholm *Town* Sweden 43 I8
Borneo *Island* Indonesia 80 G4
Bornholm *Dep. territory* Denmark 42 J7
Bosnia and Herzegovina *Country* 49
Boston *State capital* Massachusetts, USA 21 E13
Botswana *Country* 69
Bouar *Town* CAR 68 B6
Boulder *Town* Colorado, USA 27 C10
Boulogne *Town* France 47 A9
Bourges *Town* France 47 D9
Bourke *Town* Australia 91 F11
Bournemouth *Town* England, UK 41 I9
Bozeman *Town* Montana, USA 25 F8
Brahmaputra *River* Asia 77 E12
Braila *Town* Romania 55 E12
Brandenburg *Town* Germany 51 D11
Brasília *Capital* Brazil 37 D10
Brasov *Town* Romania 55 E10
Bratislava *Capital* Slovakia 56 J7
Bratsk *Town* Russian Fed. 86 G6
Braunschweig *Town* Germany 51 D10
Brazil *Country* 37
Brazzaville *Capital* Republic of the Congo 68 D6
Breda *Town* Netherlands 50 D5
Bremen *Town* Germany 51 C9
Bremerhaven *Town* Germany 51 C8
Brescia *Town* Italy 48 B5
Brest *Town* France 46 B5
Bridgeport *Town* Connecticut, USA 21 F12
Bridgetown *Capital* Barbados 35 E12
Brig *Town* Switzerland 52 G3
Brighton *Town* England, UK 41 I10
Brindisi *Town* Italy 49 F9
Brisbane *Town* Australia 91 F13
Bristol *Town* England, UK 41 H9
British Columbia *Province* Canada 28
Brive *Town* France 47 F8
Brno *Town* Czech Republic 56 H6
Broome *Town* Australia 90 C5
Brownsville *Town* Texas, USA 27 J13
Bruges *Town* Belgium 50 E4
Brunei *Country* 80
Brussels *Capital* Belgium 50 E5
Bryansk *Town* Russian Fed. 58 G6
Bucaramanga *Town* Colombia 35 G8
Bucharest *Capital* Romania 55 F11
Budapest *Capital* Hungary 54 C6
Buenaventura *Town* Colombia 34 H7
Buenos Aires *Capital* Argentina 37 G8
Buffalo *Town* New York, USA 21 F9
Bug *River* Poland 57 D10
Bujumbura *Capital* Burundi 66 H7

Bukavu *Town* DRC 69 D9
Bulawayo *Town* Zimbabwe 69 G9
Bulgaria *Country* 55
Buraydah *Town* Saudi Arabia 74 E7
Burgas *Town* Bulgaria 55 H12
Burgos *Town* Spain 45 C8
Burketown *Town* Australia 91 C10
Burlington *Town* Vermont, USA 21 D12
Burma *See Myanmar*
Burns *Town* Oregon, USA 24 G4
Burnsville *Town* Minnesota, USA 20 E3
Bursa *Town* Turkey 72 C6
Burundi *Country* 66
Butuan *Town* Philippines 79 G12
Bydgoszcz *Town* Poland 57 D8
Bytom *Town* Poland 57 G8

Cabanatuan *Town* Philippines 79 E10
Cáceres *Town* Spain 44 F6
Cádiz *Town* Spain 44 I7
Caen *Town* France 47 B8
Cagayan de Oro *Town* Philippines 79 G11
Cagliari *Town* Sardinia, Italy 48 G4
Cairns *Town* Australia 91 C11
Cairo *Capital* Egypt 63 F13
Calais *Town* France 47 A9
Calama *Town* Chile 36 E7
Calarasi *Town* Romania 55 F12
Calbayog *Town* Philippines 79 F11
Calcutta *See Kolkata*
Calgary *Town* Alberta, Canada 28 H7
Cali *Town* Colombia 34 H7
Calicut *See Kozhikode*
California, Gulf of 30 D5
California *State* USA 26
Callao *Town* Peru 36 D5
Caltanissetta *Town* Sicily, Italy 48 H7
Camagüey *Town* Cuba 35 C8
Cambodia *Country* 78
Cambrian Mountains Wales, UK 41 H8
Cambridge *Town* England, UK 41 H10
Cameroon *Country* 68
Campeche, Bay of Mexico 31 H11
Campina Grande *Town* Brazil 37 C12
Campinas *Town* Brazil 37 E10
Campobasso *Town* Italy 48 E7
Campo Grande *Town* Brazil 37 E9
Canada *Country* 28
Canary Islands Spain 64 B4
Canberra *Capital* Australia 91 H12
Cancún *Town* Mexico 31 G14
Cannes *Town* France 47 H11
Cantabrian Mountains Spain 44 B7
Can Tho *Town* Vietnam 78 H5
Canton *Town* Ohio, USA 21 G9
Cape Horn Chile 37 J8
Cape Town *Capital* South Africa 68 J7
Cape Verde Country 64
Cap-Haïtien *Town* Haiti 35 C9
Capitán Arturo Prat (Chile) *RS* Antarctica 16 D1
Caracas *Capital* Venezuela 35 F10
Cárdenas *Town* Cuba 34 B7
Cardiff *Capital* Wales, UK 41 H8
Caribbean Sea 35 E9
Carlisle *Town* England, UK 41 F9
Carlsbad *Town* New Mexico, USA 27 G10
Carnarvon *Town* Australia 90 E3
Carpathian Mountains Poland/ Romania/Slovakia 55 D11

Carrara *Town* Italy 48 C5
Carson City *State capital* Nevada, USA 26 C5
Cartagena *Town* Colombia 35 F8
Cartagena *Town* Spain 45 H11
Casablanca *Town* Morocco 62 D3
Casey (Australia) *RS* Antarctica 16 G7
Casper *Town* Wyoming, USA 25 H9
Caspian Sea 59 I9, 75 B8, 86 I2
Cassai (Kasai) *River* Angola/DRC 68 E7
Castellón de la Plana *Town* Spain 45 E11
Castries *Capital* St. Lucia 35 E12
Catania *Town* Sicily, Italy 48 H7
Catanzaro *Town* Italy 49 G8
Cayman Islands *Dep. territory* UK 34 C7
Cebu *Town* Philippines 79 G11
Cedar City *Town* Utah, USA 26 D7
Cedar Rapids *Town* Iowa, USA 20 G4
Celebes Sea 79 H11, 80 E6
Celje *Town* Slovenia 49 B8
Central African Republic (CAR) *Country* 68
Ceske Budejovice *Town* Czech Republic 56 H5
Ceuta *Town* Spain 44 J7, 62 D3
Chad, Lake Chad 65 G12
Chad *Country* 65
Châlons-en-Champagne *Town* France 47 C10
Chalon-sur-Saône *Town* France 47 E10
Chambéry *Town* France 47 F10
Champaign *Town* Illinois, USA 20 H6
Chandigarh *Town* India 77 C8
Changchun *Town* China 85 C12
Changsha *Town* China 85 G11
Channel Islands *Dep. territory* UK 41 J9
Charleroi *Town* Belgium 50 F5
Charleston *State capital* West Virginia, USA 21 I9
Charleston *Town* S Carolina, USA 23 E11
Charleville Mézières *Town* France 47 B10
Charlotte *Town* N Carolina, USA 23 C10
Charlottetown *Province capital* Prince Edward Islands, Canada 29 I13
Châteauroux *Town* France 47 D8
Chattanooga *Town* Tennessee, USA 23 D8
Cheb *Town* Czech Republic 56 G3
Chelm *Town* Poland 57 F11
Chelyabinsk *Town* Russian Fed. 86 G3
Chemnitz *Town* Germany 51 F11
Chengdu *Town* China 85 G9
Chennai (Madras) *Town* India 77 H9
Chester *Town* England, UK 41 G9
Chetumal *Town* Mexico 31 H13
Cheyenne *State capital* Wyoming, USA 25 I10
Chiang Mai *Town* Thailand 78 F3
Chiba *Town* Japan 83 G10
Chicago *Town* Illinois, USA 20 G6
Chichén Itzá Mexico 31 G13
Chiclayo *Town* Peru 36 C5
Chicoutimi *Town* Quebec, Canada 29 I12
Chihuahua *Town* Mexico 30 D7
Chile *Country* 36
Chillan *Town* Chile 36 G6
Chilpancingo *Town* Mexico 31 I9
Chimbote *Town* Peru 36 C5

Chimoio *Town* Mozambique 69 G10
China *Country* 85
Chinandega *Town* Nicaragua 34 E5
Chioggia *Town* Italy 48 C6
Chipata *Town* Zambia 69 F9
Chirripó Grande, Cerro *Mountain* Costa Rica 34 F5
Chisinau *Capital* Moldova 58 H6
Chita *Town* Russian Fed. 86 H7
Chitose *Town* Japan 83 B10
Chittagong *Town* Bangladesh 77 F12
Chitungwiza *Town* Zimbabwe 69 G9
Chon Buri *Town* Thailand 78 H4
Chongjin *Town* North Korea 85 C13
Chongqing *Town* China 85 H10
Choybalsan *Town* Mongolia 85 C10
Christchurch *Town* New Zealand 93 G8
Chukchi Sea 17 C11, 25 A10, 87 E13
Churchill *Town* Manitoba, Canada 29 G9
Cienfuegos *Town* Cuba 34 B7
Cincinnati *Town* Ohio, USA 21 H7
Ciudad Bolívar *Town* Venezuela 35 G11
Ciudad del Este *Town* Paraguay 37 F9
Ciudad Guayana *Town* Venezuela 35 G11
Ciudad Juárez *Town* Mexico 30 C7
Ciudad Madero *Town* Mexico 31 F10
Ciudad Obregón *Town* Mexico 30 D6
Ciudad Real *Town* Spain 45 F8
Ciudid Victoria *Town* Mexico 31 F9
Civitavecchia *Town* Italy 48 E6
Clarksville *Town* Tennessee, USA 22 C7
Clearwater *Town* Florida, USA 23 H10
Clermont-Ferrand *Town* France 47 E9
Cleveland *Town* Ohio, USA 21 G8
Clovis *Town* New Mexico, USA 27 F11
Cluj-Napoca *Town* Romania 55 D9
Coast Ranges California/Oregon, USA 24 F2, 26 B4
Coatzacoalcos *Town* Mexico 31 H11
Cochin *See Kochi*
Cognac *Town* France 46 E7
Coimbatore *Town* India 77 I8
Coimbra *Town* Portugal 44 E5
Colchester *Town* England, UK 41 H10
Colima *Town* Mexico 31 H8
Cologne *Town* Germany 50 E7
Colombia *Country* 35
Colombo *Capital* Sri Lanka 77 J9
Colón *Town* Panama 34 F7
Colorado *River* Mexico/USA 27 D8
Colorado *State* USA 27
Colorado Springs *Town* Colorado, USA 27 D10
Columbia *State capital* S Carolina, USA 23 D10
Columbia *Town* Missouri, USA 22 B5
Columbus *State capital* Ohio, USA 21 H8
Columbus *Town* Georgia, USA 23 F9
Como *Town* Italy 48 B5
Comodoro Rivadavia *Town* Argentina 36 H7

Comoros *Country* 69
Conakry *Capital* Guinea 64 H4
Concepción *Town* Chile 36 G6
Concord *State capital* New Hampshire, USA 21 E13
Congo *River* Western Central Africa 68 C7, 69 D8
Congo, Democratic Republic of the (DRC) *Country* 68
Congo, Republic of the *Country* 68
Connecticut *State* USA 21
Constanta *Town* Romania 55 F13
Constantine *Town* Algeria 62 D6
Coober Pedy *Town* Australia 91 F8
Cook, Mount New Zealand 92 G7
Cook Islands *Dep. territory* New Zealand 93 I13
Cook Strait New Zealand 93 F9
Cooktown *Town* Australia 91 B11
Copenhagen *Capital* Denmark 42 I7
Coquimbo *Town* Chile 36 F6
Coral Sea Islands Territory *Dep. territory* Australia 93 I11
Cordillera Central *Mountain range* Colombia/Panama 34 F6, 35 H8
Córdoba *Town* Argentina 36 F7
Córdoba *Town* Spain 45 G8
Corfu *Island* Greece 49 G10
Cork *Town* Republic of Ireland 40 H6
Corpus Christi *Town* Texas, USA 27 I13
Corrientes *Town* Argentina 37 F8
Corsica *Island* France 47 I12
Çorum *Town* Turkey 73 C9
Corvallis *Town* Oregon, USA 24 F3
Cosenza *Town* Italy 49 G8
Costa Rica *Country* 34
Côte d'Ivoire *Country* 64
Cotonou *Capital* Benin 65 I8
Cottbus *Town* Germany 51 E12
Council Bluffs *Town* Iowa, USA 20 H2
Coventry *Town* England, UK 41 H9
Craiova *Town* Romania 55 G9
Cremona *Town* Italy 48 C5
Crete, Sea of Greece 49 I12
Crete *Island* Greece 49 J12
Crimea Ukraine 58 I7
Croatia *Country* 49
Crotone *Town* Italy 49 G8
Cuba *Country* 34
Cúcuta *Town* Colombia 35 G8
Cuernavaca *Town* Mexico 31 H9
Cuito *River* Angola 68 G7
Culiacán *Town* Mexico 30 E6
Cumaná *Town* Venezuela 35 F11
Curaçao *Dep. territory* Netherlands 35 E10
Curitiba *Town* Brazil 37 F9
Cusco *Town* Peru 36 D6
Cuttack *Town* India 77 F10
Cuxhaven *Town* Germany 51 B9
Cyprus *Country* 73
Czech Republic *Country* 56
Czestochowa *Town* Poland 57 F8

Dakar *Capital* Senegal 64 F3
Dalandzadgad *Town* Mongolia 85 D8
Da Lat *Town* Vietnam 78 H6
Dalian *Town* China 85 E12
Dallas *Town* Texas, USA 27 G13
Damascus *Capital* Syria 73 H10
Dampier *Town* Australia 90 D4
Da Nang *Town* Vietnam 78 F6
Danube *River* Europe 51 I8, 40 E12, 54 D5, 55 G10, 57 J3
Danzig, Gulf of 57 B8
Dar'a *Town* Syria 73 H10
Dar es Salaam *Capital* Tanzania 67 I9

Darfur *Sudan* 66 D6
Darhan *Town* Mongolia 85 C9
Darien, Gulf of 34 F7
Darling *River* Australia 91 G10
Darmstadt *Town* Germany 51 G8
Darnah *Town* Libya 63 E10
Darwin *Town* Australia 90 B7
Davao *Town* Philippines 79 H12
Davenport *Town* Iowa, USA 20 G5
David *Town* Panama 34 F6
Davis (Australia) *RS* Antarctica 16 E7
Dayr az Zawr *Town* Syria 73 F12
Dayton *Town* Ohio, USA 21 H8
Daytona Beach *Town* Florida, USA 23 G11
Dead Sea Jordan 73 I9
Death Valley California, USA 26 E6
Debrecen *Town* Hungary 55 C8
Decatur *Town* Illinois, USA 20 H6
Delaware *State* USA 21
Delft *Town* Netherlands 50 D5
Delhi *Town* India 77 D9
Del Rio *Town* Texas, USA 27 I11
Democratic Republic of the Congo (DRC) *See* Congo, Republic of the
Den Helder *Town* Netherlands 50 C6
Denizli *Town* Turkey 72 D6
Denmark *Country* 42
Denver *State capital* Colorado, USA 27 C10
Derby *Town* England, UK 41 G9
Des Moines *State capital* Iowa, USA 20 G3
Dessau *Town* Germany 51 E11
Detroit *Town* Michigan, USA 20 F8
Devon Island Nunavut, Canada 29 D9
Dhaka *Capital* Bangladesh 77 E11
Dhanbad *Town* India 77 E10
Dieppe *Town* France 47 B8
Dijon *Town* France 47 D10
Dili *Capital* East Timor 80 H7
Dimitrovgrad *Town* Bulgaria 55 I11
Dire Dawa *Town* Ethiopia 67 D10
Diyarbakir *Town* Turkey 73 E12
Djibouti *Capital* Djibouti 67 D11
Djibouti *Country* 67
Dnieper *River* Ukraine 58 H6
Dniester *River* Ukraine 58 H6
Dnipropetrovsk *Town* Ukraine 58 H7
Dobrich *Town* Bulgaria 55 G13
Dodge City *Town* Kansas, USA 27 E12
Dodoma *Capital* Tanzania 67 I9
Doha *Capital* Qatar 75 F9
Dominica *Country* 35
Dominican Republic *Country* 35
Don *River* Russian Fed. 59 H8
Donetsk *Town* Ukraine 58 H7
Dordogne *River* France 46 F7
Dordrecht *Town* Netherlands 50 D5
Dortmund *Town* Germany 50 E7
Douala *Town* Cameroon 68 B5
Douglas *Town* Arizona, USA 27 G8
Dover *State capital* Delaware, USA 21 G12
Dover *Town* England, UK 41 I11
Drakensberg Mountains South Africa 69 J8
Drama *Town* Greece 49 F12
Drammen *Town* Norway 42 G6
Dresden *Town* Germany 51 F12
Drobeta-Turnu Severin *Town* Romania 55 F8
Drogheda *Town* Republic of Ireland 40 F7
Dubai *Town* UAE 75 F10
Dublin *Capital* Republic of Ireland 40 G7

Dubrovnik *Town* Croatia 49 E9
Duisburg *Town* Germany 50 E7
Duluth *Town* Minnesota, USA 20 D3
Dumont d'Urville (France) *RS* Antarctica 16 H5
Dunaujvaros *Town* Hungary 54 D6
Dundee *Town* Scotland, UK 41 D9
Dunedin *Town* New Zealand 92 I7
Dunkerque *Town* France 47 A9
Durango *Town* Colorado, USA 27 E9
Durango *Town* Mexico 30 F7
Durban *Town* South Africa 69 I9
Durham *Town* N Carolina, USA 23 C11
Durrës *Town* Albania 49 F9
Dushanbe *Capital* Tajikistan 86 J3
Düsseldorf *Town* Germany 50 E7

East Cape New Zealand 93 C11
East China Sea Pacific Ocean 85 G13
Eastern Ghats *Mountain range* India 77 G9
East London *Town* South Africa 69 J8
East Siberian Sea Arctic Ocean 17 C13, 87 E11
East Timor *Country* 81
Eau Claire *Town* Wisconsin, USA 20 E4
Ebetsu *Town* Japan 83 B10
Ebro *River* Spain 45 C10
Ecuador *Country* 36
Edinburgh *Capital* Scotland, UK 41 E8
Edirne *Town* Turkey 72 B5
Edmonton *Province capital* Alberta, Canada 28 H7
Edward, Lake DRC/Uganda 66 G7, 69 C9
Edwards Plateau Texas, USA 27 H12
Egypt *Country* 63
Eindhoven *Town* Netherlands 50 E6
El Aaiún *Capital* Western Sahara 64 C5
Elat *Town* Israel 73 J9
Elazig *Town* Turkey 73 D11
Elbasan *Town* Albania 49 F10
Elbe *River* Czech Republic/ Germany 51 E11, 56 G6
Elblag *Town* Poland 57 B8
Elbrus, Mount Russian Fed. 59 I8
Elche *Town* Spain 45 G11
El Fasher *Town* Sudan 66 C6
Elgin *Town* Illinois, USA 20 G6
Ellesmere Island Canada 17 F10, 29 C9
Ellsworth Land Antarctica 16 F2
El Minya *Town* Egypt 63 F13
El Obeid *Town* Sudan 66 D7
El Paso *Town* Texas, USA 27 G9
El Progreso *Town* Honduras 34 D5
El Salvador *Country* 34
Emmen *Town* Netherlands 50 C7
Empty Quarter *Desert* Saudi Arabia 75 H9
Ende *Town* Indonesia 80 H6
England *Country* UK 41
English Channel France/UK 41 I9, 46 A6
Enid *Town* Oklahoma, USA 27 E13
Enschede *Town* Netherlands 50 D7
Ensenada *Town* Mexico 30 B4
Enugu *Town* Nigeria 65 I10
Equatorial Guinea *Country* 68
Erdenet *Town* Mongolia 85 C9
Erfurt *Town* Germany 51 F10
Erie, Lake USA 21 F9
Erie *Town* Pennsylvania, USA 21 F9

Eritrea *Country* 67
Erzincan *Town* Turkey 73 D11
Erzurum *Town* Turkey 73 C13
Esbjerg *Town* Denmark 42 I5
Escuintla *Town* Guatemala 34 D4
Esfahan *Town* Iran 75 C9
Eskisehir *Town* Turkey 72 C7
Esmeraldas *Town* Ecuador 36 A5
Esperance *Town* Australia 90 H6
Esperanza (Argentina) *RS* Antarctica 16 D1
Espoo *Town* Finland 43 G10
Essen *Town* Germany 50 E7
Estonia *Country* 58
Ethiopia *Country* 67
Etna, Mount Italy 48 H7
Eugene *Town* Oregon, USA 24 F3
Euphrates *River* Iraq/Syria/Turkey 73 F12, 74 C8
Evansville *Town* Indiana, USA 20 J6
Everest, Mount China/Nepal 77 D11, 84 H6
Everett *Town* Washington, USA 24 D4
Everglades, The Florida, USA 23 J11
Évora *Town* Portugal 44 G5
Exeter *Town* England, UK 41 I8

Fairbanks *Town* Alaska, USA 25 B11
Faisalabad *Town* Pakistan 77 C8
Falkland Islands *Dep. territory* UK 37 J8
Fargo *Town* N Dakota, USA 25 F13
Fayetteville *Town* N Carolina, USA 23 C11
Feira de Santana *Town* Brazil 37 D11
Ferrara *Town* Italy 48 C6
Fes *Town* Morocco 62 D3
Feuilles *River* Quebec, Canada 29 G11
Fianarantsoa *Town* Madagascar 69 H12
Fiji *Country* 93 I12
Finland, Gulf of 58 E5
Finland *Country* 43
Firat *River* Turkey 73 E11
Fitzroy *River* Australia 90 C6
Flagstaff *Town* Arizona, USA 27 F8
Flensburg *Town* Germany 51 A9
Flint *Town* Michigan, USA 20 F7
Florence *Town* Italy 48 D6
Flores Sea 80 H6
Florianópolio *Town* Brazil 37 F9
Florida *State* USA 23
Florida Keys *Island group* Florida, USA 23 J11
Focsani *Town* Romania 55 E12
Foggia *Town* Italy 49 E8
Fontainebleau *Town* France 47 C9
Forli *Town* Italy 48 C6
Fort Albany *Town* Ontario, Canada 29 H10
Fortaleza *Town* Brazil 37 B11
Fort Collins *Town* Colorado, USA 27 C10
Fort Lauderdale *Town* Florida, USA 23 I12
Fort Myers *Town* Florida, USA 23 I11
Fort Smith *Town* Arkansas, USA 22 D4
Fort Wayne *Town* Indiana, USA 20 G7
Fort Worth *Town* Texas, USA 27 G13
Foveaux Strait New Zealand 92 J5
Fox Islands Alaska, USA 25 C9
France *Country* 46
Francistown *Town* Botswana 69 H8

Frankfurt am Main *Town* Germany 51 G8
Frankfurt an der Oder *Town* Germany 51 D12
Fraser Island Australia 91 E13
Fredericton *Province capital* New Brunswick, Canada 29 I13
Fredrikstad *Town* Norway 42 G6
Freemantle *Town* Australia 90 G4
Freetown *Capital* Sierra Leone 64 H4
Freiburg im Breisgau *Town* Germany 50 I7
French Guiana *Dep. territory* France 35 H14
French Polynesia *Dep. territory* France 93 I14
Fresno *Town* California, USA 26 D5
Fuji, Mount Japan 83 G9
Fuji *Town* Japan 83 G9
Fukui *Town* Japan 83 G8
Fukuoka *Town* Japan 82 H5
Fukushima *Town* Japan 83 F10
Fulda *Town* Germany 51 F9
Fürth *Town* Germany 51 H9
Fushun *Town* China 85 D12
Fuzhou *Town* China 85 H12

Gabon *Country* 68
Gaborone *Capital* Botswana 69 H8
Gabrovo *Town* Bulgaria 55 H11
Gainesville *Town* Florida, USA 23 G10
Gallup *Town* New Mexico, USA 27 E9
Galveston *Town* Texas, USA 27 I14
Galway *Town* Republic of Ireland 40 G6
Gambia *Country* 64
Gander *Town* Newfoundland and Labrador, Canada 29 H14
Ganges *River* India 77 D9
Gao *Town* Mali 65 F8
Gar *Town* China 84 G5
Garland *Town* Texas, USA 27 G13
Garonne *River* France 46 F7
Garoua *Town* Cameroon 68 A6
Gary *Town* Indiana, USA 20 G6
Gaspé *Town* Quebec, Canada 29 H13
Gävle *Town* Sweden 43 G8
Gaza *Town* Israel 73 I9
Gaza Strip *Disputed region* Near East 73 I9
Gaziantep *Town* Turkey 73 E10
Gdansk *Town* Poland 57 B8
Gdynia *Town* Poland 57 B8
Geelong *Town* Australia 91 I11
General Santos *Town* Philippines 79 H12
Geneva, Lake Switzerland 52 G1
Geneva *Town* Switzerland 52 G1
Genk *Town* Belgium 50 E6
Genoa *Town* Italy 48 C5
Georgetown *Capital* Guyana 35 G13
George Town *Town* Malaysia 80 E2
Georgia *Country* 59
Georgia *State* USA 23
Georg von Neumayer (Germany) *RS* Antarctica 16 C4
Gera *Town* Germany 51 F10
Germany *Country* 50
Ghana *Country* 64
Ghardaïa *Town* Algeria 62 E6
Ghent *Town* Belgium 50 E5
Gibraltar *Dep. territory* UK 44 I7
Gibraltar, Strait of Morocco/Spain 44 I7, 62 C3
Gibson Desert Australia 90 E5
Giessen *Town* Germany 51 F8
Gifu *Town* Japan 83 G8
Gijón *Town* Spain 44 B7

Gillette *Town* Wyoming, USA 25 G10

Girona *Town* Spain 45 C13

Gisborne *Town* New Zealand 93 D11

Giurgiu *Town* Romania 55 G11

Glasgow *Town* Scotland, UK 41 E8

Gliwice *Town* Poland 57 G8

Gloucester *Town* England, UK 41 H9

Gobi Desert Mongolia 85 D9

Godavari *River* India 77 F9

Godoy Cruz *Town* Argentina 36 G7

Goiânia *Town* Brazil 37 D9

Golan Heights *Mountain range* Syria 73 H9

Golmud *Town* China 84 F7

Gómez Palacio *Town* Mexico 31 E8

Gonaïves *Town* Haiti 35 C9

Gonder *Town* Ethiopia 67 D9

Gore *Town* Ethiopia 67 E9

Gorgan *Town* Iran 75 B9

Görlitz *Town* Germany 51 F12

Gorzow Wielkopolski *Town* Poland 56 D6

Gosford *Town* Australia 91 G12

Göteborg *Town* Sweden 42 H6

Gotland *Island* Sweden 43 H8

Göttingen *Town* Germany 51 E9

Gouda *Town* Netherlands 50 D6

Governador Valadares *Town* Brazil 37 E10

Grafton *Town* Australia 91 F13

Grampian Mountains Scotland, UK 41 D8

Granada *Town* Spain 45 H9

Gran Chaco Argentina 36 F7

Grand Canyon Arizona, USA 26 E7

Grand Forks *Town* N Dakota, USA 25 E13

Grand Rapids *Town* Michigan, USA 20 F7

Graz *Town* Austria 40 G12

Great Australian Bight Australia 90 G7

Great Barrier Island New Zealand 93 B9

Great Barrier Reef Australia 91 C12

Great Basin Nevada, USA 26 D6

Great Dividing Range Australia 91 D12

Great Falls *Town* Montana, USA 25 E8

Great Karoo South Africa 68 J7

Great Rift Valley Kenya 67 F9

Great Sandy Desert Australia 90 D6

Great Victoria Desert Australia 90 G5

Greece *Country* 49

Greeley *Town* Colorado, USA 27 C10

Green Bay *Town* Wisconsin, USA 20 E5

Greenland Sea 17 H11, 43 G12

Greensboro *Town* N Carolina, USA 23 C11

Greenville *Town* Mississippi, USA 22 E6

Greenville *Town* S Carolina, USA 23 D10

Greifswald *Town* Germany 51 B12

Grenada *Country* 35

Grenoble *Town* France 47 F10

Greymouth *Town* New Zealand 92 G7

Groningen *Town* Netherlands 50 C7

Grootfontein *Town* Namibia 68 G7

Grosseto *Town* Italy 48 D6

Grozny *Town* Russian Fed. 59 I8

Guadalajara *Town* Mexico 31 G8

Guadalajara *Town* Spain 45 E9

Guadeloupe *Dep. territory* France 35 D12

Guam *Dep. territory* USA 93 H11

Guanabacoa *Town* Cuba 34 B7

Guanare *Town* Venezuela 35 F9

Guangzhou *Town* China 85 I11

Guantánamo *Town* Cuba 35 C8

Guatemala *Country* 34

Guatemala City *Capital* Guatemala 34 D4

Guayaquil *Town* Ecuador 36 B5

Guaymas *Town* Mexico 30 D5

Guernsey *Island* Channel Islands, UK 41 J9

Guiana Highlands *Mountain range* Guyana/Venezuela 35 G12

Guinea, Gulf of 64 J7

Guinea *Country* 64

Guinea-Bissau *Country* 64

Guiyang *Town* China 85 H10

Gujranwala *Town* Pakistan 77 C8

Guwahati *Town* India 77 E12

Guyana *Country* 35

Gwadar *Town* Pakistan 76 D5

Gyor *Town* Hungary 54 C5

Haarlem *Town* Netherlands 50 D6

Hachinohe *Town* Japan 83 D10

Hadera *Town* Israel 73 H9

Haifa *Town* Israel 73 H9

Haikou *Town* China 85 J11

Hailar *Town* China 85 B11

Haiphong *Town* Vietnam 78 E5

Haiti *Country* 35

Hakodate *Town* Japan 83 C10

Halifax *Province capital* Nova Scotia, Canada 29 I13

Halle *Town* Germany 51 E10

Halley (UK) *RS* Antarctica 16 D3

Halmstad *Town* Sweden 42 I7

Hamadan *Town* Iran 75 C8

Hamah *Town* Syria 73 F10

Hamamatsu *Town* Japan 83 G9

Hamar *Town* Norway 42 G6

Hamburg *Town* Germany 51 C9

Hamhung *Town* North Korea 85 D13

Hamilton *Town* New Zealand 93 C9

Hamilton *Town* Ontario, Canada 29 J11

Hamm *Town* Germany 51 E8

Hanamaki *Town* Japan 83 E10

Hangzhou *Town* China 85 G12

Hannover *Town* Germany 51 D9

Hanoi *Capital* Vietnam 78 E5

Harare *Capital* Zimbabwe 69 G9

Harbel *Town* Liberia 64 I5

Harbin *Town* China 85 C12

Harer *Town* Ethiopia 67 E10

Hargeisa *Town* Somalia 67 D11

Harrisburg *State capital* Pennsylvania, USA 21 G11

Hartford *State capital* Connecticut, USA 21 F12

Hasselt *Town* Belgium 50 E6

Hastings *Town* New Zealand 93 E10

Hat Yai *Town* Thailand 78 J4

Haugesund *Town* Norway 42 G5

Havana *Capital* Cuba 34 B7

Hawaii *State* USA 26

Hefei *Town* China 85 F12

Heidelberg *Town* Germany 51 G8

Heilbronn *Town* Germany 51 H8

Helena *State capital* Montana, USA 24 E7

Helsingborg *Town* Sweden 42 I7

Helsinki *Capital* Finland 43 G10

Hengyang *Town* China 85 H11

Henzada *Town* Myanmar (Burma) 78 F2

Herat *Town* Afghanistan 76 A6

Hermosillo *Town* Mexico 30 D5

Hilversum *Town* Netherlands 50 D6

Himalayas Asia 77 D10, 84 H6

Hims *Town* Syria 73 G10

Hirosaki *Town* Japan 83 D10

Hiroshima *Town* Japan 82 H6

Hitachi *Town* Japan 83 F10

Ho Chi Minh City *Town* Vietnam 78 H6

Hofu *Town* Japan 82 H6

Hohhot *Town* China 85 E10

Hokkaido *Island* Japan 83 B11

Holguín *Town* Cuba 35 C8

Homyel *Town* Belarus 58 G6

Honduras *Country* 34

Hong Kong *Town* China 85 I11

Honolulu *State capital* Hawaii, USA 26 H3

Honshu *Island* Japan 83 F9

Hormuz, Strait of Iran/Oman 75 E10

Houston *Town* Texas, USA 27 H14

Hradec Kralove *Town* Czech Republic 56 G6

Hrodna *Town* Belarus 58 G5

Huacho *Town* Peru 36 C5

Huambo *Town* Angola 68 F6

Huancayo *Town* Peru 36 D6

Huang *River* China 85 F11

Hudson Bay Canada 29 G10

Hué *Town* Vietnam 78 F6

Huelva *Town* Spain 44 H6

Hull *Town* England, UK 41 F10

Hungary *Country* 54

Huntington *Town* West Virginia, USA 21 I9

Huntsville *Town* Alabama, USA 23 D8

Huron, Lake USA 20 E8

Hyderabad *Town* India 77 G8

Hyderabad *Town* Pakistan 76 D7

Hyesan *Town* North Korea 85 D13

Iasi *Town* Romania 55 C12

Ibadan *Town* Nigeria 65 I9

Ibagué *Town* Colombia 35 H8

Ibarra *Town* Ecuador 36 A5

Ibiza *Balearic Islands*, Spain 45 F12

Ibiza *Town* Ibiza, Spain 45 F12

Ica *Town* Peru 36 D5

Iceland *Country* 43

Idaho *State* USA 24

Idaho Falls *Town* Idaho, USA 24 G7

Illinois *River* Illinois, USA 20 H5

Illinois *State* USA 20

Iloilo *Town* Philippines 79 G11

Ilorin *Town* Nigeria 65 I9

Imperatriz *Town* Brazil 37 B10

Imphal *Town* India 77 E12

Inchon *Town* South Korea 85 E13

Independence *Town* Missouri, USA 22 B4

India *Country* 77

Indiana *State* USA 20

Indianapolis *State capital* Indiana, USA 20 H7

Indian Ocean 67, 69, 76, 90

Indonesia *Country* 80

Indore *Town* India 77 E8

Indus *River* Pakistan 76 D7

Ingolstadt *Town* Germany 51 H10

Inhambane *Town* Mozambique 69 H10

Innsbruck *Town* Austria 52 F7

In Salah *Town* Algeria 62 F5

Invercargill *Town* New Zealand 92 J6

Inverness *Town* Scotland, UK 41 C8

Ioánnina *Town* Greece 49 G10

Ionian Sea 49 H9

Iowa *State* USA 20

Ipoh *Town* Malaysia 80 E2

Ipswich *Town* England, UK 41 H10

Iqaluit *Province capital* Nunavut, Canada 29 F11

Iquique *Town* Chile 36 E6

Iquitos *Town* Peru 36 B6

Iráklion *Town* Crete, Greece 49 I12

Iran *Country* 75

Iraq *Country* 74

Irbid *Town* Jordan 73 H9

Ireland, Republic of *Country* 40

Iringa *Town* Tanzania 67 I9

Irish Sea 40 F7

Irkutsk *Town* Russian Fed. 86 H6

Irrawaddy *River* Myanmar (Burma) 78 F2

Ishinomaki *Town* Japan 83 E10

Islamabad *Capital* Pakistan 77 B8

Isle of Man *Dep. territory* UK 41 F8

Isparta *Town* Turkey 72 E7

Israel *Country* 73

Istanbul *Town* Turkey 72 B6

Itabuna *Town* Brazil 37 D11

Italy *Country* 48

Iwaki *Town* Japan 83 F10

Izhevsk *Town* Russian Fed. 59 F9

Izmir *Town* Turkey 72 D5

Izmit *Town* Turkey 72 C7

Jackson *State capital* Mississippi, USA 22 F6

Jacksonville *Town* Florida, USA 23 G10

Jaén *Town* Spain 45 H8

Jaffna *Town* Sri Lanka 77 I9

Jaipur *Town* India 77 D8

Jakarta *Capital* Indonesia 80 H3

Jamaica *Country* 35

Jambi *Town* Indonesia 80 F2

Jamnagar *Town* India 76 E7

Jamshedpur *Town* India 77 E10

Janesville *Town* Wisconsin, USA 20 G5

Japan, Sea of 82 F7, 85 D13

Japan *Country* 82

Java *Island* Indonesia 80 H4

Java Sea 80 H4

Jayapura *Town* Indonesia 81 F11

Jefferson City *State capital* Missouri, USA 22 B5

Jena *Town* Germany 51 F10

Jersey *Island* Channel Islands, UK 41 J9

Jerusalem *Capital* Israel 73 I9

Jiddah *Town* Saudi Arabia 74 G5

Jihlava *Town* Czech Republic 56 H6

Jilin *Town* China 85 C12

Jima *Town* Ethiopia 67 E9

Jinan *Town* China 85 E11

Jinzhou *Town* China 85 D11

João Pessoa *Town* Brazil 37 C12

Jodhpur *Town* India 77 D8

Johannesburg *Town* South Africa 69 J9

John o'Groats *Town* Scotland, UK 41 C9

Johor Baharu *Town* Malaysia 80 F2

Joliet *Town* Illinois, USA 20 G6

Jönköping *Town* Sweden 42 H7

Jordan *Country* 73

Jordan *River* Jordan 73 H9

Jorhat *Town* India 77 D12

Joseph Bonaparte Gulf 90 B7

Juazeiro *Town* Brazil 37 C11

Juazeiro do Norte *Town* Brazil 37 C11

Juba *Town* Sudan 67 F8

Judenburg *Town* Austria 40 G11

Juliaca *Town* Peru 36 D6

Juneau *State capital* Alaska, USA 25 C11

Jyväskylä *Town* Finland 43 F10

K2 *Mountain* China/Pakistan 77 B9

Kabul *Capital* Afghanistan 76 B7

Kabwe *Town* Zambia 69 F9

Kachchh, Rann of India 76 E7

Kaduna *Town* Nigeria 65 H10

Kagoshima *Town* Japan 82 I5

Kairouan *Town* Tunisia 62 D7

Kaiserslautern *Town* Germany 50 G7

Kalahari Desert Namibia 68 H7

Kalamata *Town* Peleponnese, Greece 49 I11

Kalamazoo *Town* Michigan, USA 20 G7

Kalemie *Town* DRC 69 E9

Kalgoorlie *Town* Australia 90 G5

Kaliningrad *Town* Russian Fed. 58 G5

Kalisz *Town* Poland 56 E7

Kamina *Town* DRC 69 E8

Kamloops *Town* British Columbia, Canada 28 H6

Kampala *Capital* Uganda 67 G8

Kampong Cham *Town* Cambodia 78 H5

Kananga *Town* DRC 69 E8

Kanazawa *Town* Japan 83 F8

Kandy *Town* Sri Lanka 77 J9

Kankan *Town* Guinea 64 H5

Kano *Town* Nigeria 65 G10

Kanpur *Town* India 77 D9

Kansas *River* Kansas, USA 27 D13

Kansas *State* USA 27

Kansas City *Town* Missouri, USA 22 B4

Kansk *Town* Russian Fed. 86 G6

Kaposvár *Town* Hungary 54 D5

Karabük *Town* Turkey 73 B8

Karachi *Town* Pakistan 76 D6

Kara Sea 17 G14, 59 B10, 86 D4

Karbala *Town* Iraq 74 C7

Kardhitsa *Town* Greece 49 G11

Karlovac *Town* Croatia 49 C8

Karlovy Vary *Town* Czech Republic 56 G4

Karlskrona *Town* Sweden 42 I7

Karlsruhe *Town* Germany 50 H7

Karlstad *Town* Sweden 42 G7

Kars *Town* Turkey 73 C13

Kasai (Cassai) *River* Angola/DRC 68 D7

Kashi *Town* China 84 E4

Kassala *Town* Sudan 67 C9

Kassel *Town* Germany 51 E9

Katherine *Town* Australia 91 B8

Kathmandu *Capital* Nepal 77 D10

Katowice *Town* Poland 57 G8

Katsina *Town* Nigeria 65 G10

Kattegat *Sea* 42 H6

Kaunas *Town* Lithuania 58 G5

Kaválla *Town* Greece 49 F12

Kawasaki *Town* Japan 83 G10

Kayseri *Town* Turkey 73 D9

Kazakhstan *Country* 86

Kazan *Town* Russian Fed. 59 F9

Kecskemét *Town* Hungary 54 D6

Kelang *Town* Malaysia 80 E2

Kemerovo *Town* Russian Fed. 86 G5

Kemi *Town* Finland 43 D9

Kénitra *Town* Morocco 62 D3

Kentucky *State* USA 23

Kenya *Country* 67

Kerman *Town* Iran 75 D10

Kesennuma *Town* Japan 83 E10

Kettering *Town* Ohio, USA 21 H8

Key West *Town* Florida, USA 23 J11

Khabarovsk *Town* Russian Fed. 87 H9

Kharkiv *Town* Ukraine 58 H7

Khartoum *Capital* Sudan 67 C8

Khaskovo *Town* Bulgaria I11

Khon Kaen *Town* Thailand 78 G4

Khulna *Town* Bangladesh 77 F11
Kiel *Town* Germany 51 B10
Kiev *Capital* Ukraine 58 G6
Kigali *Capital* Rwanda 66 G7
Kigoma *Town* Tanzania 66 H7
Kikwit *Town* DRC 68 D7
Kilimanjaro, Mount Tanzania
   67 H9
Kimberley *Town* South Africa 69 I8
Kimberley Plateau Australia 90 C6
Kingston *Capital* Jamaica 35 D8
Kingstown *Capital* St. Vincent
   35 E12
Kinshasa *Capital* DRC 68 D6
Kiribati *Country* 93 I13
Kirikkale *Town* Turkey 73 C9
Kirkuk *Town* Iraq 74 B7
Kirov *Town* Russian Fed. 58 G6
Kiruna *Town* Sweden 43 C8
Kisangani *Town* DRC 69 C8
Kismaayo *Town* Somalia 67 G10
Kisumu *Town* Kenya 67 G8
Kitakyushu *Town* Japan 82 H5
Kitchener *Town* Ontario, Canada
   29 J11
Kitwe *Town* Zambia 69 F9
Kivu, Lake DRC/Rwanda 66 H7,
   69 D9
Klagenfurt *Town* Austria 40 H11
Klamath Falls *Town* Oregon, USA
   24 G3
Knoxville *Town* Tennessee, USA
   23 C9
Kobe *Town* Japan 82 H7
Koblenz *Town* Germany 50 F7
Kochi (Cochin) *Town* India 77 I8
Kochi *Town* Japan 82 H7
Kodiak *Town* Alaska, USA 25 C10
Kofu *Town* Japan 83 G9
Kokshetau *Town* Kazakhstan 86 H3
Kolhapur *Town* India 76 G7
Kolkata (Calcutta) *Town* India
   77 F11
Kolwezi *Town* DRC 69 E8
Komatsu *Town* Japan 83 F8
Komsomol'sk-na-Amure *Town*
   Russian Fed. 87 H9
Konya *Town* Turkey 73 E8
Koper *Town* Slovenia 48 B7
Korçë *Town* Albania 49 F10
Korea, North *Country* 85
Korea, South *Country* 85
Korea Strait Japan/South Korea
   82 H4, 85 E13
Koriyama *Town* Japan 83 F10
Korla *Town* China 84 E6
Kortrijk *Town* Belgium 50 E4
Kosice *Town* Slovakia 57 I10
Kosovo *Country* 49
Kosovska Mitrovica *Town* Serbia
   49 D10
Koszalin *Town* Poland 56 B6
Kotka *Town* Finland 43 G10
Kotte *Capital* Sri Lanka 77 J9
Kotto *River* CAR 68 B7
Kozáni *Town* Greece 49 F11
Kozhikode (Calicut) *Town* India
   77 H8
Kragujevac *Town* Serbia 49 D10
Kraków *Town* Poland 57 G9
Krasnodar *Town* Russian Fed.
   58 I7
Krasnoyarsk *Town* Russian Fed.
   86 G5
Krefeld *Town* Germany 50 E7
Kristiansand *Town* Norway 42 H5
Krusevac *Town* Serbia 49 D11
Kryyvy Rih *Town* Ukraine 58 H6
Kuala Lumpur *Capital* Malaysia
   80 E2
Kuala Terengganu *Town* Malaysia
   80 E2
Kuching *Town* Malaysia 80 F4

Kugluktuk *Town* Nunavut, Canada
   28 E7
Kumamoto *Town* Japan 82 I5
Kumanovo *Town* Macedonia
   49 E11
Kumasi *Town* Ghana 64 I7
Kunlun Shan *Mountain range*
   China 84 F6
Kunming *Town* China 85 I9
Kuopio *Town* Finland 43 E10
Kupang *Town* Indonesia 80 H7
Kure *Town* Japan 82 H6
Kushiro *Town* Japan 83 B11
Kütahya *Town* Turkey 72 D7
Kuwait *Country* 75
Kuwait City *Capital* Kuwait 75 D8
Kwangju *Town* South Korea 85 E13
Kwango *River* DRC 68 E6
Kwilu *River* DRC 68 D7
Kyoto *Town* Japan 83 G8
Kyrgyzstan *Country* 86
Kyushu *Island* Japan 82 I5
Kyustendil *Town* Bulgaria 55 I9

Labrador Sea 29 F12
La Ceiba *Town* Honduras 34 D5
La Coruña *Town* Spain 44 B5
La Crosse *Town* Wisconsin, USA
   20 F4
Ladoga, Lake Russian Fed. 58 E6
Lafayette *Town* Louisiana, USA
   22 H5
Lagos *Town* Nigeria 65 I8
Lagos *Town* Portugal 44 H5
Lahore *Town* Pakistan 77 C8
Lahti *Town* Finland 43 F10
Lake Charles *Town* Louisiana, USA
   22 H5
Lakewood *Town* Colorado, USA
   27 D10
Lalitpur *Town* India 77 E9
Lamía *Town* Greece 49 G11
Lansing *State capital* Michigan,
   USA 20 F7
Lanzhou *Town* China 85 F9
Laoag *Town* Philippines 79 D10
Laos *Country* 78
La Paz *Capital* Bolivia 36 D7
La Paz *Town* Mexico 30 F5
La Plata *Town* Argentina 37 G8
Laptev Sea 17 D13, 87 D8
Laredo *Town* Texas, USA 27 I12
Larissa *Town* Greece 49 G11
Larkana *Town* Pakistan 76 C7
La Rochelle *Town* France 46 E6
La Romana *Town* Dominican
   Republic 35 D10
Las Cruces *Town* New Mexico, USA
   27 G9
La Serena *Town* Chile 36 F6
La Spezia *Town* Italy 48 C5
Las Vegas *Town* Nevada, USA
   26 E6
Latina *Town* Italy 48 E6
Latvia *Country* 58
Launceston *Town* Australia 91 J11
Lausanne *Town* Switzerland 52 G1
Laval *Town* France 46 C7
Lawton *Town* Oklahoma, USA
   27 F12
Lebanon *Country* 73
Lecce *Town* Italy 49 F9
Leeds *Town* England, UK 41 F9
Leeuwarden *Town* Netherlands
   50 C7
Legnica *Town* Poland 56 F6
Le Havre *Town* France 47 B8
Leicester *Town* England, UK 41 G9
Leiden *Town* Netherlands 50 D6
Leipzig *Town* Germany 51 F11
Le Mans *Town* France 47 C8
Lena *River* Russian Fed. 86 G7
León *Town* Mexico 31 G8

León *Town* Nicaragua 34 E5
León *Town* Spain 44 C7
Lerwick *Town* Scotland, UK 41 A9
Leskovac *Town* Serbia 49 D11
Lesotho *Country* 69
Lethbridge *Town* Alberta, Canada
   28 I7
Leuven *Town* Belgium 50 E5
Lewis *Island* Scotland, UK 40 C7
Lewiston *Town* Idaho, USA 24 E5
Lewiston *Town* Maine, USA 21 D13
Lexington *Town* Kentucky, USA
   23 B8
Lhasa *Town* China 84 H7
Lianyungang *Town* China 85 F12
Liberec *Town* Czech Republic 56 F5
Liberia *Country* 64
Libreville *Capital* Gabon 68 C5
Libya *Country* 63
Libyan Desert Egypt/Libya/Sudan
   63 G11, 66 A6
Liechtenstein *Country* 52
Liège *Town* Belgium 50 F6
Liepaja *Town* Latvia 58 F5
Likasi *Town* DRC 69 F8
Lille *Town* France 47 A10
Lillehammer *Town* Norway 42 F6
Lilongwe *Capital* Malawi 69 F10
Lima *Capital* Peru 36 D5
Limassol *Town* Cyprus 73 G8
Limerick *Town* Republic of Ireland
   40 G6
Limoges *Town* France 47 E8
Limón *Town* Costa Rica 34 F6
Limpopo *River* South Africa 69 H9
Linares *Town* Spain 45 G9
Lincoln *State capital* Nebraska,
   USA 21 I14
Lincoln Sea 17 G11
Lindi *Town* Tanzania 67 J10
Linköping *Town* Sweden 42 H7
Linz *Town* Austria 40 E11
Lipetsk *Town* Russian Fed. 58 G7
Lisbon *Capital* Portugal 44 G4
Lithuania *Country* 58
Little Rock *State capital* Arkansas,
   USA 22 E5
Liuzhou *Town* China 85 I10
Liverpool *Town* England, UK 41 G8
Livingstone *Town* Zambia 69 G8
Livorno *Town* Italy 48 D5
Ljubljana *Capital* Slovenia 48 B7
Lleida *Town* Spain 45 C11
Lobamba *Capital* Swaziland 69 I9
Lobito *Town* Angola 68 F6
Lodz *Town* Poland 57 E8
Logroño *Town* Spain 45 C9
Loire *River* France 46 D7
Lomami *River* DRC 69 D8
Lomas de Zamora *Town* Argentina
   37 G8
Lomé *Capital* Togo 65 I8
London *Capital* England, UK
   41 H10
London *Town* Ontario, Canada
   29 J11
Londonderry *Town* Northern
   Ireland, UK 40 E7
Long Beach *Town* California, USA
   26 F5
Long Island New York, USA 21 F12
Longview *Town* Texas, USA 27 G14
Lorca *Town* Spain 45 H10
Lorient *Town* France 46 C6
Los Angeles *Town* California, USA
   26 F5
Los Angeles *Town* Chile 36 H6
Los Mochis *Town* Mexico 30 E6
Louisiana *State* USA 22
Louisville *Town* Kentucky, USA
   23 B8
Lowell *Town* Massachusetts, USA
   21 E13

Lower Hutt *Town* New Zealand
   93 F9
Luanda *Capital* Angola 68 E6
Lubango *Town* Angola 68 F6
Lubbock *Town* Texas, USA 27 F11
Lübeck *Town* Germany 51 B10
Lublin *Town* Poland 57 F11
Lubumbashi *Town* DRC 69 F9
Lucknow *Town* India 77 D9
Lüderitz *Town* Namibia 68 I6
Ludhiana *Town* India 77 C8
Ludwigshafen *Town* Germany
   51 G7
Luena *Town* Angola 68 F7
Lugano *Town* Switzerland 52 H4
Lugo *Town* Spain 44 B6
Luleå *Town* Sweden 43 D9
Lund *Town* Sweden 42 I7
Lüneburg *Town* Germany 51 C10
Luoyang *Town* China 85 F10
Lusaka *Capital* Zambia 69 F9
Luxembourg *Capital* Luxembourg
   50 G6
Luxembourg *Country* 50 G6
Luxor *Town* Egypt 63 G13
Luzon *Island* Philippines 79 E10
Lviv *Town* Ukraine 58 H5
Lynchburg *Town* Virgina, USA
   23 B11
Lyon *Town* France 47 F10

Maas (Meuse) *River* Belgium/
   France/Netherlands 50 E6
Maastricht *Town* Netherlands
   50 E6
Macapá *Town* Brazil 37 B9
Macau *Town* China 85 I11
Macdonnell Ranges Australia 91 E8
Macedonia *Country* 49
Maceio *Town* Brazil 37 C11
Mackay *Town* Australia 91 D12
Macon *Town* Georgia, USA 23 E9
Ma'daba *Town* Jordan 73 I10
Madagascar *Country* 69
Madeira *River* Brazil 37 B8
Madison *State capital* Wisconsin,
   USA 20 F5
Madras *See Chennai*
Madrid *Capital* Spain 45 E8
Madurai *Town* India 77 I8
Magadan *Town* Russian Fed. 87 G11
Magdeburg *Town* Germany 51 D10
Magnitogorsk *Town* Russian Fed.
   59 G10
Mahajanga *Town* Madagascar
   69 G12
Maiduguri *Town* Nigeria 65 H11
Main *River* Germany 51 G10
Maine, Gulf of 21 D14
Maine *State* USA 21
Mainz *Town* Germany 51 G8
Maitri (India) *RS* Antarctica 16 C5
Malabo *Capital* Equatorial Guinea
   68 C5
Málaga *Town* Spain 45 I8
Malakal *Town* Sudan 67 D8
Malang *Town* Indonesia 80 H4
Malatya *Town* Turkey 73 D11
Malawi *Country* 69
Malaysia *Country* 80
Mali *Country* 64
Mallorca Balearic Islands, Spain
   45 E13
Malmö *Town* Sweden 42 I7
Malta *Country* 48
Manado *Town* Indonesia 80 F7
Managua *Capital* Nicaragua 34 E5
Manama *Capital* Bahrain 75 E8
Manaus *Town* Brazil 37 B8
Manchester *Town* England, UK
   41 G9
Manchester *Town* New Hampshire,
   USA 21 E13

Mandalay *Town* Myanmar (Burma)
   78 E2
Mangalore *Town* India 76 H7
Manila *Capital* Philippines 79 F10
Manisa *Town* Turkey 72 D5
Manitoba *Province* Canada 29
Manizales *Town* Colombia 35 H8
Mankato *Town* Minnesota, USA
   20 F3
Mannheim *Town* Germany 51 G8
Manta *Town* Ecuador 36 B5
Maputo *Capital* Mozambique 69 I9
Marabá *Town* Brazil 37 B9
Maracaibo *Town* Venezuela 35 F9
Maradi *Town* Niger 65 G10
Marajo Island Brazil 37 B9
Marbella *Town* Spain 45 I8
Mardan *Town* Pakistan 77 B8
Mar del Plata *Town* Argentina
   37 G8
Maribor *Town* Slovenia 49 B8
Marie Byrd Land Antarctica 16 F3
Marka *Town* Somalia 67 G11
Marmara, Sea of 72 C6
Marquette *Town* Michigan, USA
   20 D5
Marrakech *Town* Morocco 62 E2
Marseille *Town* France 47 H10
Marshall Islands *Country* 93 H12
Martin *Town* Slovakia 57 H8
Martinique *Dep. territory* France
   35 E12
Maryland *State* USA 21
Masaka *Town* Uganda 67 G8
Maseru *Capital* Lesotho 69 I8
Mashhad *Town* Iran 75 B11
Massa *Town* Italy 48 C5
Massachusetts *State* USA 21
Massawa *Town* Eritrea 67 C9
Massif Central France 47 F9
Matadi *Town* DRC 68 D6
Matamoros *Town* Mexico 31 E10
Mataram *Town* Indonesia 80 H5
Mataró *Town* Spain 45 C13
Matsue *Town* Japan 82 G6
Matsumoto *Town* Japan 83 G9
Matsuyama *Town* Japan 82 H6
Matterhorn, Mount Switzerland
   52 H2
Maun *Town* Botswana 69 G8
Mauritania *Country* 64
Mauritius *Country* 69
Mawson (Australia) *RS* Antarctica
   16 E6
Mayotte *Dep. territory* France
   69 F12
Mazar-e Sharif *Town* Afghanistan
   76 A7
Mazatlán *Town* Mexico 30 F7
Mbabane *Capital* Swaziland 69 I9
Mbandaka *Town* DRC 68 C7
Mbeya *Town* Tanzania 67 I9
Mbuji-Mayi *Town* DRC 69 E8
McKinley, Mount Alaska, USA
   25 B11
McMurdo (US) *RS* Antarctica
   16 H5
Mecca *Town* Saudi Arabia 74 G5
Mechelen *Town* Belgium 50 E5
Medan *Town* Indonesia 80 E1
Medellín *Town* Colombia 35 G8
Medicine Hat *Town* Alberta,
   Canada 28 I7
Medina *Town* Saudi Arabia 74 G5
Mediterranean Sea 45, 47, 62, 73
Meerut *Town* India 77 D9
Mekong *River* Asia 78 G5, 85 I9
Melbourne *Town* Australia 91 I11
Melilla *Town* Spain 45 J9, 62 D4
Melville Island Canada 17 E9
Memphis *Town* Tennessee, USA
   22 D6
Mendoza *Town* Argentina 36 G7

Menorca Balearic Islands, Spain
45 E14
Mérida Town Mexico 31 G13, 44 F7
Mérida Town Spain 44 F7
Mesa Town Arizona, USA 26 F7
Messina Town Sicily, Italy 48 H7
Metairie Town Louisiana, USA
22 H6
Metz Town France 47 C11
Meuse (Maas) River Belgium/
France/Netherlands 50 F5
Mexicali Town Mexico 30 B4
Mexico, Gulf of 23 H8, 27 J14,
31 F11
Mexico Country 30
Mexico City Capital Mexico 31 H9
Miami Town Florida, USA 23 I12
Michigan, Lake USA 20 E6
Michigan State USA 20
Micronesia Country 93 H11
Middlesbrough Town England, UK
41 F9
Midland Town Texas, USA 27 G11
Milan Town Italy 48 B5
Miles City Town Montana, USA
25 F10
Milwaukee Town Wisconsin, USA
20 F6
Mindanao Island Philippines
79 G12
Mindoro Strait South China Sea
79 G10
Minneapolis Town Minnesota, USA
20 E3
Minnesota State USA 20
Minot Town N Dakota, USA 25 E12
Minsk Capital Belarus 58 G6
Mirny (Russian Federation) RS
Antarctica 16 F7
Mirpur Khas Town Pakistan 76 D7
Miskolc Town Hungary 54 B7
Mississippi River USA 20 F4, 22 E6
Mississippi State USA 22
Missouri River Montana, USA
25 E10
Missouri State USA 22
Mito Town Japan 83 F10
Miyako Town Japan 83 D10
Miyakonojo Town Japan 82 I5
Miyazaki Town Japan 82 I6
Mobile Town Alabama, USA 22 G7
Modesto Town California, USA
26 C4
Mogadishu Capital Somalia 67 F11
Moldova Country 58
Molodezhnaya (Russian
Federation) RS Antarctica 16 D6
Molucca Sea 80 F7
Mombasa Town Kenya 67 H10
Monaco Capital Monaco 47 H11
Monaco Country 47
Monclova Town Mexico 31 E9
Mongolia Country 85
Monroe Town Louisiana, USA
22 F5
Monrovia Capital Liberia 64 I4
Mons Town Belgium 50 F5
Montana State USA 25
Montana Town Bulgaria 55 H9
Montauban Town France 46 G7
Mont Blanc Mountain France
47 F11
Mont-de-Marsan Town France
46 F7
Montego Bay Town Jamaica 35 C8
Montélimar Town France 47 G10
Montenegro Country 49
Monterey Town California, USA
26 D4
Montería Town Colombia 35 F8
Monterrey Town Mexico 31 E9
Montevideo Capital Uruguay
37 G8

Montgomery State capital
Alabama, USA 23 F8
Montluçon Town France 47 E9
Montpelier State capital Vermont,
USA 21 D12
Montpellier Town France 47 H9
Montreal Town Quebec, Canada
29 I12
Montserrat Dep. territory UK
35 D12
Monza Town Italy 48 B5
Moorhead Town Minnesota, USA
20 D2
Mopti Town Mali 64 G6
Morelia Town Mexico 31 H8
Morocco Country 62
Moroni Capital Comoros 69 F12
Moscow Capital Russian Fed. 58 F7
Mosselbaai Town South Africa
68 J7
Mossoró Town Brazil 37 B11
Mostar Town Bosnia and Herz.
49 D9
Mosul Town Iraq 74 B6
Moulmein Town Myanmar
(Burma) 78 G3
Moundou Town Chad 65 I12
Mount Isa Town Australia 91 D10
Mozambique Country 69
Mufulira Town Zambia 69 F9
Mulhouse Town France 47 D12
Multan Town Pakistan 77 C8
Mumbai (Bombay) Town India
76 F7
Muncie Town Indiana, USA 20 H7
Munich Town Germany 51 I10
Münster Town Germany 50 D7
Murcia Town Spain 45 G10
Murmansk Town Russian Fed.
58 C7
Muroran Town Japan 83 C10
Murray River Australia 91 H11
Muscat Capital Oman 75 F11
Mwanza Town Tanzania 67 H8
Mweru, Lake DRC 69 E9
Myanmar (Burma) Country 78
Myrtle Beach Town S Carolina,
USA 23 D11
Mysore Town India 77 H8
Myvatn Lake Iceland 43 H13

Nacala Town Mozambique 69 F11
Nagano Town Japan 83 F9
Nagaoka Town Japan 83 F9
Nagasaki Town Japan 82 I5
Nagoya Town Japan 83 G8
Nagpur Town India 77 F9
Nain Town Newfoundland and
Labrador, Canada 29 G12
Nairobi Capital Kenya 67 G9
Nakhon Ratchasima Town
Thailand 78 G4
Nakhon Sawan Town Thailand
78 G4
Nakhon Si Thammarat Town
Thailand 78 I4
Nakuru Town Kenya 67 G9
Nam Dinh Town Vietnam 78 E5
Namib Desert Namibia 68 H6
Namibe Town Angola 68 F6
Namibia Country 68
Nampula Town Mozambique
69 F11
Namur Town Belgium 50 F5
Nanchang Town China 85 G11
Nanchong Town China 85 G9
Nancy Town France 47 C11
Nanjing Town China 85 F12
Nanning Town China 85 I10
Nantes Town France 46 D6
Napier Town New Zealand 93 D10
Naples Town Italy 48 F7
Narvik Town Norway 43 C8

Nashville State capital Tennessee,
USA 23 C8
Nassau Capital Bahamas 35 A8
Nasser, Lake Egypt 63 H13
Natal Town Brazil 37 C12
Nauru Country 93 H12
Naypyidaw Capital Myanmar
(Burma) 78 F2
Nazareth Town Israel 73 H9
Nazilli Town Turkey 72 D6
Nazret Town Ethiopia 67 E10
N'Djamena Capital Chad 65 H12
Ndola Town Zambia 69 F9
Neápolis Town Greece 49 I11
Near Islands Alaska, USA 25 B8
Nebitdag Town Turkmenistan
86 J2
Nebraska State USA 25
Negev Desert Israel 73 I9
Negotin Town Serbia 49 C11
Negro River Brazil 36 B7
Nellore Town India 77 H9
Nelson Town New Zealand 93 F8
Nepal Country 77
Netanya Town Israel 73 H9
Netherlands Country 50
Neubrandenburg Town Germany
51 C11
Neuchâtel Town Switzerland 52 F2
Neuquén Town Argentina 36 H7
Nevada State USA 26
Newark Town New Jersey, USA
21 F12
New Brunswick Province Canada
29
New Caledonia Dep. territory
France 93 J12
Newcastle Town Australia 91 G12
Newcastle upon Tyne Town
England, UK 41 E9
New Delhi Capital India 77 D9
Newfoundland and Labrador
Province Canada 29
New Guinea Island Indonesia
81 G10
New Hampshire State USA 21
New Haven Town Connecticut,
USA 21 F12
New Jersey State USA 21
New Mexico State USA 27
New Orleans Town Louisiana, USA
22 H6
New Plymouth Town New Zealand
93 D9
Newport Town Vermont, USA
21 C12
Newport News Town Virginia, USA
23 B12
New South Wales State Australia
91
New York State USA 21
New York City Town New York,
USA 21 F12
New Zealand Country 92
Nha Trang Town Vietnam 78 H7
Niagara Falls USA 21 F9
Niamey Capital Niger 65 G8
Nicaragua Country 34
Nice Town France 47 H11
Nicobar Islands India 77 J12
Nicosia Capital Cyprus 73 F8
Niger Country 65
Niger River West Africa 65 I9
Nigeria Country 65
Niigata Town Japan 83 F9
Niksic Town Montenegro 49 D9
Nile River East Africa 63 F13, 66 B7
Nîmes Town France 47 G9
Ningbo Town China 85 G12
Nis Town Serbia 49 D11
Nitra Town Slovakia 57 I8
Niue Dep. territory New Zealand
93 I13

Nizhnevartovsk Town Russian Fed.
86 G4
Nizhniy Novgorod Town Russian
Fed. 59 F8
Nobeoka Town Japan 82 I6
Norfolk Town Nebraska, USA
25 H13
Norfolk Town Virginia, USA 23 B12
Noril'sk Town Russian Fed. 86 E5
Norman Town Oklahoma, USA
27 F13
Norrköping Town Sweden 43 H8
Northampton Town England, UK
41 H9
North Cape New Zealand 93 A8
North Cape Norway 43 A9
North Carolina State USA 23
North Dakota State USA 25
Northern Ireland Country UK 40
Northern Mariana Islands Dep.
territory USA 93 G11
Northern Territory State Australia
91
North Island New Zealand 93
North Korea See Korea, North
North Sea 41, 42, 50
Northwest Territories Province
Canada 28
Norway Country 42
Norwegian Sea 17 I11, 43 J13
Norwich Town England, UK 41 G10
Nottingham Town England, UK
41 G9
Nouakchott Capital Mauritania
64 E3
Nova Iguaçu Town Brazil 37 E10
Novara Town Italy 48 B4
Nova Scotia Province Canada 29
Novaya Zemlya Island Russian
Fed. 17 G13, 59 B10
Novgorod Town Russian Fed. 58 F6
Novi Sad Town Serbia 49 C10
Novokuznetsk Town Russian Fed.
86 H5
Novosibirsk Town Russian Fed.
86 H5
Nubian Desert Sudan 67 A8
Nueva Gerona Town Cuba 34 B6
Nuevo Laredo Town Mexico 31 D9
Nunavut Province Canada 29
Nuremberg Town Germany 51 H10
Nyala Town Sudan 66 D6
Nyíregyháza Town Hungary 55 C8

Oakland Town California, USA
26 C4
Oamaru Town New Zealand 92 I7
Oaxaca Town Mexico 31 I10
Ob River Russian Fed. 86 G4
Obihiro Town Japan 83 B11
Oceanside Town California, USA
26 F5
Odense Town Denmark 42 I6
Oder River Poland 56 F7
Odessa Town Texas, USA 27 G11
Odessa Town Ukraine 58 H6
Offenbach Town Germany 51 G8
Ogaden Plateau Ethiopia 67 E11
Ogbomosho Town Nigeria 65 I9
Ogden Town Utah, USA 27 C8
Ohio State USA 21
Ohrid, Lake Albania/Macedonia
49 F10
Oita Town Japan 82 H6
Okavango Delta Botswana 68 G7
Okayama Town Japan 82 H7
Okeechobee, Lake Florida, USA
23 I11
Okhotsk, Sea of 87 G10
Oklahoma State USA 27
Oklahoma City State capital
Oklahoma, USA 27 F13
Öland Island Sweden 43 I8

Oldenburg Town Germany 51 C8
Olomouc Town Czech Republic
56 H7
Olsztyn Town Poland 57 C9
Olympia State capital Washington,
USA 24 D3
Olympus, Mount Greece 49 F11
Omaha Town Nebraska, USA
25 I14
Oman, Gulf of 75 F11
Oman Country 75
Omdurman Town Sudan 67 C8
Omsk Town Russian Fed. 86 H4
Onega, Lake Russian Fed. 58 E7
Onega Town Russian Fed. 58 D7
Onitsha Town Nigeria 65 I9
Ontario, Lake USA 21 E10
Ontario Province Canada 29
Opole Town Poland 56 F7
Oradea Town Romania 55 C8
Oran Town Algeria 62 D5
Orange River South Africa 69 I8
Orcadas (Argentina) RS Antarctica
16 C1
Ordu Town Turkey 73 C11
Örebro Town Sweden 42 G7
Oregon State USA 24
Orenburg Town Russian Fed.
59 G10, 86 H2
Orense Town Spain 44 C6
Orkney Islands Scotland, UK 41 B9
Orlando Town Florida, USA 23 H11
Orléans Town France 47 D8
Örnsköldsvik Town Sweden 43 E8
Orsk Town Russian Fed. 59 G10
Oruro Town Bolivia 36 D7
Osaka Town Japan 83 H8
Oshawa Town Ontario, Canada
29 J11
Oshkosh Town Wisconsin, USA
20 F5
Osijek Town Croatia 49 B9
Oslo Capital Norway 42 G6
Osmaniye Town Turkey 73 E10
Osnabrück Town Germany 51 D8
Osorno Town Chile 36 H6
Ostend Town Belgium 50 E4
Östersund Town Sweden 42 E7
Ostrava Town Czech Republic
57 H8
Otago Peninsula New Zealand
92 I7
Otaru Town Japan 83 B10
Ottawa Capital Canada 29 I12
Ouagadougou Capital Burkina
Faso 64 G7
Oujda Town Morocco 62 D4
Oulu Town Finland 43 D10
Outer Hebrides Island group
Scotland, UK 40 C7
Oviedo Town Spain 44 B7
Owensboro Town Kentucky, USA
22 B7
Oxford Town England, UK 41 H9
Oxnard Town California, USA 26 E5

Pachuca Town Mexico 31 G9
Pacific Ocean 24, 25, 26, 28, 30,
36, 79, 83, 85, 87, 91, 93
Padang Town Indonesia 80 F2
Paderborn Town Germany 51 E8
Paducah Town Kentucky, USA
22 C7
Pakistan Country 76
Pakxe Town Laos 78 G5
Palau Country 93 H10
Palawan Passage South China Sea
79 H9
Palembang Town Indonesia 80 G3
Palencia Town Spain 45 C8
Palermo Town Sicily, Italy 48 H6
Palma Town Mallorca, Spain 45 E13
Palmer (US) RS Antarctica 16 D1

Palmerston North *Town* New Zealand 93 E9
Palo Alto *Town* California, USA 26 D4
Palu *Town* Indonesia 80 F6
Pamplona *Town* Spain 45 B10
Panama, Gulf of 34 G7
Panama *Country* 34
Panama Canal Panama 34 F6
Panama City *Capital* Panama 34 F7
Pancevo *Town* Serbia 49 C10
Papua New Guinea *Country* 93
Paraguay *Country* 37
Paramaribo *Capital* Suriname 35 G13
Pardubice *Town* Czech Republic 56 G6
Paris *Capital* France 47 C9
Parma *Town* Italy 48 C5
Parnaíba *Town* Brazil 37 B11
Pasadena *Town* California, USA 26 F5
Pasadena *Town* Texas, USA 27 H14
Pasco *Town* Washington, USA 24 E5
Passau *Town* Germany 51 I11
Pasto *Town* Colombia 34 I7
Patagonia Argentina 36 I7
Paterson *Town* New Jersey, USA 21 F12
Patna *Town* India 77 E10
Pátrai *Town* Greece 49 H11
Pau *Town* France 46 G6
Pavlodar *Town* Kazakhstan 86 H4
Pearl *River* Mississippi, USA 22 G6
Pec *Town* Serbia 49 E10
Pechora *River* Russian Fed. 59 D9
Pécs *Town* Hungary 54 E5
Pedro Juan Caballero *Town* Paraguay 37 E8
Pegu *Town* Myanmar (Burma) 78 G2
Pekanbaru *Town* Indonesia 80 F2
Pennines *Hills* England, UK 41 F9
Pennsylvania *State* USA 21
Penza *Town* Russian Fed. 59 G8
Peoria *Town* Illinois, USA 20 H5
Pereira *Town* Colombia 35 H8
Perm *Town* Russian Fed. 59 F9
Pernik *Town* Bulgaria 55 I9
Persian Gulf 75 E8
Perth *Town* Australia 90 G4
Perth *Town* Scotland, UK 41 D8
Peru *Country* 36
Perugia *Town* Italy 48 D6
Pescara *Town* Italy 48 E7
Peshawar *Town* Pakistan 77 B8
Peterborough *Town* England, UK 41 G10
Petropavlovsk-Kamchatskiy *Town* Russian Fed. 87 H11
Petrozavodsk *Town* Russian Fed. 58 E7
Pforzheim *Town* Germany 51 H8
Philadelphia *Town* Pennsylvania, USA 21 G12
Philippines *Country* 79
Phnom Penh *Capital* Cambodia 78 H5
Phoenix *State capital* Arizona, USA 26 F7
Phuket *Town* Thailand 78 I3
Piacenza *Town* Italy 48 C5
Pierre *State capital* S Dakota, USA 25 G12
Pietermaritzburg *Town* South Africa 69 I9
Pietersburg *Town* South Africa 69 H9
Pinar del Río *Town* Cuba 34 B6
Pine Bluff *Town* Arkansas, USA 22 E5

Piraeus *Town* Greece 49 H12
Pisa *Town* Italy 48 D5
Pistoia *Town* Italy 48 C6
Pitesti *Town* Romania 55 F10
Pittsburgh *Town* Pennsylvania, USA 21 G9
Piura *Town* Peru 36 B5
Plano *Town* Texas, USA 27 G13
Platte *River* Nebraska, USA 25 I12
Plauen *Town* Germany 51 F10
Plenty, Bay of New Zealand 93 C10
Pleven *Town* Bulgaria 55 H10
Plock *Town* Poland 57 D9
Ploiesti *Town* Romania 55 F11
Plovdiv *Town* Bulgaria 55 I10
Plymouth *Town* England, UK 41 I8
Plzen *Town* Czech Republic 56 G4
Podgorica *Capital* Montenegro 49 E9
Pointe-Noire *Town* Republic of the Congo 68 D5
Poitiers *Town* France 46 D7
Poland *Country* 56
Pontianak *Town* Indonesia 80 F4
Poona See Pune
Popayán *Town* Colombia 34 H7
Pori *Town* Finland 43 F9
Port Arthur *Town* Texas, USA 27 H14
Port Augusta *Town* Australia 91 G9
Port-au-Prince *Capital* Haiti 35 D9
Port Elizabeth *Town* South Africa 69 J8
Port-Gentil *Town* Gabon 68 C5
Port Harcourt *Town* Nigeria 65 J9
Portland *Town* Maine, USA 21 D13
Portland *Town* Oregon, USA 24 E3
Port Louis *Capital* Mauritius 69 H14
Port Macquarie *Town* Australia 91 G13
Porto *Town* Portugal 44 D5
Porto Alegre *Town* Brazil 37 F9
Port-of-Spain *Capital* Trinidad and Tobago 35 F12
Porto-Novo *Capital* Benin 65 I8
Porto Velho *Town* Brazil 36 C7
Portoviejo *Town* Ecuador 36 B5
Port Said *Town* Egypt 63 E13
Portsmouth *Town* England, UK 41 I9
Portsmouth *Town* New Hampshire, USA 21 D13
Portsmouth *Town* Virginia, USA 23 B12
Port Sudan *Town* Sudan 67 B9
Portugal *Country* 44
Potosí *Town* Bolivia 36 E7
Potsdam *Town* Germany 51 D11
Poznan *Town* Poland 56 E7
Prague *Capital* Czech Republic 56 G5
Praia *Capital* Cape Verde 64 F1
Prato *Town* Italy 48 D6
Presov *Town* Slovakia 57 H10
Prespa, Lake Macedonia 49 F10
Presque Isle *Town* Maine, USA 21 B13
Pretoria *Capital* South Africa 69 H9
Préveza *Town* Greece 49 G10
Prichard *Town* Alabama, USA 22 G7
Prilep *Town* Macedonia 49 E11
Prince Edward Islands *Province* Canada 29
Prince George *Town* British Columbia, Canada 28 H6
Pristina *Capital* Kosovo 49 D10
Prizren *Town* Serbia 49 E10
Prome *Town* Myanmar (Burma) 78 F2
Providence *State capital* Rhode Island, USA 21 E13

Provo *Town* Utah, USA 27 C8
Pucallpa *Town* Peru 36 C6
Puducherry *Town* India 77 H9
Puebla *Town* Mexico 31 H10
Pueblo *Town* Colorado, USA 27 D10
Puerto Ayacucho *Town* Venezuela 35 G10
Puerto Montt *Town* Chile 36 H6
Puerto Princesa *Town* Philippines 79 G10
Puerto Rico *Dep. territory* USA 35 D11
Pula *Town* Croatia 48 C7
Pune (Poona) *Town* India 76 F7
Puno *Town* Peru 36 D6
Punta Alta *Town* Argentina 37 H8
Punta Arenas *Town* Chile 36 J7
Puntarenas *Town* Costa Rica 34 F5
Pusan *Town* South Korea 85 E13
Putrajaya *Capital* Malaysia 80 E2
Pyongyang *Capital* North Korea 85 D12
Pyrenees *Mountain range* France/Spain 45 C11, 46 H7

Qamdo *Town* China 85 H8
Qatar *Country* 75
Qattara Depression Egypt 63 F12
Qena *Town* Egypt 63 G13
Qilian Shan *Mountain range* China 85 F8
Qingdao *Town* China 85 E12
Qom *Town* Iran 75 C8
Quebec *Province* Canada 29
Quebec *Province capital* Quebec, Canada 29 I12
Queen Elizabeth Islands Canada 17 F9
Queensland *State* Australia 91
Queenstown *Town* Australia 91 J11
Quelimane *Town* Mozambique 69 G10
Querétaro *Town* Mexico 31 G9
Quetta *Town* Pakistan 76 C7
Quezaltenango *Town* Guatemala 34 D4
Quibdó *Town* Colombia 34 G7
Quimper *Town* France 46 B5
Qui Nhon *Town* Vietnam 78 G7

Rabat *Capital* Morocco 62 D3
Radom *Town* Poland 57 F10
Ragusa *Town* Sicily, Italy 48 H7
Rainier, Mount Washington, USA 24 D4
Raipur *Town* India 77 F9
Rajshahi *Town* Bangladesh 77 E11
Raleigh *State capital* N Carolina, USA 23 C11
Rancagua *Town* Chile 36 G7
Randers *Town* Denmark 42 I6
Rapid City *Town* S Dakota, USA 25 G11
Rasht *Town* Iran 75 B8
Rat Islands Alaska, USA 25 C8
Ravenna *Town* Italy 48 C6
Rawalpindi *Town* Pakistan 77 B8
Reading *Town* England, UK 41 H9
Reading *Town* Pennsylvania, USA 21 G11
Recife *Town* Brazil 37 C12
Red *River* USA 22 G5
Red Deer *Town* Alberta, Canada 28 H7
Redding *Town* California, USA 26 B4
Red Sea 63 G14, 67 B9, 74 G5
Regensburg *Town* Germany 51 H10
Reggio di Calabria *Town* Italy 49 H8
Reggio nell' Emilia *Town* Italy 48 C5

Regina *Province capital* Saskatchewan, Canada 29 I8
Reims *Town* France 47 C10
Rennes *Town* France 46 C7
Reno *Town* Nevada, USA 26 C5
Republic of Ireland See Ireland, Republic of
Republic of the Congo See Congo, Republic of
Resistencia *Town* Argentina 37 F8
Resita *Town* Romania 55 E8
Réunion *Dep. territory* France 69 H14
Reus *Town* Spain 45 D12
Reutlingen *Town* Germany 51 I8
Reykjavik *Capital* Iceland 43 I11
Reynosa *Town* Mexico 31 E10
Rhine *River* Europe 50 F7, 52 E4
Rhode Island *State* USA 21
Rhódes *Town* Rhodes, Greece 49 I14
Rhodope Mountains Bulgaria 55 J10
Rhône *River* France 47 F10
Richmond *State capital* Virginia, USA 23 B12
Richmond *Town* Kentucky, USA 23 B9
Riga, Gulf of 58 F5
Ríga *Capital* Latvia 58 F5
Rijeka *Town* Croatia 48 C7
Rimini *Town* Italy 48 C6
Riobamba *Town* Ecuador 36 B5
Río Cuarto *Town* Argentina 37 G7
Rio de Janeiro *Town* Brazil 37 E10
Rio Gallegos *Town* Argentina 36 J7
Rio Grande *Town* Brazil 37 G9
Rivera *Town* Uruguay 37 F8
Riverside *Town* California, USA 26 F5
Riyadh *Capital* Saudi Arabia 74 F7
Roanoke *Town* Virginia, USA 23 B11
Rochester *Town* Minnesota, USA 20 F4
Rochester *Town* New York, USA 21 E10
Rockford *Town* Illinois, USA 20 G5
Rockhampton *Town* Australia 91 E12
Rocky Mountains Canada/USA 24 F7, 27 D9, 28 G6
Roeselare *Town* Belgium 50 E4
Romania *Country* 55
Rome *Capital* Italy 48 E6
Ronne Ice Shelf Antarctica 16 E3
Rosario *Town* Argentina 37 G8
Roseau *Capital* Dominica 35 D12
Ross Ice Shelf Antarctica 16 G4
Ross Sea 16 H4
Rostock *Town* Germany 51 B11
Rostov-na-Donu *Town* Russian Fed. 58 H7
Roswell *Town* New Mexico, USA 27 G10
Rothera (UK) *RS* Antarctica 16 E1
Rotorua *Town* New Zealand 93 C10
Rotterdam *Town* Netherlands 50 D5
Roubaix *Town* France 47 A10
Rouen *Town* France 47 B8
Rukwa, Lake Tanzania 67 I8
Ruse *Town* Bulgaria 55 G11
Rushmore, Mount S Dakota, USA 25 H11
Russian Federation *Country* 59, 86
Rwanda *Country* 66
Ryazan *Town* Russian Fed. 58 G7
Rybinsk *Town* Russian Fed. 58 F7
Rzeszow *Town* Poland 57 G11

Saarbrücken *Town* Germany 50 G7
Saba *Dep. territory* Netherlands 35 D12
Sabac *Town* Serbia 49 C10
Sabah *Region* Malaysia 80 E5
Sabha *Town* Libya 63 F8
Sacramento *State capital* California, USA 26 C4
Safi *Town* Morocco 62 E2
Saginaw *Town* Michigan, USA 20 F7
Sagunto *Town* Spain 45 F11
Sahara Desert North Africa 62 H5, 64 E7
Saiki *Town* Japan 82 I6
St. Augustine *Town* Florida, USA 23 G11
St. Barthélémy *Dep. territory* France 35 D12
St. Eustatius *Dep. territory* Netherlands 35 D12
St. Étienne *Town* France 47 F9
St. George's *Capital* Grenada 35 E12
St. George's Channel 40 G7
St. John *Town* New Brunswick, Canada 29 I13
St. John's *Capital* Antigua and Barbuda 35 D12
St. John's *Province capital* Newfoundland and Labrador, Canada 29 H14
St. Joseph *Town* Missouri, USA 22 B4
St. Kitts and Nevis *Country* 35
St. Lawrence Island Alaska, USA 25 B10
St. Louis *Town* Missouri, USA 22 B6
St. Louis *Town* Senegal 64 F3
St. Lucia *Country* 35
St. Malo *Town* France 46 B7
St. Martin *Dep. territory* France, Netherlands 35 D12
St. Moritz *Town* Switzerland 52 G5
St. Nazaire *Town* France 46 C6
St. Paul *State capital* Minnesota, USA 20 E3
St. Petersburg *Town* Florida, USA 23 H10
St. Petersburg *Town* Russian Fed. 58 E6
St. Pierre and Miquelon *Dep. territory* France 29 H14
St. Quentin *Town* France 47 B10
St. Vincent and the Grenadines *Country* 35
Sakai *Town* Japan 83 H8
Sakata *Town* Japan 83 E10
Salamanca *Town* Spain 44 D7
Salem *State capital* Oregon, USA 24 F3
Salerno *Town* Italy 48 F7
Salina *Town* Kansas, USA 27 D13
Salinas *Town* California, USA 26 D4
Salta *Town* Argentina 36 E7
Saltillo *Town* Mexico 31 E8
Salt Lake City *State capital* Utah, USA 27 C8
Salto *Town* Uruguay 37 F8
Salvador *Town* Brazil 37 D11
Salzburg *Town* Austria 40 F9
Samara *Town* Russian Fed. 59 G9
Samarkand *Town* Uzbekistan 86 J3
Samoa *Country* 93 I13
Samsun *Town* Turkey 73 C10
Sanaa *Capital* Yemen 74 I7
Sanae (South Africa) *RS* Antarctica 16 C4
San Angelo *Town* Texas, USA 27 H11
San Antonio *Town* Texas, USA 27 I12

San Bernardino *Town* California, USA 26 F5
San Cristóbal *Town* Venezuela 35 G9
Sancti Spíritus *Town* Cuba 34 B7
Sandakan *Town* Malaysia 80 E6
Sand Hills Nebraska, USA 25 H12
San Diego *Town* California, USA 26 F5
San Francisco *Town* California, USA 26 C4
San Francisco de Macorís *Town* Dominican Republic 35 C10
San José *Capital* Costa Rica 34 F5
San Jose *Town* California, USA 26 D4
San Juan *Town* Argentina 36 F7
Sankt Pölten *Town* Austria 40 E12
San Luis Potosí *Town* Mexico 31 F9
San Marino *Capital* San Marino 48 D6
San Marino *Country* 48
San Martin (Argentina) *RS* Antarctica 16 E2
San Miguel de Tucumán *Town* Argentina 36 F7
San Miguelito *Town* Panama 34 F7
San Pedro Sula *Town* Honduras 34 D5
San Remo *Town* Italy 48 C4
San Salvador *Capital* El Salvador 34 D4
San Salvador de Jujuy *Town* Argentina 36 E7
Santa Barbara *Town* California, USA 26 E5
Santa Clara *Town* Cuba 34 B7
Santa Cruz *Town* Bolivia 36 D7
Santa Fe *State capital* New Mexico, USA 27 E10
Santa Fe *Town* Argentina 37 G8
Santa Marta *Town* Colombia 35 F8
Santander *Town* Spain 45 B8
Santarém *Town* Brazil 37 B9
Santa Rosa *Town* California, USA 26 C4
Santiago *Capital* Chile 36 G7
Santiago *Town* Dominican Republic 35 C10
Santiago de Cuba *Town* Cuba 35 C8
Santo Domingo *Capital* Dominican Republic 35 D10
Santos *Town* Brazil 37 E10
São Luis *Town* Brazil 37 B10
São Paulo *Town* Brazil 37 E10
São Tomé *Capital* São Tomé and Príncipe 68 C4
São Tomé and Príncipe *Country* 68
Sapporo *Town* Japan 83 B10
Sarajevo *Capital* Bosnia and Herz. 49 D9
Saratov *Town* Russian Fed. 59 G8
Sarawak Malaysia 80 F4
Sardinia *Island* Italy 48 F4
Sarh *Town* Chad 65 H13
Sariwon *Town* North Korea 85 D12
Sasebo *Town* Japan 82 H5
Saskatchewan *Province* Canada 29
Saskatoon *Town* Saskatchewan, Canada 29 H8
Sassari *Town* Sardinia, Italy 48 F4
Satu Mare *Town* Romania 55 C8
Saudi Arabia *Country* 74
Savannah *Town* Georgia, USA 23 F11
Savona *Town* Italy 48 C4
Saynshand *Town* Mongolia 85 D10
Scheldt *River* Belgium 50 E4
Schenectady *Town* New York, USA 21 E12
Schwaz *Town* Austria 40 F8

Schwerin *Town* Germany 51 C10
Scotland *Country* UK 41
Scott Base (New Zealand) *RS* Antarctica 16 G4
Scranton *Town* Pennsylvania, USA 21 F11
Seattle *Town* Washington, USA 24 D4
Ségou *Town* Mali 64 G6
Segovia *Town* Spain 45 D8
Seine *River* France 47 B9
Sekondi-Takoradi *Town* Ghana 64 I7
Semarang *Town* Indonesia 80 H4
Sendai *Town* Japan 83 E10
Senegal *Country* 64
Senegal *River* Senegal 64 F4
Seoul *Capital* South Korea 85 E13
Serbia *Country* 49
Serov *Town* Russian Fed. 86 G3
Sète *Town* France 47 H9
Setúbal *Town* Portugal 44 G5
Sevastopol *Town* Crimea, Ukraine 58 I7
Severn *River* England, UK 41 H9
Severnaya Zemlya Russian Fed. 17 F13, 86 C6
Seville *Town* Spain 44 H7
Seychelles *Country* 69
Sfax *Town* Tunisia 62 D7
Shanghai *Town* China 85 F12
Shannon *River* Republic of Ireland 40 G6
Sheberghan *Town* Afghanistan 76 A7
Sheffield *Town* England, UK 41 G9
Shenyang *Town* China 85 D12
Sherbrooke *Town* Quebec, Canada 29 I12
's-Hertogenbosch *Town* Netherlands 50 D6
Shetland Islands Scotland, UK 41 A9
Shimonoseki *Town* Japan 82 H5
Shinyanga *Town* Tanzania 67 H8
Shiraz *Town* Iran 75 D9
Shizuoka *Town* Japan 83 G9
Shkodër *Town* Albania 49 E10
Shreveport *Town* Louisiana, USA 22 F4
Shumen *Town* Bulgaria 55 H12
Sibenik *Town* Croatia 49 D8
Siberia Russian Fed. 86 F7
Sibiu *Town* Romania 55 E10
Sicily *Island* Italy 48 H7
Sidi Bel Abbès *Town* Algeria 62 D5
Siegen *Town* Germany 51 F8
Siena *Town* Italy 48 D6
Sierra de Gredos *Mountain range* Spain 44 E7
Sierra Leone *Country* 64
Sierra Nevada *Mountain range* California, USA 26 C5
Sierra Nevada *Mountain range* Spain 45 H9
Signy (UK) *RS* Antarctica 16 C1
Silver City *Town* New Mexico, USA 27 G9
Sincelejo *Town* Colombia 35 F8
Singapore *Capital* Singapore 80 F2
Singapore *Country* 80
Sinuiju *Town* North Korea 85 D12
Sioux City *Town* Iowa, USA 20 G2
Sioux Falls *Town* S Dakota, USA 25 H14
Siracusa *Town* Sicily, Italy 48 H7
Sittwe *Town* Myanmar (Burma) 78 E1
Sivas *Town* Turkey 73 D10
Skagerrak *Sea* Norway 42 H6
Skellefteå *Town* Sweden 43 D9
Skopje *Capital* Macedonia 49 E11
Slavonski Brod *Town* Croatia 49 C9

Sligo *Town* Republic of Ireland 40 F6
Sliven *Town* Bulgaria 55 H12
Slovakia *Country* 57
Slovenia *Country* 48
Smederevo *Town* Serbia 49 C10
Smolensk *Town* Russian Fed. 58 F6
Snake *River* Idaho/Oregon, USA 24 H6
Snowdon *Mountain* Wales, UK 41 G8
Socotra *Island* Yemen 75 J10
Söderhamn *Town* Sweden 43 F8
Södertälje *Town* Sweden 43 G8
Sofia *Capital* Bulgaria 55 I9
Soledad *Town* Colombia 35 F8
Solingen *Town* Germany 50 E7
Solomon Islands *Country* 93 I12
Solomon Sea 81 G13
Somalia *Country* 67
Songea *Town* Tanzania 67 J9
Songkhla *Town* Thailand 78 J4
Soria *Town* Spain 45 C9
Sorong *Town* Indonesia 81 F9
Sousse *Town* Tunisia 62 D7
South Africa *Country* 68
Southampton *Town* England, UK 41 I9
Southampton Island Nunavut, Canada 29 F7
South Australia *State* Australia 91
South Bend *Town* Indiana, USA 20 G6
South Carolina *State* USA 23
South China Sea 79 G8, 85 J12
South Dakota *State* USA 25
Southern Ocean 16, 90
South Georgia *Dep. territory* UK 37 J10
South Island New Zealand 92
South Korea *See* Korea, South
South Orkney Islands Antarctica 16 C1
Soweto *Town* South Africa 69 I8
Spain *Country* 44
Spanish Town *Town* Jamaica 35 D8
Spartanburg *Town* S Carolina, USA 23 D10
Split *Town* Croatia 49 D8
Spokane *Town* Washington, USA 24 D5
Springfield *State capital* Illinois, USA 20 I5
Springfield *Town* Massachusetts, USA 21 E12
Springfield *Town* Missouri, USA 22 C4
Srebrenica *Town* Bosnia and Herz. 49 C9
Sri Lanka *Country* 77
Stamford *Town* Connecticut, USA 21 F12
Stara Zagora *Town* Bulgaria 55 I11
Stavanger *Town* Norway 42 G5
Stavropol *Town* Russian Fed. 59 I8
Stewart Island New Zealand 92 J6
Stockholm *Capital* Sweden 43 G8
Stockton *Town* California, USA 26 C4
Stockton Plateau Texas, USA 27 H10
Stoke-on-Trent *Town* England, UK 41 G9
Strasbourg *Town* France 47 D12
Stuttgart *Town* Germany 51 H8
Subotica *Town* Serbia 49 B10
Suceava *Town* Romania 55 C11
Sucre *Capital* Bolivia 36 E7
Sudan *Country* 66
Sudbury *Town* Ontario, Canada 29 I11
Suez, Gulf of 63 F13
Suez *Town* Egypt 63 F13

Sühbaatar *Town* Mongolia 85 C9
Sukkur *Town* Pakistan 76 C7
Sulu Archipelago Philippines 79 I10
Sulu Sea 79 H10
Sumatra *Island* Indonesia 80 F2
Sunderland *Town* England, UK 41 F9
Sundsvall *Town* Sweden 43 F8
Sunnyvale *Town* California, USA 26 D4
Superior, Lake USA 20 C5
Sur *Town* Oman 75 F11
Surabaya *Town* Indonesia 80 H4
Surakarta *Town* Indonesia 80 H4
Surat *Town* India 76 E7
Surgut *Town* Russian Fed. 86 G4
Suriname *Country* 35
Surt *Capital* Libya 63 E9
Suwalki *Town* Poland 57 B11
Svalbard *Dep. territory* Norway 17 H12
Swansea *Town* Wales, UK 41 H8
Swaziland *Country* 69
Sweden *Country* 43
Swindon *Town* England, UK 41 H9
Switzerland *Country* 52
Sydney *Town* Australia 91 H12
Syktyvkar *Town* Russian Fed. 59 E9
Sylhet *Town* Bangladesh 77 E12
Syowa (Japan) *RS* Antarctica 16 D6
Syracuse *Town* New York, USA 21 E11
Syria *Country* 73
Syrian Desert Syria 73 G11, 74 C6
Szczecin *Town* Poland 56 C5
Szeged *Town* Hungary 54 D6
Székesfehérvár *Town* Hungary 54 D5
Szombathely *Town* Hungary 54 D4

Tabora *Town* Tanzania 67 H8
Tabriz *Town* Iran 74 B7
Tacoma *Town* Washington, USA 24 D3
Taegu *Town* South Korea 85 E13
Taejon *Town* South Korea 85 E13
Taguatinga *Town* Brazil 37 D9
Taipei *Capital* Taiwan 85 H13
Taiwan *Country* 85
Taiyuan *Town* China 85 E10
Ta'izz *Town* Yemen 74 I7
Tajikistan *Country* 86
Takasaki *Town* Japan 83 F9
Taklimakan Desert China 84 F5
Talcahuano *Town* Chile 36 G6
Taldyqorgan *Town* Kazakhstan 86 I4
Tallahassee *State capital* Florida, USA 23 G9
Tallinn *Capital* Estonia 58 E5
Tamale *Town* Ghana 64 H7
Tamanrasset *Town* Algeria 62 H6
Tampa *Town* Florida, USA 23 H10
Tampere *Town* Finland 43 F9
Tampico *Town* Mexico 31 G10
Tamworth *Town* Australia 91 G12
Tanami Desert Australia 91 D8
Tanga *Town* Tanzania 67 H9
Tanganyika, Lake DRC/Tanzania 66 I7, 69 G9
Tangier *Town* Morocco 62 D3
Tanzania *Country* 67
Taranto *Town* Italy 49 F8
Tarbes *Town* France 46 G7
Târgu Mures *Town* Romania 55 D10
Tarija *Town* Bolivia 36 E7
Tarim Basin China 84 E6
Tarnow *Town* Poland 57 G10
Tarragona *Town* Spain 45 D12
Tarsus *Town* Turkey 73 E9
Tartu *Town* Estonia 58 F6

Tartus *Town* Syria 73 G10
Tashkent *Capital* Uzbekistan 86 I3
Tasmania *State* Australia 91
Tasman Sea 91 I12, 92 F6
Tatra Mountains Slovakia 57 H9
Taupo, Lake New Zealand 93 D10
Tauranga *Town* New Zealand 93 C10
Taurus Mountains Turkey 73 E8
Tavoy *Town* Myanmar (Burma) 78 G3
Tbilisi *Capital* Georgia 59 I8
Tegucigalpa *Capital* Honduras 34 D5
Tehran *Capital* Iran 75 B9
Tehuantepec, Gulf of 31 I11
Tekirdag *Town* Turkey 72 B6
Tel Aviv *Town* Israel 73 H9
Temuco *Town* Chile 36 H6
Tennessee *River* Alabama/ Tennessee, USA 23 D8
Tennessee *State* USA 23
Tepic *Town* Mexico 30 G7
Teramo *Town* Italy 48 D7
Teresina *Town* Brazil 37 B10
Terni *Town* Italy 48 D6
Terrasa *Town* Spain 45 C12
Terre Haute *Town* Indiana, USA 20 H6
Teruel *Town* Spain 45 E10
Tete *Town* Mozambique 69 G10
Tétouan *Town* Morocco 62 D3
Texas *State* USA 27
Thailand, Gulf of 78 H4
Thailand *Country* 78
Thai Nguyen *Town* Vietnam 78 E5
Thames *River* England, UK 41 H10
Thanh Hoa *Town* Vietnam 78 E5
The Hague *Capital* Netherlands 50 D5
Thessaloníki *Town* Greece 49 F11
Thimphu *Capital* Bhutan 77 D11
Thiruvananthapuram (Trivandrum) *Town* India 77 I8
Thun *Town* Switzerland 52 G3
Thunder Bay *Town* Ontario, Canada 29 I10
Tianjin *Town* China 85 E11
Tibesti Mountains Chad 65 E13
Tibet China 84 G6
Tibet, Plateau of China 84 G7
Tigris *River* Iraq 74 C7
Tijuana *Town* Mexico 30 B3
Tilburg *Town* Netherlands 50 E6
Timaru *Town* New Zealand 92 H7
Timisoara *Town* Romania 54 E7
Tindouf *Town* Algeria 62 F2
Tiranë *Capital* Albania 49 F10
Tiraspol *Town* Moldova 58 H6
Tiruchchirappalli *Town* India 77 I8
Tisza *River* Central Europe 54 D7
Titicaca, Lake Peru 36 D6
Tocantins *River* Brazil 37 C10
Togo *Country* 65
Tokelau *Dep. territory* New Zealand 93 I13
Tokushima *Town* Japan 82 H7
Tokyo *Capital* Japan 83 G10
Toledo *Town* Ohio, USA 21 G8
Toledo *Town* Spain 45 E8
Toluca *Town* Mexico 31 H9
Tolyatti *Town* Russian Fed. 59 G9
Tomakomai *Town* Japan 83 C10
Tombouctou *Town* Mali 64 F7
Tomsk *Town* Russian Fed. 86 G5
Tonga *Country* 93 I13
Tonkin, Gulf of 78 E5, 85 J10
Tonopah *Town* Nevada, USA 26 D6
Toowoomba *Town* Australia 91 F13
Topeka *State capital* Kansas, USA 27 D13
Toronto *Province capital* Ontario, Canada 29 J11

Torun *Town* Poland 57 D8
Tottori *Town* Japan 82 G7
Toubkal, Mount Morocco 63 E2
Toulon *Town* France 47 H10
Toulouse *Town* France 46 G7
Tournai *Town* Belgium 50 E4
Tours *Town* France 47 D8
Townsville *Town* Australia 91 D11
Toyama *Town* Japan 83 F8
Toyota *Town* Japan 83 G8
Trabzon *Town* Turkey 73 C12
Transylvanian Alps Romania 55 E9
Trapani *Town* Sicily, Italy 48 H6
Trencin *Town* Slovakia 56 I7
Trent *River* England, UK 41 G10
Trento *Town* Italy 48 B6
Trenton *State capital* New Jersey,
USA 21 G12
Treviso *Town* Italy 48 B6
Trier *Town* Germany 50 G6
Trieste *Town* Italy 48 B7
Trincomalee *Town* Sri Lanka 77 I9
Trinidad and Tobago *Country* 35
Tripoli *Capital* Libya 63 E8
Tripoli *Town* Lebanon 73 G10
Trivandrum *See*
    Thiruvananthapuram
Trnava *Town* Slovakia 56 I7
Trois-Rivières *Town* Quebec,
Canada 29 I12
Tromsø *Town* Norway 43 B8
Trondheim *Town* Norway 42 E6
Troy *Town* New York, USA 21 E12
Troyes *Town* France 47 C10
Trujillo *Town* Peru 36 C5
Tshikapa *Town* DRC 68 E7
Tubruq *Town* Libya 63 E11
Tucson *Town* Arizona, USA 27 G8
Tuguegarao *Town* Philippines
79 E10
Tula *Town* Russian Fed. 58 G7
Tulcea *Town* Romania 55 E13
Tulsa *Town* Oklahoma, USA 27 E13
Tunis *Capital* Tunisia 62 D7
Tunisia *Country* 62
Tunja *Town* Colombia 35 G8
Turin *Town* Italy 48 B4
Turkana, Lake Kenya 67 F9
Turkey *Country* 73
Turkmenistan *Country* 86
Turks and Caicos Islands *Dep.*
territory UK 35 B9
Turku *Town* Finland 43 G9
Tuvalu *Country* 93 I12
Tuxtla Gutiérrez *Town* Mexico
31 I12
Tuz, Lake Turkey 73 D8
Tuzla *Town* Bosnia and Herz. 49 C9
Tver *Town* Russian Fed. 58 F7
Twin Falls *Town* Idaho, USA 24 H6
Tyler *Town* Texas, USA 27 G14
Tyrrhenian Sea 48 G6

Uberaba *Town* Brazil 37 E10
Uberlândia *Town* Brazil 37 D10
Ubon Ratchathani *Town* Thailand
78 G5
Uchiura Bay Japan 83 C10
Udaipur *Town* India 77 E8
Udine *Town* Italy 48 B7
Udon Thani *Town* Thailand 78 F4
Uele *River* DRC 69 C9
Ufa *Town* Russian Fed. 59 G10
Uganda *Country* 67
Ukhta *Town* Russian Fed. 59 D9
Ukraine *Country* 58
Ulaanbaatar *Capital* Mongolia
85 C9
Ulaangom *Town* Mongolia 84 C7
Ulan-Ude *Town* Russian Fed. 86 H7
Ulm *Town* Germany 51 I9
Umeå *Town* Sweden 43 E8
Umtata *Town* South Africa 69 J8

Ungava Peninsula Quebec,
Canada 29 F11
United Arab Emirates (UAE)
Country 75
Uppsala *Town* Sweden 43 G8
Ural Mountains Russian Fed.
59 F10, 86 G2
Urganch *Town* Uzbekistan 86 I3
Uruguay *Country* 37
Urumqi *Town* China 84 D6
Usak *Town* Turkey 72 D6
Ushuaia *Town* Argentina 36 J7
Usol'ye-Sibirskoye *Town* Russian
Fed. 86 H6
Ust'Ilimsk *Town* Russian Fed.
86 G6
Ústí nad Labem *Town* Czech
Republic 56 G5
Ustyurt Plateau Uzbekistan 86 I2
Utah *State* USA 27
Utica *Town* New York, USA 21 E11
Utrecht *Town* Netherlands 50 D6
Utsunomiya *Town* Japan 83 F10
Uzbekistan *Country* 86

Vaal *River* South Africa 69 I9
Vaasa *Town* Finland 43 E9
Vadodara *Town* India 76 E7
Vadsø *Town* Norway 43 A10
Vaduz *Capital* Liechtenstein 52 F5
Valdivia *Town* Chile 36 H6
Valdosta *Town* Georgia, USA
23 F10
Valence *Town* France 47 G10
Valencia, Gulf of 45 F11
Valencia *Town* Spain 45 F11
Valencia *Town* Venezuela 35 F10
Valladolid *Town* Spain 45 D8
Valletta *Capital* Malta 48 I7
Valparaíso *Capital* Chile 36 G6
Van *Town* Turkey 73 D13
Vancouver *Town* British Columbia,
Canada 28 I6
Vancouver Island British Columbia,
Canada 28 H5
Vantaa *Town* Finland 43 G10
Vanuatu *Country* 93 I12
Varanasi *Town* India 77 E10
Varna *Town* Bulgaria 55 H13
Västerås *Town* Sweden 43 G8
Vatican City *Country* 48
Växjö *Town* Sweden 42 I7
Venezuela *Country* 35
Venice, Gulf of 48 C7
Venice *Town* Italy 48 C6
Veracruz *Town* Mexico 31 H10
Verkhoyanskiy Mountains Russian
Fed. 87 F9
Vermont *State* USA 21
Verona *Town* Italy 48 B6
Versailles *Town* France 47 C9
Verviers *Town* Belgium 50 F6
Viareggio *Town* Italy 48 D5
Vicenza *Town* Italy 48 B6
Victoria, Lake Kenya/Tanzania/
Uganda 67 G8
Victoria *Province capital* British
Columbia, Canada 28 I6
Victoria *State* Australia 91
Victoria *Capital* Seychelles 69 D14
Victoria Falls Zimbabwe 69 G8
Victoria Island Canada 17 E8, 29 E8
Vidin *Town* Bulgaria 55 G9
Vienna *Capital* Austria 40 E13
Vientiane *Capital* Laos 78 F4
Vietnam *Country* 78
Vigo *Town* Spain 44 C5
Vijayawada *Town* India 77 G9
Villach *Town* Austria 40 H10
Villahermosa *Town* Mexico 31 H12
Villavicencio *Town* Colombia
35 H8
Vilnius *Capital* Lithuania 58 G5

Vina del Mar *Town* Chile 36 G6
Vineland *Town* New Jersey, USA
21 G12
Vinh *Town* Vietnam 78 F5
Virginia *State* USA 23
Virginia Beach *Town* Virginia, USA
23 B12
Virgin Islands *Dep. territory* USA
35 C11
Vishakhapatnam *Town* India
77 G10
Vitoria *Town* Brazil 37 E11
Vitória-Gasteiz *Town* Spain 45 B9
Vitsyebsk *Town* Belarus 58 F6
Vladikavkaz *Town* Russian Fed.
59 I8
Vladivostok *Town* Russian Fed.
87 I9
Vlissingen *Town* Netherlands
50 D5
Vlorë *Town* Albania 49 F10
Volga *River* Russian Fed. 59 F8
Volgograd *Town* Russian Fed.
59 H8
Vólos *Town* Greece 49 G11
Volta, Lake Ghana 64 I7
Vorkuta *Town* Russian Fed. 59 C11,
86 E3
Voronezh *Town* Russian Fed. 58 G7
Vosges Mountains France 47 D11
Voss *Town* Norway 42 F5
Vostok (Russian Federation) *RS*
Antarctica 16 F5
Vratsa *Town* Bulgaria 55 H9
Vyborg *Town* Russian Fed. 58 E6

Waal *River* Netherlands 50 D6
Waco *Town* Texas, USA 27 H13
Waddenzee *Sea* Netherlands
50 B7
Wadi Halfa *Town* Sudan 66 A7
Wad Medani *Town* Sudan 67 C8
Wagga Wagga *Town* Australia
91 H11
Wakayama *Town* Japan 82 H7
Wakkanai *Town* Japan 83 A10
Walbrzych *Town* Poland 56 F6
Wales *Country* UK 41
Wallis and Futuna *Dep. territory*
France 93 I13
Walvis Bay *Town* Namibia 68 H6
Wandel Sea 17 G11
Warren *Town* Michigan, USA 20 F8
Warsaw *Capital* Poland 57 E10
Washington, Mount USA 21 D12
Washington *State* USA 24
Washington D.C. *Capital* USA
21 H11
Waterford *Town* Republic of
Ireland 40 H6
Waterloo *Town* Iowa, USA 20 G4
Watertown *Town* New York, USA
21 E10
Wau *Town* Sudan 66 E7
Weddell Sea 16 D2
Weimar *Town* Germany 51 F10
Wellington *Capital* New Zealand
93 F9
Wels *Town* Austria 40 E10
Wenzhou *Town* China 85 G12
West Bank *Disputed region*
Near East 73 H9
Western Australia *State* Australia
90
Western Ghats *Mountain range*
India 76 F7
Western Sahara *Territory* 64
West Palm Beach *Town* Florida,
USA 23 I12
West Virginia *State* USA 21
Whitehorse *Province capital* Yukon
Territory, Canada 28 F5
White Nile *River* Sudan 67 D8

White Sea 58 D7
Whitney, Mount California, USA
26 D5
Wichita *Town* Kansas, USA 27 E13
Wichita Falls *Town* Texas, USA
27 F12
Wieliczka *Town* Poland 57 G9
Wiener Neustadt *Town* Austria
40 F13
Wiesbaden *Town* Germany 51 G8
Wilhelmshaven *Town* Germany
51 C8
Wilkes Land Antarctica 16 G6
Williston *Town* N Dakota, USA
25 E11
Wilmington *Town* Delaware, USA
21 G11
Wilmington *Town* N Carolina, USA
23 D12
Windhoek *Capital* Namibia 68 H7
Windsor *Town* Ontario, Canada
29 J11
Winnipeg *Province capital*
Manitoba, Canada 29 I9
Winston-Salem *Town* N Carolina,
USA 23 C10
Winterthur *Town* Switzerland
52 F4
Wisconsin *State* USA 20
Wloclawek *Town* Poland 57 D8
Wolfsberg *Town* Austria 40 H11
Wolfsburg *Town* Germany 51 D10
Wollongong *Town* Australia 91 H12
Wonsan *Town* North Korea 85 D13
Worcester *Town* Massachusetts,
USA 21 E13
Worms *Town* Germany 51 G8
Wroclaw *Town* Poland 56 F7
Wuhan *Town* China 85 G11
Wuppertal *Town* Germany 50 E7
Würzburg *Town* Germany 51 G9
Wyoming *State* USA 25

Xiamen *Town* China 85 H12
Xi'an *Town* China 85 F10
Xining *Town* China 85 F8
Xuzhou *Town* China 85 F11

Yakima *Town* Washington, USA
24 E4
Yakutsk *Town* Russian Fed. 87 F9
Yambol *Town* Bulgaria 55 I12
Yamoussoukro *Capital* Côte
d'Ivoire 64 I6
Yanbu *Town* Saudi Arabia 74 F5
Yangon (Rangoon) *Town* Myanmar
(Burma) 78 G2
Yangtze *River* China 85 G10
Yantai *Town* China 85 E12
Yaoundé *Capital* Cameroon 68 C5
Yaroslavl *Town* Russian Fed. 58 F7
Yazd *Town* Iran 75 D9
Yekaterinburg *Town* Russian Fed.
86 G3
Yellowknife *Province capital*
Northwest Territories, Canada
28 F7
Yellow Sea 85 E12
Yemen *Country* 75
Yenisey *River* Russian Fed. 86 F5
Yerevan *Capital* Armenia 59 J8
Yinchuan *Town* China 85 E9
Yining *Town* China 84 D5
Yokohama *Town* Japan 83 G10
Yonago *Town* Japan 82 G7
York *Town* England, UK 41 F9
Youngstown *Town* Ohio, USA 21 G9
Yucatán Peninsula Mexico 31 G13
Yukon *River* Alaska, USA 25 B10
Yukon Territory *Province* Canada
28
Yuma *Town* Arizona, USA 26 G6
Yumen *Town* China 85 E8

Yuzhno-Sakhalinsk *Town* Russian
Fed. 87 I10
Zadar *Town* Croatia 49 D8
Zagreb *Capital* Croatia 49 B8
Zagros Mountains Iran 75 C8
Zahedan *Town* Iran 75 D11
Zajecar *Town* Serbia 49 D11
Zambezi *River* Southern Africa
69 G8
Zambia *Country* 69
Zamboanga *Town* Philippines
79 H11
Zamora *Town* Spain 44 D7
Zanzibar *Town* Tanzania 67 I9
Zanzibar Island Tanzania 67 I10
Zaporizhzhya *Town* Ukraine 58 H7
Zaria *Town* Nigeria 65 H10
Zeebrugge *Town* Belgium 50 E4
Zenica *Town* Bosnia and Herz.
49 C9
Zhangjiakou *Town* China 85 E11
Zhanjiang *Town* China 85 I11
Zhengzhou *Town* China 85 F11
Zhezkazgan *Town* Kazakhstan
86 I3
Zhongshan (China) *RS* Antarctica
16 E7
Zibo *Town* China 85 E11
Zielona Gora *Town* Poland 56 E6
Zilina *Town* Slovakia 57 H8
Zimbabwe *Country* 69
Zinder *Town* Niger 65 G10
Zlin *Town* Czech Republic 56 H7
Zomba *Town* Malawi 69 F10
Zonguldak *Town* Turkey 73 B8
Zrenjanin *Town* Serbia 49 C10
Zug *Town* Switzerland 52 F4
Zürich *Town* Switzerland 52 F4
Zwettl Stadt *Town* Austria 40 D12
Zwickau *Town* Germany 51 F11
Zwolle *Town* Netherlands 50 C7

Index

ACKNOWLEDGEMENTS

The publishers would like to thank Richard Burgess for his contribution to this book.

All other artworks are from the Miles Kelly Artwork Bank.

The publishers would like to thank the following source for the use of their photographs:

Fotolia.com 10(b) Andrey Mirzoyants, Jean Luc Bohin, Giovanni Catalani, Kárpáti Gábor, Matt Ireland; 20 David Ruderman; 22 Daren Whitaker; 25 Sascha Burkard; 27 Tomasz Kawka; 28 Melissa Schalke; 29 Roman Krochuk; 30 Beatrice Preve; 31(t) Lein De Leon; 34 Françoise Bro; 35 pixphoto; 36(t) urbanhearts; 41(b) C J Photography; 43 Marco Regalia; 44 Hugues Argence; 48 Dubravko Grakalic; 50 Jarno Gonzalez/Fotolia.com; 51 Philip Lange; 52(t) Renato Francia; 54(b) Jozsef Szasz-fabian; 56(b) Bartlomiej Kwieciszewski; 57 Martin Džumela; 58(b) Salazkin Vladimir; 59 Jacek Malipan 65(t) Natasha Owen; 74(t) Richard Connors, (b) MaxFX; 79(c) Dmitry Ersler; 80 Stuart Taylor; 81(b) TAOLMOR/; 83(t) Anna Cseresnjes; 87(b) NFive; 91 Flavia Bottazzini; 92(b) Rico Leffanta; 93 Adam Booth

All other photographs are from: Corel, digitalSTOCK, digitalvision, istock.com, John Foxx, PhotoAlto, PhotoDisc, PhotoEssentials, PhotoPro, Stockbyte

Every effort has been made to acknowledge the source and copyright holder of each picture. Miles Kelly Publishing apologises for any unintentional errors or omissions.